THAT TIME, THAT PLACE, THAT WAR

MARGARET BROWN

To order additional copies of this book, contact:
Xlibris Corporation
1-888-795-4274
www.Xlibris.com
Orders@Xlibris.com
89070

Marines riding on an M-48 tank.

*Two soldiers wading through a muddy hole
while on a search mission.*

Dedication

To Earl, still my go-to guy.
To Emily, our daughter, and my personal IT.
To Rosie, our jealous 18-pound tabby.
She pushed books out of her way, tore keys off my laptop
but stayed up late with me while I wrote without my "delete" key.

Without their love, encouragement, and company,
I could not have attempted this book.
My tour is over, although I re-upped more than once
because of brain surgery.
My Freedom Bird is on the way.
One day and a wake-up.

CONTENTS

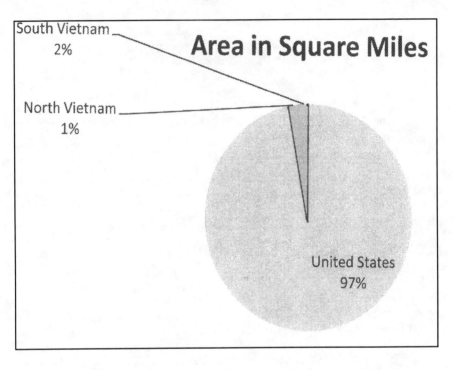

Area in Square Miles

South Vietnam
2%

North Vietnam
1%

United States
97%

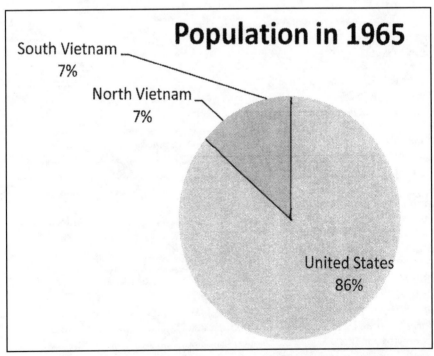

Population in 1965

South Vietnam
7%

North Vietnam
7%

United States
86%

PREFACE

WEAR A T-SHIRT, jacket, or cap that says "Vietnam Vet" and you might find a young woman or young man headed right for you. Scattered about are 120 graduates of Radford University in Radford, Virginia who want to shake your hand and say "Welcome home." Thanks to the members of the Vietnam Veterans of America, Chapter 138, we know how much that means and why there was no parade for you when you came home, back to the World.

Those graduates enrolled in one of my courses on the Vietnam War that I taught out of the Department of English and RU's Honors Program. The topic, the Vietnam War, was my choice. In 1968, the year that saw a huge troop build-up, I was a college senior living at home. Like so many other families, we watched the news and video footage of the war over dinner. I knew I wouldn't be drafted; no females in combat. If the war lasted too long, my brother could get a college deferment or maybe he'd get a good draft number. Running to Canada was not an option. Much later, I heard some bizarre stories. One young man lost 60 pounds taking him down to 155. Another young man showed up at his draft board wrapped in Christmas tree lights powered by some kind of battery clipped to his belt. Another put one leg in a cast from knee to ankle and exercised his *other* leg. When he chipped off his homemade cast, his legs appeared to belong to two different people; one leg was pale with no muscle tone, and the other leg was tanned and strong. These ideas didn't come from the Internet, that's for sure. Not in 1968.

Chapter 138 advertised my course in its newsletter in 1993 that I was looking for Vietnam vets to talk informally with my college students and anyone else who showed up. (The biggest complaint came from my students who were missing *Seinfeld*.)

That first Thursday, one Vietnam vet showed up and introduced himself. Bobby Ward. One? Had I made a dreadful mistake? I found out later that Bobby came just to check us out. Who was I, and why did I want the vets to come? Did I have an agenda? Did the students want them to be there? What would be the students' reactions to these former soldiers?

That Thursday program with Bobby could have lasted all night, although I wouldn't have believed it when the first question was "How many people did you kill?" Well, I didn't expect that one. Bobby didn't seem surprised. He said that he didn't know. When his unit was fired upon, he shot back into the jungle. "I wasn't going looking for no dead bodies. No tellin' what was in there." Four hours later I asked everyone to save some questions for next week. (If there was to be a program next week.) Students followed Bobby out, reluctant to let him go. One of my former students, Chris, hesitant about enrolling in an honors course made his best friend Joe take it, too. Chris was hooked that Thursday. He wrote in his journal, "Last night was Magic." Indeed it was.

We must have passed inspection because the next Thursday, Bobby brought along another Vietnam vet from the chapter, and a few newcomers trickled in. But Johnny was spared what we began to call the Terrible Questions—"How many people did you kill" and "How does it feel to kill someone?" My students were prepared to jump in with a question of their own if someone's question sounded as if it were going to be Terrible.

Thursday nights brought more vets, different vets, two or three or four. I never knew who was coming. Eventually we had a core of four men with others dropping in for a Thursday or two. Halfway through the semester, the wives of the vets contacted me. Could they sit in? They were jealous, they said, because apparently my students were hearing about *their* husbands' tours when the wives themselves knew very little. They also wanted to talk with my students, to have their own Thursday night as long as their husbands didn't come. One night, we had a family: Johnny, one of our regulars, his wife Diane, and their daughter Dee who had just joined the Army. We learned so much from all of them because we just talked—no lectures, no handouts, no ties and jackets. Our vets, as we came to call them, were gracious with their time, their energy, and their patience. Going to the Wall with them is something all of us will treasure. One of our vets who couldn't make himself go for years walked through holding the hand of one of my students. "I did it, I did it," he said to my student—and both were in tears. Me, too.

Thank you, Heather Casto, for asking Johnny how she could get her father, a veteran, to talk with her about the war. "Welcome him home." She then walked over to Johnny and welcomed him home. The emotion they showed will stay with me forever. Thank you, Chris Armes, for asking the same question of each vet: "How do you think the war changed you?" We learned so much from the different answers each gave. Thank you, our vets and families: George Albright, Jim Bowman, Kathy Bowman, Al Davis, Randall Fletcher, Frank Longaker, Carolyn Parsons, Diane Phillips, Johnny Phillips, Dee Phillips, James Ratcliff, Lee Thacker, Bobby Ward, Joyce Ward, and Banjo Williams. They gave up their Thursday evenings to teach us. Welcome home.

INTRODUCTION

HOW DO WE talk about a war? In the United States, wars are won, never lost. The government issues reports on the money spent, the jobs created, the number of troops sent, and the number brought home. The government issues reports on technical improvements to weapons, equipment, armored vehicles, and airplanes. The government seems busy collecting information and churning out information. No matter what we face, no matter what the cost, we will win.

What happens, however, if who won and who lost is in dispute? One Vietnam vet told me that of course we won the war. "You don't see a Vietnam flag flying at the White House, do you?" His buddy, another Vietnam vet, frowned and said the government didn't let us win because it was all politics. The military watched Washington run the war. So we couldn't shut down the Ho Chi Minh Trail that was North Vietnam's supply route because it bordered Laos and Cambodia giving easy entrance. No, we had our hands tied. We didn't take territory and hold it; we took some prisoners and killed others; we didn't know who the enemy was so we couldn't shoot unless we were fired upon; in Saigon, people we thought were innocent civilians had booby-trapped baby carriages and tossed grenades and stole what they could.

Everybody's got an opinion. So whom can we trust? Soldiers. The people who were there. They watched, listened, talked, fought, hid, and killed. Many died doing what the government asked of them, so they can't tell their stories. But others can.

Let's listen to them. Yes, it's been over forty years. They come to us as strangers, but perhaps they won't always be. After all, one of them might be your uncle who flies an American flag every day. One of them might be your mechanic who wears a POW button on his uniform. One might be your bank's president who has a vanity license plate that says *Semper Fi*. Once a Marine, always a Marine. One could be your ex-husband who took his secrets from the war with him when he left. One could be your mother who teaches nursing. Many questions may be answered here.

This book is written in code. Our American soldiers learned the code from the soldiers around them. So here's the code that I hope unlocks the door that separates the soldiers who went to war from those who love them and from those who want to know about history. The code is infantry-speak, grunt style. Their words, their photos, and their poetry are all history to respect, to remember, and to pass on to others.

A grunt in country.

The grunt was an infantryman, Army or Marine, drafted or more-likely a volunteer. One tour was 12 months for the Army infantry, 12 months plus an extra 20 days for being a Marine. One Vietnam vet told me he could count down how much longer until his tour was over down to the minute. Soldiers planning for one and done kept count on what they called their short-timer's stick or cartoon or girlie-girlie poster. Break off part of the stick after the day is over whenever that happens to be, or tear off a piece of poster, saving the funniest or sexiest for last. No more stick, a final rip on the poster, and you knew you could head back to the World on your Freedom Bird, the plane that takes you away from Vietnam; some soldiers thought it didn't exist, that it wasn't part of any world. They will explain that and more, maybe more than we thought we wanted to know.

A NOTE ON LANGUAGE

We are now infantrymen, grunts, with some drop-ins such as reporters, photographers, a television crew, movie stars, and a general now and then. Coming to support the troops, we know. Our language conveys violence in a violent world: ("Get that motha-fucker"); sexual words used in non-sexual situations show violence and aggression ("Fuck you"); language can show indifference when the real feeling is exactly the opposite. ("It don't mean nothing") said over one of our dead soldiers is a survival technique; we toss it off and go on about our business. Language comforts when the absurdity of Vietnam comes at us. ("There it is") when a body bag tumbles out of a helicopter. What else can we expect in this crazy war that other grunts say it isn't real, doesn't exist, is a dream. Language also puts icing on a shit cake: neutralize not kill; navigational misdirection for bombing errors. Military operations hide behind their names: search and destroy means go find some gooks and kill them; Operation Apache means drop defoliants and herbicides to destroy trees, grasses, and bushes over at least 1.7 million acres of land possibly destroyed forever.

We personalize our equipment and use nicknames, all to create a familiarity with everything around us in this strange country. Puff the Magic Dragon (a big helicopter), Freedom Bird, White Mice (Saigon police and their white gloves), shake-and-bake (an instant lieutenant, barely through basic), Monopoly money (we're not paid in money but in certificates), the Jolly Green Giant (a bigger helicopter), Mad Minute (fire like crazy), WHAM (Winning Hearts and Minds), and Ho Chi Minh sandals (made from cast-off rubber). We can laugh at these because laughter and humor are natural impulses; why should they disappear in a war? Why can't we laugh at a grunt that sleeps with his M16 that somehow goes off? There it is. That's the 'Nam.

A machine gunner and a rifleman fire at the enemy.

An infantry patrol moving up to assault Viet Cong.

THAT TIME, THAT PLACE, THAT WAR

"War is an ugly thing, but not the ugliest of things. The decayed and degraded state of moral and patriotic feeling which thinks that nothing is worth war is much worse. The person who has nothing for which he is willing to fight, nothing which is more important than his own personal safety, is a miserable creature and has no chance of being free unless made and kept so by the exertions of better men than himself."

—John Stuart Mill

Winning hearts and minds.

Winning hearts and minds.

ALPHA (A)

> "There's nothing so embarrassing as when
> things go wrong in a war."
> —Michael Herr, *Dispatches*

○ **A-Team.** Twelve-man team of US Special Forces known as Green Berets. These elite soldiers mostly fought alone in remote places accessible only by helicopter. They were trained to fight guerillas through unconventional warfare, including political subversion and psychological operations. "Nicknamed the 'Green Berets,' the Special Forces had been created in the early 1950s with the mission of organizing guerrilla forces behind enemy lines. As a natural corollary to their guerrilla mission, they also began to develop a counter-guerrilla doctrine" (Dunnigan and Nofi 168).

Reporter Michael Herr saw a sign in the Special Forces A Camp that read, "If you kill for money you're a mercenary. If you kill for pleasure you're a sadist. If you kill for both you're a Green Beret" (257). President Kennedy, upon watching increased Vietcong guerilla activity, ordered anti-guerilla training for US troops. The Special Forces also included the Navy SEALS, LRRPS (pronounced Lurps), and CIA operatives. In the Vietnam War, the "most successful operations against the Viet Cong and the North Vietnamese were by small groups of specialists in irregular warfare. These were the Army Special Forces, the Navy SEALS, CIA operatives, and several other groups" (Dunnigan and Nofi 168).

○ **Ace of Spades.** Vietnam was not the first war where the ace of spades was used by American soldiers—this time as a psychological weapon in the Vietnam War. "US troops believed that Vietnamese traditions held the symbolism of the spade to mean death and ill-fortune and in a bid to scare away NLF [VC] soldiers without a firefight, it was common practice to leave an ace of spades on the bodies of killed Vietnamese and even to litter the forested grounds and fields with the card" (Wikipedia).

Bicycle Secret Weapon.

"This custom was believed to be so effective, that the United States Playing Card Company was asked by Charlie Company, 2nd Battalion 35th Infantry Regiment, and 25th Infantry Division to supply crates of that single card in bulk. The crates were often marked with '*Bicycle Secret Weapon*'" (Wikipedia).

A Japanese reporter, Katsuichi Honda noticed, "Those things most precious to peasants were not worth a straw in the eyes of these soldiers. But, there was one thing which one of them put into his pocket. It was a pack of playing cards found in a shelter. Strangely enough, however, all the cards of the pack were aces" (42-43).

A lot of soldiers "believed that the ace of spades was a bad omen to the Vietnamese, so . . . many others decorated their helmet covers with them" (Ebert 204). Many grunts put messages on their helmets, too. Michael Herr reports seeing, "Yea, though I walk through the Valley of the Shadow of Death I shall fear no Evil, because I am the meanest motherfucker in the Valley!" (87); "HELL SUCKS"; "TIME IS ON MY SIDE"; "JUST YOU AND ME, GOD—RIGHT?" (74). "FAR FROM FEARLESS"; "AVENGER V"; "BORN TO LOSE"; "BORN TO DIE" (74).

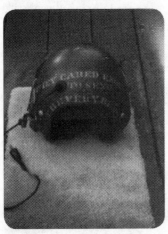

US borrows Hallmark Card motto: "We care enough to send the very best."

"Antimilitary slogans became common later in the war: 'Re up?—Throw up' or FTA (fuck the army). Peace symbols were literally everywhere" (Ebert 204).

The symbols and slogans personalized the uniform each had to wear. "The peace symbol surprised me in a way, but was understandable. I don't really know why it surprised me, but it seemed soldiers would carry something, maybe from home. But I know they wanted peace" (Erin, Vet Program 1/28/93). "Home states and the names of girlfriends or wives were prevalent. Other slogans on helmets included: 'Home is where you dig it' or 'God Bless Du Pont Chemicals' or 'Defoliate and Napalm' or 'Just You and Me Lord' or 'If You Can Read This You're Too Close'" (Ebert 204).

○ **AFRVN—Armed Forces Radio in Vietnam.** "More than the Vietnam War, music defined the 1960s, and the music followed the troops to Vietnam" (Dunnigan and Nofi 157). "Those songs provided the war with its own distinctive music; but they provided more than that. They offered the men who were there a rhetoric and a set of attitudes—brash, anti-establishment, often explicitly anti-war. Armies are traditionally and necessarily authoritarian and disciplined; but the music this army moved to was neither of those, was indeed the opposite (Hynes 185). Rock 'n Roll Forever.

Adrian Cronauer, an Airman from Roanoke, Virginia, who was in Vietnam beginning in 1962, found himself a radio announcer on AFRVN in May of 1965. In a speech at Radford University, Radford, Virginia in 1992, Cronauer said, "I tried to make AF radio sound like a stateside radio station." First of all, he said, he wanted music to be a morale factor. "Many of our young men, just in their teens, had never even been out of their own state. The music I hoped would be an antidote to culture shock." Cronauer is the soldier who began what became a ritual:

G-O-O-D M-O-R-N-I-N-G *V-I-E-T-N-A-M!*

Cronauer brought music, ads, and gimmicks to Vietnam. Two of his public service announcements: "Malaria pill, special, Tuesday only" or "Mail Christmas packages by November 1 to beat the rush" or "New fatigues on the way. Reserve yours now." He also sponsored gag contests; for example: "send $37.50 plus eight copies of orders for a free getaway to Point Barrow, Alaska."

Was it appropriate for the AFRVN to have humor? Cronauer said yes—"How can you ignore this aspect of our lives—all aspects, even humor in a war, exist over a year's time." Cronauer's favorite compliment came from an Air Force pilot who, on hearing the station, thought he was back home. "Thanks for getting me through 'Nam" the pilot told Cronauer.

Since the AFRVN paid no royalties, there were copyright problems. To solve them, record companies sent a master tape to LA; a master record was cut on an AFR label, and then sent overseas. Any DJ could play any record; there was no censorship in the music. The military did have material censored. Certain events had to be cleared by the military before Cronauer could broadcast it. Cronauer said there were some legitimate reasons why some information wasn't on the radio: a one-person guerilla incident in Saigon; the bombing of a popular restaurant in Saigon; General Westmoreland has called for an additional 200,000 troops. Don't give them news they can use, he was told. Not even the weather.

The AFR bureaucracy wouldn't allow him to share over the network anything that might prove embarrassing to the United States. He wasn't permitted to warn the soldiers about prostitutes. He couldn't even broadcast the Pope's message for peace because it might be interpreted as anti-war. The military also changed words for him to report. He gave this example: a pilot just back from a raid when interviewed said he was exhilarated; it was changed to gratified. What the bureaucracy didn't realize was that its own network was passing on information to the troops; its DJs between the rock music used double-entendres that went right over the heads of the censors: be on the lookout for roaches in the walls—which meant get your marijuana cigarettes (roaches) someplace safe.

Cronauer said that what serves the United States well is that the military doesn't trust the media and the media doesn't trust the military. In ideas, he said, freedom works best; in wartime the military rules by fiat. The best solution, however, he said was more free speech, more free media that can be accurate. Then he explained that not every soldier was in the field. Support troops did the work that allowed enlisted combat soldiers to serve out in the field and be resupplied when needed. Cronauer said it took 12-15 people—cooking, cleaning, resupplying, checking choppers, servicing vehicles, putting in gas, unloading planes—to keep one combat soldier in the field. He predicted there would be billions of different stories of the war in the future— "like a mosaic, billions of tiles, to represent the billions of stories" (Speech at Radford University, September 16, 1992).

Dr. Byron Holley, drafted in late 1967 as a surgeon, wrote on April 10, 1969 to his girlfriend, later to become his wife: "Well, Baby, I am lying around the old aid station tonight, listening to AFRVN radio, and they are playing *'Please Release Me'* by Engelbert Humperdinck. It really reminds me of you and just how much I love you and miss you. Music is such an important morale factor over here. Between mail call and the music from AFRVN, I somehow manage to avoid going out of my tree. There is one real crazy DJ over here who starts off each morning show with a long-drawn-out 'Good morning, Viet-nam!' and then he starts cracking on the place and what a bummer it is for us to have to be over here, halfway around the world away from our loved ones. I don't know how he gets away with it, but the troops really love him" (154). Herr reports hearing "moving right along here with our fabulous Sounds of the Sixties, AFRVN, Armed Forces Radio Network, Vietnam, and for all you guys in the First of the Forty-fourth, and especially for the Soul Brother in the Orderly Room, here's Otis Redding—the *immortal* Otis Redding, singing *'Dock of the Bay'''* (137). Another DJ was Pat Sajak, now host of a popular game show "Wheel of Fortune." Sajak joined the Army, was assigned to be a finance clerk, a job in the rear, but managed to get transferred to AFRVN in Saigon as a morning disk jockey. He said "The Good Morning thing was already in place" (e-mail to writer Nov. 8, 2010).

THE MUSIC

Without the context of war, the popular music chosen by the disk jockeys was simply groovy or hip. At the senior proms back home, girls with pink carnation corsages, boys yanking at ties that didn't fit, chaperones with arms crossed, shaking their heads while watching the kids do the monkey and the boogaloo to the rock 'n roll music, a boy slipping cheap vodka into the punch of orange sherbet and ginger ale, couples slipping out of the gym to make out in cars in the parking lot, a few fast girls smoking joints outside with an English teacher, celebrating with McDonald's hamburgers, the new fast food chain. Few at the prom were thinking about college, student deferments, or the war.

So thousands and thousands of miles away, it was a rock-and-roll war (Hynes 185). Those same songs put grunts in a Jeep in Vietnam singing along, poking each other, one grunt standing, bopping to the music. "These were last year's football players, pool-playing dropouts from down the block, drag-racing steelworkers' sons who got their girls in trouble at the drive-in movie on warm summer nights, crew-cut ranchers' sons from Kansas" (Anderson *The Grunts* 74). But the music was part of them and part of the war. "The music said much about the war, and the troops knew it" (Dunnigan and Nofi 159). You listen to the lyrics differently when you're in a war. Even the song titles suggest something about war.

'*The Letter*' (the Box Tops) indicated how important mail from home was. '*Leaving on a Jet Plane*' (Peter, Paul, and Mary) was all about the most important event in a soldier's experience, the end of his tour and his trip home on a Freedom Bird. '*We've Gotta Get Out of This Place*' (the Animals) expressed a widely held sentiment about life in the bush, as did '*Paint It Black*' (the Rolling Stones). '*The Dock of the Bay*' (Otis Redding) was popular because of the way it referred to San Francisco, the last part of America many soldiers saw before being flown to Vietnam . . . . Creedence Clearwater Revival (CCR) produced numerous songs that were very popular with the troops. Among the most heard were '*Proud Mary*' and '*Bad Moon Rising*.' Tunes with a driving beat were often favored. Most popular of these types was '*Wooly Bully*' (Sam the Sham & the Pharaohs). And then, '*W A R—What is it good for?*' (Edwin Starr) chanted by the troops.

"Filling out the Vietnam hit parade were: '*A Whiter Shade of Pale*' (Procol Harum), '*All Along the Watchtower*' (Jimi Hendrix), '*Aquarius/Let the Sunshine In*' (the Fifth Dimension), '*As Tears Go By*' (the Rolling Stones), '*Babe, I'm Gonna Leave You*' (Led Zepplin), '*Baby Love*' (Diana Ross and the Supremes), '*Ballad of Ira Hayes*' (Johnny Cash), '*Billy and Sue*' (B.J. Thomas), '*Black is Black*' (Los Bravos), '*Black Magic Woman*' (Santana), '*Bobby McGee*' (Bobby Gentry and Glen Campbell), '*Born on the Bayou*' (CCR), '*Burning Bridges*' (the Mike Curb Congregation), '*Coming Home Soldier*' (Bobby Vinton), '*Crimson and Clover*' (Tommy James and the Shondells), '*Darling Be Home Soon*' (the Lovin' Spoonful), '*Dazed and Confused*' (Jake Holmes), '*Different Drum*' (Linda Ronstadt and the Stone Poneys), '*Do You Believe in Magic*' (the Lovin' Spoonful), '*Don't Worry, Baby*' (the Beach Boys), '*Draft Dodger Rag*' (Phil Ochs), '*Drive On*' (Johnny Cash), '*Eve of Destruction*' (Barry McGuire),

'*For What It's Worth*' (Buffalo Springfield), '*Fortunate Son*' (CCR), '*Galveston*' (Glen Campbell), '*Get Off of My Cloud*' (the Rolling Stones), '*Good Morning Starshine*' (Oliver), '*Goodnight Saigon*' (Billy Joel), '*Hang on Sloopy*' (the McCoys), '*Have You Ever Seen The Rain*' (CCR), '*Heartbreaker*' (the Crystals), '*Hey Joe*' (Jimi Hendrix), '*Hey Jude*' (the Beatles), '*House of the Rising Sun*' (the Animals), '*I Heard It Through the Grapevine*' (Marvin Gaye), '*I Wish It Would Rain*' (the Temptations), '*I Feel Like I'm Fixin' to Die Rag*' (Country Joe McDonald & the Fish), '*I'm a Believer*' (the Monkees), '*In the Year 2525*' (Zager & Evans), '*Is There Anybody Here*' (Phil Ochs), '*Judy in Disguise*' (John Fred & the Playboys), '*Let's Spend the Night Together*' (the Rolling Stones), '*Light My Fire*' (the Doors), '*Long As I Can See the Light*' (CCR), '*Lookin' Out My Back Door*' (CCR), '*Louie Louie*' (the Kingsmen), '*Love the One You're With*' (Stephen Stills), '*Me and You and a Dog Named Boo*' (Lobo), '*Monday, Monday*' (Mamas & the Papas), '*Mr. Lonely*' (Bobby Vinton), '*My Girl*' (the Temptations), '*Nowhere Man*' (the Beatles), '*Ode to Billy Joe*' (Bobbie Gentry), '*Okie from Muskogee*' (Merle Haggard), '*One*' (Three Dog Night), '*Positively 4th Street*' (Bob Dylan), '*Presence of the Lord*' (Blind Faith), '*Proud Mary*' (Ike and Tina Turner), '*Purple Haze*' (Jimi Hendrix), '*Radio V-I-E-T-N-A-M*' (Bell & Shore), '*Reach Out, I'll Be There*' (the Four Tops), '*Rescue Mission*' (Kris Kristofferson), '*Ruby, Don't Take Your Love to Town*' (Kenny Rogers), '*Run Through the Jungle*' (CCR), '*(I Can't Get No) Satisfaction*' (the Rolling Stones), '*Sgt. Pepper's Lonely Hearts Club Band*' (the Beatles), '*Sherry*' (the Four Seasons), '*Silver Medals and Sweet Memories*' (the Statler Brothers), '*Snoopy Vs. the Red Baron*' (the Royal Guardsman), '*Soldier Boy*' (the Shirelles), '*Soul Deep*' (the Box Tops), '*Stand By Your Man*' (Tammy Wynette), '*Star-Spangled Banner*' (Jimi Hendrix), '*Still in Saigon*' (the Charlie Daniels Band), '*Sugar Pie, Honey Bunch*' (the Four Tops), '*Susie Q*' (CCR), '*These Boots Are Made for Walkin*' (Nancy Sinatra), '*Tighten Up*' (Archie Bell & the Drells), '*Unchained Melody*' (Righteous Brothers), '*Up Around The Bend*' (CCR), '*Veterans Day*' (Tom Russell), '*Vietnam Blues*' (Dave Dudley), '*Walk Like a Man*' (the Four Seasons), '*What's Going On*' (Marvin Gaye), '*When a Man Loves a Woman*' (Percy Sledge), '*Whole Lotta Love*' (Led Zeppelin), '*You Didn't Have to Be So Nice*' (the Lovin' Spoonful)" (Dunnigan and Nofi 157-159). (Note: song titles were bolded to make reading easier.)

"And then there was Vietnam veteran and Special Forces NCO S. SGT Barry Sadler who had three hit songs, all of them hitting a responsive chord with the troops in the bush: '*The Ballad of the Green Berets,*' '*I'm a Lucky One*' and '*Trooper's Lament*'" (Dunnigan and Nofi 159).

Of course, opinions about the rock 'n roll show differ. Back in Vietnam after a quick trip home for a funeral, Ed Emanuel, a member of an all-black LRRP team called the

Soul Patrol, woke up his first morning to the "Gooooooood Morning Vietnam!" He was thinking, not that again. "The Armed Forces Radio disc jockeys felt a need to entertain the troops in Vietnam with a cheerful beginning to the day. The 'goooooooood morning' commentary was for those 'REMF' (rear echelon motherfuckers) who didn't have to go to the boonies and fight the war. Each morning that we had to listen to that noise, other [LRRPS] and I routinely responded to the expression with a loud and vocal chorus of 'Kiss my ass!' Yeah, it was easy for those REMF to have a good morning; they didn't have to face Charlie" (77-78). Bobby Ward, Vietnam vet, thought that the music was not entertaining, that instead it was a great divider. "There were the **Heads**—who smoked pot and listened to rock. Then there were the **Juicers**—who drank and listened to country music" (Vet Program 02/04/93).

○ *Agent Blue, Agent Orange, and Agent White.* When the United States realized how at risk its soldiers were going to be because the VC could maneuver unseen under the protection of the triple canopy jungle, it instigated Operation Ranch Hand. "*Only you can prevent forests.* That was the motto of Operation Ranch Hand, perhaps the world's largest deliberate destruction of a natural environment for military purposes.... The operation began proper in 1962. C-123 aircrafts swooped over the jungle, each aircraft carrying enough Agent Orange to reduce 300 acres of virgin forest to a desolate brown

The effect of defoliant on nature.

wasteland full of dead and decaying plants. The operation peaked in 1967 when 1.7 million acres of land were doused in the defoliant" (Daugherty and Mattson 197). "It was chemical warfare pure and simple. Its defenders had the arrogance to maintain that what would kill trees would not hurt people, or American people anyway" (Safer 106). Our troops, however, waded in water that had been affected and drank water in-country purified by iodine tablets—with no proof or any thought to what could purify water contaminated by various defoliants.

"The United States appears to have used about 90,000 tons of herbicide in Vietnam to clear away the undergrowth alongside roads and around base camps, so the enemy would not be able to get in close for attacks or ambushes. The use of herbicides in Vietnam undoubtedly saved American lives" (Dunnigan and Nofi 136). It is crucial to note that the "use of herbicides for defoliation and crop destruction was primarily an operation of the government of South Vietnam, supported by US assets and expertise" (Hay 90). Unfortunately, the military results were negligible because the VC quickly adjusted to this destruction and changed tactics.

(Note: the names of these chemicals came from the color markings banded on the containers in which they were shipped (Hay 90). One of our veterans rolled barrels with *orange* banding into C-123s; sometimes ugly red bumps and splotches pop up on one arm. In pain, he goes to a local VA hospital. The diagnosis is different each time. Poison ivy, poison oak, fungal infection, allergies—but nothing connected to Agent Orange (Vet Program 02/25/93).)

Agent Blue was a drying agent that caused "leaves to drop off but [would] not necessarily kill the plant itself. In Vietnam new foliage may grow back within thirty to ninety days after applying Blue" (Hay 90). Purple and Blue reached Vietnam in 1962 (Hay 90).

Agent Orange was probably the worst: "a known carcinogen [and] ... the most widely used. About 90 percent of it was used for defoliation, about 8 percent for crop destruction, and about 2 percent to clear base perimeters, roads and so forth" (Dunnigan and Nofi 136). Orange eventually kills the plant because [the plant] absorbs the agent (Hay 90). Defoliation was about 90% of the sorties [a single flying mission is one sortie]; crop destruction, 10%. Each sortie could drop 700-800 gallons (Hay 90). Years later, Brownmiller, a news writer for ABC during the war, discovered the irony of Agent Orange:

Agent Orange kills.

"Vietnam's doctors and scientists placed a low priority on rigorous, expensive studies of the lasting effects of Agent Orange. They had more pressing national health problems to deal with. Vietnam is an impoverished tropical country beset by malaria, malnutrition, hepatitis B, encephalitis, dengue fever, and parasites, and hampered by a polluted water supply, a Third World sanitation system, and an almost total lack of antibiotics" (139).

Agent Purple was both a defoliant and an herbicide. It was ten times more dangerous than Agent Orange. Even in 1973, the VA recognized Agent Purple caused soft tissue cancer (Johnny Phillips, Vet Program 02/04/93).

Agent White was an herbicide and the second in use behind Agent Orange.

○ *Airborne.* Soldiers with parachutes trained to jump from a chopper/plane that has taken them on a mission.

Parachute
by Randy Cribbs

Floating, suspended
By soft billowy wings,
Held together by only
Silken strings.

Silence, as in a chasm,
Vast, deep, wide;
Billowing canopy,
Rolling, like the tide;
Other like you,
Side by side.

That brief time when
Noise does not exist
And clouds touch
With a soft kiss.

Man preparing to jump from helicopter.

Then, too soon,
Coming quickly,
The ground;
And with it,
Sound.
Changed,
This warm summer day
And this meadow
Sweet with hay.
No longer a sea of green;
Gone,
With my collapsing wings. (47)

Airborne dropping men into battle.

◦ **Airmobile.** Soldiers helicopter-borne. They jump to the ground with no parachutes usually with chopper hovering over the site. They hope the chopper has gotten them there faster than the VC could find them. Or that they didn't jump on a mine.

One soldier, Gene Woodley, during Airmobile jumped off a chopper about ten feet right on a punji stake, a pointed stake of bamboo well hidden. "It was about two feet long, sticking up in the ground. I don't know if my weight or whatever pulled the stake loose. But I just kept running because there was no use stopping. It went right through my boot, my foot, everything. It just protruded through the top of the boot.

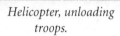

Helicopter, unloading troops.

Soldiers jumping out of helicopter.

I couldn't get the boot off. And I was told not to pull it through the leather . . . . They would get me out as soon as possible, but not immediately, 'cause they couldn't jeopardize the mission by comin' back out and get us. They didn't get me out for three days. My foot swell up inside my boot. They had to cut the boot off. It just happened that I was lucky that it wasn't human urine on the stake, or my foot would've been amputated from infection" (Terry 244-245).

◦ **AIT.** "Advanced infantry training, which usually follows basic training for enlisted personnel" (Terry 299). But it's more than that. Being trained to leave base camps and pursue the enemy wasn't enough, so advanced meant being proficient in light weapons and military tactics. "They were [also] taught to kill close up and would witness firsthand the results of doing so. Thus soldiers bound for AIT tended to undergo an accompanying shift in mood" (Ebert 54). To kill close up required overcoming "the average individual's deep-seated-resistance to killing" (Grossman 252). Special Forces were trained to kill face-to-face.

So in training, soldiers were rewarded for shooting at man-shaped targets that popped up sporadically. The target fell backwards (as if shot) and the shooter was praised. Soldiers not firing quickly enough to engage (that is, kill) the target were punished lightly. This training was called "quick shoot" (Grossman 253). Through training and rehearsal of this process, the soldier "when he does kill in combat he is able to, at one level, deny to himself that he is actually killing another human being . . . he has only 'engaged' another target" (Grossman 255-256). As one of our vets said, he was brainwashed by the Army (Vet Program, Bobby Ward 01/14/93).

○ **AK-47.** "Soviet-made assault rifle copied by Chinese and used by Communist forces in Vietnam" (Terry 299). This weapon was also known as the Kalashnikov, and it was "sturdy, reliable, compact, and relatively lightweight" (Olson 16). The AK-47 could fire like a machine gun as long as the trigger was held down. It also had a "high muzzle velocity (speed of the bullet after firing) and the tumbling action of the bullet" (16) which caused massive damage to a human body.

○ **Allied Forces.** From 1964-1972, we were assisted with military personnel from Australia, Korea, Thailand, New Zealand, and the Philippines. Each year, Korea sent the most; from 1966-1972, Korea sent about 47,500 personnel. Far greater than Thailand's high of 11,586 in 1970; New Zealand's high of 552 in 1969; the Philippines' high of 2,061 in 1966. Australian support, given its resources, was a high of 7,661.

Canada was a quiet ally. About 40,000 enlisted in the US armed forces. Other supporters may have been observers, technical advisors, relief workers, and medical personnel: Argentina, Britain, the Republic of China, Spain, and West Germany. (All information from Dunnigan and Nofi 64-65.)

○ **Aluminum boxes.** Bodies returned to the US in aluminum boxes. "In the last possible hour of the last possible day in the least sensible of all ways to do it, Roland Epps had won his plastic body bag with the big long zipper. About one hundred twenty of their son's one hundred seventy-two pounds were sent home to Mr. and Mrs. Epps" (Anderson *The Grunts* 165). A military man in dress uniform comes to the door to break the news.

○ **Amerasian.** Chuck, new to his unit, learned about a different dark side of the war from Thanh, his Vietnamese female interpreter. She introduced him "to the most shameful facet of the American involvement in Vietnam, the side of the war that never made it on the evening news. The unmentioned result of sending over two and a half million Americans to Vietnam without wives were several hundred thousand illegitimate children. Very few fathers of such children acknowledged and helped support them. Most fathers simply deserted by following their transfer orders back to the States. Mothers left with mixed-blood illegitimate children [called *bui doi* for 'dust of life'] were usually ill-equipped to support young children—the only job 'skills' most had were those required by bar hostesses and prostitutes. More devastating was the humiliation and discrimination to which unmarried mothers and their illegitimate offspring were subjected. Children born of white or black Western men and Vietnamese women stand out in a Vietnamese crowd. They are immediately noticed, pointed at, and gossiped about for their 'strange' looks, and rejected for their racial 'impurity.' Their mothers are shunned for prostituting themselves to foreign soldiers. Under such severe social pressure many mothers abandoned their children, and every Vietnamese city had its colony of mixed-blood orphans living in the streets" (Anderson *Other War* 97-98).

Later Thanh took me to visit a Catholic church in a part of town off-limits to Americans. More than 300 children lived there, Thanh told me.

Amerasian & Asian orphans attend USO Easter party, March 28, 1970.

Chuck tries to put this into perspective. "So here it is, another kind of Body Count. More than three hundred. Most Americans in Vietnam were interested in the body count of dead enemy troops. But here was another kind of body count, produced by Americans, a body count of the living, not the dead. The living and the rejected—rejected by all the world except a handful of French Catholic priests and nuns" (Anderson *Other War* 99).

Spec. 5 Emmanuel J. Holloman married a Vietnamese woman, Tran Thi Saly, in 1968. The papers required to allow her to come to America were not completed by the end of Holloman's tour. He says, "When the paper work did get approved, it was too late. I was shipped home." He didn't get back to Vietnam until 1971, but couldn't find her right away. About all he could do was buy gifts for her and her mother. But after 1974, he didn't hear from the mother again. "I'm told that they mistreat or maybe killed a lot of kids that, you know, were black. I just hope the baby was able to pass for Cambodian. Then she won't have a problem" (Terry 84-85).

○ ***Anti-war demonstrators.*** This was the 60s, and a whole generation heard turn on (do drugs), tune in (connect, listen), and drop out (do whatever). Anti-war songs that went to #1: '***The Eve of Destruction***' (Barry McGuire), one week in 1965; '***Ballad of the Green Berets***' (Sgt. Barry Sadler), five weeks in 1966; '***People Got to be Free***' (The Rascals), five weeks in 1968; '***Aquarius/Let the Sun Shine in***' (The Fifth Dimension), for six weeks in 1969; '***War***' (Edwin Starr), three weeks in 1970; '***Give me Love/Give me Peace on Earth***' (George Harrison), one week in 1973. Other popular anti-war songs were Stephen Still's '***For What it's Worth***' and Buffy St. Marie's '***Universal Soldier***' and '***Where Have All the Flowers Gone?***'

One song that stayed around forever was Country Joe and the Fish's '***I'm Fixing to Die Rag***.' It was played at Woodstock and was also played on AFRVN, a surprise because of its powerful anti-war lyrics. What follows is the opening stanza.

I-Feel-Like-I'm-Fixin'-To-Die-Rag

Oh this is, this is just a try out. It's not . . .
'Fixin'-To-Die-Rag', 'Fixin'-To-Die-Rag', Take 1.
One, two, three, four.

Well, come on all of you, big strong men,
Uncle Sam needs your help again.
Yeah, he's got himself in a terrible jam
Way down yonder in Vietnam
So put down your books and pick up a gun,
Gonna have a whole lotta fun.
And it's one, two, three,
What are we fighting for?
Don't ask me, I don't give a damn,
Next stop is Vietnam;
And it's five, six, seven,
Open up the pearly gates,
Well there ain't no time to wonder why,
Whoopee! we're all gonna die.

Dr. Lifton in working with Vietnam veterans learned many went into service with the image of John Wayne as soldier. It was a powerful image to take into battle. "All men in battle require elements of that imagery, having to do with courage and male group loyalty, or bonding, in order to cope with their fear of death, the concern with manhood, and the quest for higher purpose" (220). The wicked satire in the lyrics points to a war nobody understands—unless it's Uncle Sam. And he's keeping it a secret. Then there's the prediction that death is unavoidable followed by a contradictory "Whoopee!" That's hardly the war-time response. In the Vietnam War, "It don't mean nothing" was hug-yourself time. Shake off the horror and go on. In Basic Training, soldiers were taught to keep focused, to have eyes at the back of their heads, and to never stop to think. React. Do what you've been taught to do: quick kill; call in artillery; stay off the trail, and stay alert for your own protection and for the protection of your buddies counting on you.

One of the veterans Dr. Lifton worked with in his rap sessions (his term) said he listened to the song all the time, but it took him some time to really *hear* it (221). Once you *heard* it, you could face "the actuality of death [that] severely threatens the playful romance of the John Wayne image" (223).

John Wayne—Everybody's hero in war.

Professor Hung, a former NVA soldier, reported, "We had radios.... It was forbidden to listen to the stations in the South. At night we would listen to the news from Hanoi. Of course it always reported victories . . . and the student demonstrations in the United States were all reported in great detail. I know the names of the American universities just from listening to the war news" (Safer 102).

Most of the anti-war demonstrators were not countercultural or sexually promiscuous—they were just ordinary people. They were not cowards, afraid to fight. Many were harassed, put under surveillance, put on trial, or sent to jail (Zaroulis and Sullivan xii). One form of the protest against the war was to burn your draft card in public with others tossing their draft cards into the fire, too. That was illegal since a man was supposed to have his draft card at all times.

The protestors were not organized groups; "groups" tended to be campus-based, sometimes only ten or twenty core members; they were not "anti-American" (Zaroulis and Sullivan xiii)—they wanted to know what the government was doing and why. One of the Vietnam veterans from SW Virginia said when he came home, he thought he'd been fighting for the government; he didn't know he *wasn't* fighting for the American people as well. This distinction between the government's policy and the citizens' eventual understanding of that policy was made by Johnny who was 17 when he enlisted. Later, he sat with his daughter who joined the Army in 1993. Dee Phillips, Johnny's daughter, said, "I have a lot of resentment towards the peace movement during the war, and towards those who dodged the draft." Her father had a different view: "A lot *did* want to stop war. A lot didn't want to go. That was their right. I wasn't no hero for going when I got drafted. I was there to survive" (Vet Program 3/1/93).

Lynda Van Devanter, nurse in Vietnam, writes, "It hurts so much sometimes to see the paper full of demonstrators, especially people burning the flag. Fight fire with fire, we ask here. Display the flag, Mom and Dad, please, every day. And tell your friends to do the same. It means so much to us to know we're supported, to know not everyone feels we're making a mistake being here" (Edelman 233).

From PFC Stephen W. Pickett: "We were well informed about the demonstrations by both sides. Even though I'm here, I still have an open mind—realizing, of course, that an immediate pullout or anything of the sort is out of the question. It would degrade the heroic deaths of those who never returned because it would mean going back on everything that we have done. There are many here who feel as I do, but we will continue to fight for the country in which we believe" (Edelman 222).

Although grunts served in different parts of South Vietnam, they knew about the protestors. After all, television at base camps and USO havens showed what was happening, and they heard from home about them. "To the proud grunts, the loudmouth hippies back in the World were the most obvious of adversaries—they were guilty of two unforgivable acts. First, by their constant demonstrating they had poisoned the minds of many civilians, thereby preventing the latter from uniting behind the President so the war could be won or at least ended as fast as possible. Second, by their draft card burning and constant screaming, 'Ho, Ho, Ho Chi Minh, Viet Cong are gonna win,' the hippies had encouraged the North Vietnamese and Viet Cong to fight instead of seeing the light and surrendering. They had thus made the grunts' job of fighting those enemies infinitely more difficult; they had stabbed grunts in the back . . . . Small wonder the proud grunts came home aching to 'get my hands on one of them fucking hippy-bastards who was hiding behind his college deferment and waving a VC flag while my buddies was getting blowed all to hell, all to hell!'" (Anderson *The Grunts* 226-227).

Marine Lewis Puller, Jr. with devastating wounds, many surgeries, struggles with prostheses, was angry both with the protestors and also at himself. "It made me angry to see these college kids, with no frame of reference outside a classroom, second-guessing the decisions that had almost cost me my life, and it made me angrier still to think that they might be right" (269). Both groups shared, however, the same problem: their government's apparent lack of will. "Those who were bloodied in the hundreds of demonstrations against the war were also lied to and deceived, and tasted disillusion. They and the veterans have resolved to tolerate less abuse of authority and deception in life than previous generations" (Anderson *The Grunts* 233).

Some researchers after the war saw a different picture. "Critics of the war claimed that their opposition was a principled one, rooted in pacifism, respect for human dignity, and anti-imperialism. Many were. But not all. In fact, many of them seem to have been conscious supporters of the Communists, some were freelance agents of the Soviet Union, and some were on the KGB payroll. For example, in December 1976 a group of prominent former war protestors . . . publicly censured the Socialist Republic of Vietnam for violations of human rights. This elicited a swift and quite vicious reaction from many of their erstwhile allies in the anti-war movement, who severely criticized them for attacking a 'democratic socialist' government" (Dunnigan and Nofi 261).

Protestors were seen as "Communist dupes who took orders from Moscow, Peking, and Hanoi" . . . . The connection between the anti-war movement and any foreign power (especially any Communist country) was investigated a number of times. "No such link was ever found, despite intensive investigations by the Central Intelligence Agency (investigations illegal under its charter), the Federal Bureau of Investigation, and other government agencies" (Zaroulis and Sullivan xii).

Some were quiet protestors who felt guilty because they didn't know what to do. A high school student wrote the following poem identifying with the grunts while at the same regretting what she saw.

I Am A Veteran of Vietnam
by Sue Halpern

> I
> am a veteran
> of Vietnam
> I've been from
> Hamburger Hill to the DMZ
> and back again
> with a mere flick
> of my wrist.
> Through my own eyes
> I've seen people
> Tortured.
> Bombed.
> Burned.
> Destroyed.
> Beyond hope of recovery
> While I
> sit contently
> watching . . .
> and let it
> go on. (Rottmann 113)

○ *Ao baba.* Normal dress for male peasants. To American soldiers, the *ao baba* looked like black pajamas.

A male peasant, thought to be a Viet Cong.

Memorial For Man In Black Pajamas
by Jan Barry

Trinh Vo Man was a poet
in his own land a scholar
to his own people a venerable
and wise old man
in his village
throughout his native land
a warm and kind man
to his wife and children
and grandchildren
a humorous and tolerant man
to his neighbors
an hospitable man to all

til the blue-eyed visitors
came uninvited
and shot him

because a Man wearing
black pajamas.
to them
was just a slope, a dink, a gook
was 'Vietcong.' (Rottmann 94)

Little Man in Black
by Randy Cribbs

Minutes ago, my enemy;
Probably neither of us knew why.
Just two soldiers trying to survive,
And it was he to die.

Strange that I feel sad
For this little man in black,
Just another number
In the body count,
Added to the stack.

But I do mourn him.
As I hope others will,
And pray he is at heavens door;
This little man in black
Is my enemy no more. (13)

∘ **Ao dai.** A Vietnamese woman's dress. "The *ao dai* is fitted tight around the waist and over the hips and makes these slim, fragilely constructed women even more willowy. A street filled with them, their hair falling down their backs to their waists . . . is a remarkable sight. The swaying hair, glistening black in the sun, the gentle flapping of the *ao dai* make the street shimmer, as if seen through a heat haze" (Safer 204).

∘ **Apache Snow.** Name given to the operation to take Hill 937 (Kutler 47b). A vicious battle that raged

Vietnamese woman wearing traditional Ao Dai.

from May 10-20, 1969. It came to be called "Hamburger Hill" because of the specially-bloody, ten-day, up-hill battle.

"The US forces eventually took Hamburger Hill, but not without 272 support sorties (assignments) by the USAF, 450 tons of bombs, 69 tons of napalm, five infantry battalions of eighteen hundred men, and 10 batteries of artillery. Seventy Americans were killed, 372 wounded while 630+ soldiers in the North Vietnamese Army were killed. Another two fresh battalions were air-lifted in on May 19. Although US Forces took this hill (Ap Bia) near the Laotian border in the A Shau Valley, they abandoned it on June 5, 1969 (36 days later). The North Vietnamese retook the hill one month after we abandoned it" (Wikipedia).

"Troops in the 101st Airborne Division (Airmobile) even offered $10,000 to anyone who would kill the officer who ordered the bloody and pointless attack on Hamburger Hill" (Kutler 175). The outrage reached home as well. "Soon afterwards as a grim reminder that the war was far from over, *Life* published photographs of the two hundred and forty-two young Americans slain in a single week" (Karnow 601).

An American soldier tried to put this battle into the perspective of war: "It was the bare determination, not to take this hill or that one, but to survive this hell, to outlast that little slant-eyed, rice-powered bastard they chased no matter how many hills had to be humped or how many monsoons or 118° days had to be endured" (Anderson *The Grunts* 158).

One North Vietnam soldier, Bao Ninh, one of ten to survive from a brigade of 500 men, writes: "Often in the middle of a busy street, in broad daylight, I've suddenly become lost in a daydream. On smelling the stink of rotten meat I've suddenly imagined I was back crossing Hamburger Hill in [1969]. Walking over strewn corpses. The stench of death is often so overpowering I have to stop in the middle of the pavement, holding my nose . . ." (46).

Spec. 5 Light Bulb Bryant was never in the fight over Hill 937, but he could see the lunacy of fighting for territory, then letting it go. "And we weren't gaining any ground. We would fight for a hill all day, spend two days or two nights there, and then abandon the hill. Then maybe two, three months later, we would have to come back and retake the same piece of territory. Like this Special Forces camp outside Dak To. The camp was attacked one evening. Maybe two or three platoons flew up to give them some assistance. Then somehow headquarters decided we should close down that camp. So they ended up closing down. Two or three months later, we went back to the same area to retake it. We lost 20 men the first time saving it, 30-40 men the next time retaking it" (Terry 21).

US news reporting focused on a military strategy that appeared to have no purpose. Why take a hill then abandon it at a tremendous loss of life?

10 May 1969
Troops of the 101 Airborne Division
Engaged the enemy at the base
of Hill 937 in the Ashau Valley
10 days, 11 bloody assaults later,
Troops called it Hamburger Hill
****

If you are able
save for them a place
inside of you
and save one backward glance
when you are leaving
for the places they can
no longer go.

Be not ashamed to say
you loved them,
though you may
or may not have always.

Take what they have left
and what they have taught you
with their dying
and keep it with your own.

And in that time
when men decide and feel safe
to call the war insane
take one moment to embrace
those gentle heroes
you left behind.
> —Major Michael Davis O'Donnell
> Dak To, South Vietnam, Jan 1970
> (From *Hamburger Hill,* Dir John Irvin, Paramount 1987.)

The military was sensitive about an operation that became known as Hamburger Hill. So there were other word changes and restrictions as well: no more "hearts and minds"—instead, we're developing community spirit; "Search and destroy" became "search and clear" so as to protect the civilians; 22 common terms were dropped, including the much-abused body count. And no more "Five O'clock Follies" (Herr 99) instead, reporters are briefed. Herr had to shake his head at the new jargon: "frontier sealing, census grievance, black operations (pretty good, for jargon), revolutionary development, and armed propaganda. I asked a spook [spy] what that one meant and he just smiled. Surveillance, collecting and reporting, was like a carnival bear now, broken and dumb, an Intelligence beast, our own" (52).

○ **APC.** Armored personnel carrier. APCs ran on tank-tracks. One of the APCs, the M113, was the most versatile and valuable. It carried ten troops, a driver, an assistant, and a machine gun on top. It could be a defensive or offensive vehicle. Bobby drove an APC until his MOS, his military occupation specialty, was changed and he became a cook. "When we were part of a convoy, we had to stop sometimes. I slept in that APC a lot of times" (Vet Program 2/4/93).

○ **ARS. Army Ranger School.** Training for combat. Graduates were usually LRRPs (pronounced LURPS) that did long range reconnaissance. In a monograph written by the Department of the Army, "long-range patrol (LRP) was a particularly significant aspect of US operations in Vietnam. Such patrols were not new to the US Army, but they were used in increasing density and were now operating at division level. Long-range patrols were needed in Vietnam because of the difficult terrain assigned to the divisions and the elusiveness of the enemy. The helicopter and effective communications enabled the patrols to be more densely dispersed" (Hay 123).

○ **Article 15.** Non-judicial punishment for enlisted personnel. Since an Article 15 lowered the rank and pay of the soldier, it was taken seriously. Dr. Holley, with about four months left in his tour, was transferred to the 229th General Dispensary at Tan Son Nhut Air Base, headquarters of the MACV (MacVee), the Military Assistance Command Vietnam. He finds himself the replacement for a CO who "didn't give a damn, and he let things go pretty far" (177). Dr. Holley's efforts to yank the place back in shape meant that he became "a very unpopular person" (192). After three months, he and his new first sergeant do some kicking ass together.

Holley says, "All these assholes care about is getting stoned and screwing gooks, seven nights a week! I have issued more Article 15s in the past three months than were issued by all the COs over the past one-and one-half years. They really seem to hate my guts, and I have gone back to sleeping with my door locked and my .45 under my pillow. I don't think any of them have the guts to try anything, but I'm getting too short [too close to leaving] to take any chances" (192). His replacement CO arrived as scheduled in October, so Holley knows his Freedom Bird will take him back to the World and to Sondra, his girlfriend, in only five days.

○ **Artillery (or arty).** Sergeant Robert L. Daniels, from Chicago, served fifteen consecutive months as a Howitzer gunner and radio wireman (RTO) from September 1967-November 1967 and November 1967-November 1968. "I spend most of my time on the 105 howitzers. There were six guys around it. Each guy has a different job. One guy tilts the artillery. One guy might be on the telephone runnin' from one gun to another. My job was either cleanin' it or help loadin' it" (Terry 231).

"[The US Army] used several million tons of artillery shells . . . [they] were only 10 percent explosive but they threw off metal fragments . . . . and individual infantry battalions would often be given the exclusive use of one or more artillery battalions for some operations" (Dunnigan and Nofi 70).

Sgt Daniels said, "In November '68 I had about a month left. When I think about it now, I should have been gone since I was out there 14 months already. They were tellin' me to go to the field. I told 'em that I didn't wanna go . . . . It was dangerous out there, and I didn't know what might happen . . . . [But they needed me to drive out on this amtrac, that I was the only sergeant out there.] "We hit this mine. Got blew up. Blew the track straight up in the air. I thought it was all over" (Terry 232).

Daniels came away "with third-degree burns everywhere" (Terry 233) and lost his right hand to gangrene. Back in the World, he was a black amputee from a despised war. He actually thought he'd be of better use to his family dead with his life insurance to live on (Terry 234-235).

Captain Joseph B. Anderson, Jr., a newbie and just a lieutenant, found himself in charge of a platoon outnumbered ten to one; he just didn't know it. Anderson, soon learned "very quickly how to call in artillery, how to put aircraft over me to drop flares and keep the area lighted up so they couldn't sneak up on me.

"I was calling artillery in within 35, 40 yards of my own people, as tight as I could without hitting us.

"I can't remember wondering if I was ever gonna get out of this. I just did not have time to think about it. I was too busy directing fire to be scared" (Terry 220).

Artillery fire. Notice the men covering their ears.

○ **ARVN.** Pronounced ar-vin—the Army of the Republic of Vietnam. In April 1968 an ARVN private earned $467-US per year; generals $2,500-US per year; not matching standard of living; many deserted because of money; ARVN's enemy was not NV (North Vietnam); the Vietnamese would have preferred to handle its civil war itself (Kutler 52, 54).

ARVN TROOPS. Trained at National Training Center 1970,
to help South Vietnamese help themselves.

Wage and tax statement 1966 for American infantryman

Federal income tax withheld	$86.48
Wages paid subject to withholding in 1966	$1,432.92
F.I.C.A. employee tax withheld	$60.22
Total F.I.C.A. wages paid in 1966	**$1,432.92**

(Note: this was provided by a Vietnam vet who wishes to remain anonymous.)

"The ARVN were terrible," said Johnny Phillips. "Not behind us. They were doing what they had to do to survive, I was, too. We got to go home to America; they had to stay in rice paddies. They were scared the US would pull out. They knew that if they were captured, they were killed. I couldn't trust them. I didn't know if they were VC or not—they ran from us, maybe because they didn't want to be recognized" (Vet Program 2/4/93).

The official numbers after the war don't tell the story. According to Fitzgerald, over 165,268 ARVN soldiers and about 380,000 civilians were killed. She writes that those awful numbers in proportion to the United States would mean we would have lost 20 million Americans in the war (537).

○ **Atrocities.** These made the news because there weren't long, protracted battles for the print or television news to follow. In addition to beatings and rapes, there were Zippo raids that destroyed whole villages. Some cut off ears or carved something on the chest or forehead of their victims. Tom Magedanz couldn't understand why "[B]ack home people were always appalled by stories of taking ears, but not about killing" (Ebert 361). Some in Vietnam didn't know that was happening. After the war, CBS reporter Morley Safer was speaking with a Vietnamese professor who had been a soldier about hearing war news at the time. He said he'd heard on the radio about Americans' cruelty. In his explanation, he said he'd heard about Americans cutting ears off dead enemy soldiers. When Safer confirmed this, the professor said, "Then it's true? They did cut the ears off our soldiers?" I told him "this was not a policy. That something happens to ordinary men during and after battle. That for the most part American soldiers were decent men who did what was asked of them" (102-103).

"Most of the mutilation, however, probably resulted from frustration, a desire for revenge, or outright callousness .... After the death of [a popular] machine-gunner, a member of his squad carved their unit designation across the chest of a nearby corpse and tacked an Ace of Spades to his forehead" (Ebert 359).

Vietnam Vet Charles R. Anderson shares his perceptive thoughts on atrocities. "There were several physical and cultural characteristics about the Vietnamese which set the foundation for an environment in which atrocities could occur. The first thing any Westerner notices about the Vietnamese is their small physical size. Half the adult population appears to be under five feet tall and weigh less than 120 pounds. Also ... the Vietnamese were unarmed. Those two observations together invited the impression that the Vietnamese were unable to effectively answer injustices done them" (Anderson *The Grunts* 204).

"The language difference between Vietnamese civilians and American troops did much to increase the probability of atrocities. Effective communication between the two groups was prevented for all but the few willing to learn a foreign language in a short time. The two groups thus remained for the most part unintelligible to each other; neither was able to ask the other for explanations of superficial traits that may have provoked wonder, irritation or outright anger. Instead, misunderstanding compounded misunderstanding until the general reaction of each to the other was at least a constant suspicion and at worst a deep anger and hatred. When an American on patrol walked into a village and saw two Vietnamese talking, he assumed they were discussing the best time to shoot him in the back or trigger the booby trap that lay just ahead, not the best time to plant the next crop or the chances of rain during the next week.

"The American was confirmed in his belief that Orientals have always been a sly and cunning race, 'just like the Japs showed at Pearl Harbor.' When Americans expressed their frustration or anger against the Vietnamese, the language difference worked to the benefit of the former. No matter how loudly the Vietnamese might protest, the grunts couldn't understand; according to the perverted logic of which the latter were sometimes capable, the complaint then wasn't a complaint. Thus, whatever feelings of guilt that might follow an atrocity were either considerably lessened or completely precluded" (Anderson *The Grunts* 205).

David Gelman in *Newsweek* 28 August 1989, 62-64 blames ethnocentrism. A student in one of the Vet Programs, Paul, agreed. "Whether 'Gooks' in Vietnam or 'Yellow monkeys' in Japan, the less we know, the more we hate." His priest told him, "There is no way to kill unless you hate . . . . and that it's not as simple as it may seem: 'How much hate does it take to fly in an airplane, and press a button that drops thousands of bombs?'" In one of the Vet Programs, Al said that units determined behavior if they could. Some of the guys were like animals (02/25/93). Combat Engineer Bryant would agree. After a firefight, they went looking for a body count, shot two wounded VC until they were dead, and then "this guy—one of the white guys—cut off the VC's dick and stuck it in his mouth as a reminder that the 1st Cavs had been through there. And he left the ace of spaces on the body" (Terry 24).

Atrocities occurred throughout the war.

○ **AWL.** Permission to be absent.

○ **AWOL.** Absent without official leave; absent for more than thirty days, the American soldier (usually white) became a deserter. That rates a dishonorable discharge. The numbers grew each year:

> 1967 = 27,000 deserters
> 1968 = 29,234 deserters
> 1969 = 56,608 deserters
> 1970 = 65,643 deserters (Kutler 175).

Grunts leaving by helicopter. Mission accomplished.

Grunts picked up by a Huey.

BRAVO (B)

"Now we have a problem in making our power credible,
and Vietnam is the place."
—John F. Kennedy (1961)

○ **"Baby-Killer."** One of the worst names returning soldiers were called. Vietnam vet Johnny Phillips said to a group of university students, "Soldiers were just like you—kids—forced into it. Not child-killers" (Vet Program 1/28/1973).

"The Vietnam veteran's defensive response to a nation accusing him of being a baby killer and murderer is consistently [denial.] 'No, it never really bothered me . . . You get used to it.' This defensive repression and denial of emotions appear to have been one of the major causes of post-traumatic stress disorder" (Grossman 279).

Jim Gray, a Vietnam vet from Athens, GA, served in the First Air Cav in 1967 and 1968. He found his voice after the war in poetry.

Frozen in the Now
by Jim Gray

Murderer! Baby Killer!
I haven't heard that in awhile.
But then, I don't listen anymore
Frozen in the Now.

Returned and readjusted
To exist with proper style.
Discarded dreams of coming home
Frozen in the Now.

Gratitude and honor
Wreaths for the warrior's brow.
Belated gifts to the ambivalent
Frozen in the Now.

Take heed of me my son
While still your dreams can smile.
A believer of empty promises
Frozen in the Now. (23)

○ **Bad Paper.** Anything other than an honorable discharge from service (Dickson 261). A dishonorable discharge occurs for serious offenses while in the military: sexual assault; murder or manslaughter; AWOL which includes desertion; sedition which includes mutiny and spying. A dishonorable discharge has major consequences: loss of benefits such as VA educational benefits, housing loans, medical and funeral benefits; not considered for any federal job and many state jobs; no possession of a gun; can be legally discriminated against by banks and companies (because you're not considered a "class" such as handicapped, gender/age discrimination). You also lose your "veteran" status. If you are convicted of domestic violence or found abusing drugs, you may have a bad conduct discharge. Source: <*www.ehow.com/ about_6674442_impact-dishonorable-discharge_html*>. According to author Tim O'Brien, "[O]nly 3 percent of the nation's Vietnam-era veterans received bad paper. For veterans of the Korean War era, the rate was exactly the same. For veterans of the World War II era, the bad-paper rate was considerably *higher*" (*Esquire* Dec. 1979: 99).

○ **Bagged and Tagged.** Processing a dead body at Graves Registration.

○ **Band-Aid.** Dr. Holley, drafted precisely because he *was* a doctor, arrives in Vietnam: "My call sign is Band-Aid 6 or Big Band-Aid. My medics are Band-Aid—Charlie 1 or Band-Aid—Alpha 1, etc. depending which company and platoon they are assigned to" (40).

○ **Bao Chi! Bao Chi!** Vietnamese for journalist; **Bao chi fap!** Vietnamese for French journalist, but according to Herr, it also meant "Don't shoot! Don't shoot!" (135).

○ **Base camp.** Brigade or division-sized headquarters. Johnny said there was not a lot of motivation or morale. Soldiers were coming in from base camp every two months. "Base camps were generally permanent and were larger than most firebases. Some base camps, especially division headquarters, were huge, covering hundreds of acres and containing thousands of troops. Many were pretty rough affairs, but most of the combat troops were always anxious to secure a job that kept them there and not out in the bush. Base camps for combat units had about half their troops constantly going out into the bush, while the other half generally stayed at the base to provide support (clerks, supply, maintenance, cooks, etc.)" (Dunnigan and Nofi 154-155).

○ **Battalion.** Headed by a Lt. Col; usually 900 infantry, 500 artillery; battalions were smaller in Vietnam War.

○ **Battery.** Artillery unit with self-propelled howitzers at 105mm, 155mm, or 175mm.

○ **BCD.** Bad Conduct Discharge; it stays on record forever. A bad conduct discharge may occur "when somebody is convicted of a serious crime. But, in my experience it's more commonly given for court-martial incidents related to desertion, assaulting an officer or theft" (Tully). "About 550,000 troops were absent without leave or absent over leave during the Vietnam War. Of these, some 92,000 were declared deserters . . . of these 92,000 some 83,000 were given less than honorable discharges" (Dunnigan and Nofi 339). "81 percent of those who deserted had **not** seen service in Vietnam" (Dunnigan and Nofi 340).

○ **BDA.** Bomb Damage Assessment. One of the ways was to count craters.

○ **Beaucoup.** "*Boo-coo.*" French for "many" or "a lot"; "boo-coo" became a much-used term in Vietnam, as in "boo-coo money."

○ **Believer.** A dead Vietnamese (Herr 42). Hundreds of ways to die. One of the worst was a white phosphorous grenade. "White phosphorus is a very potent, caustic, and deadly agent, which will burn straight through any human tissue it comes into contact with. It will also burn through most manmade materials as well" (Holley 133). Both sides of the war used it even though it was banned by the Geneva Convention. Herr was told this while riding in a chopper that encountered a misty white smoke: "Willy Peter/ Make you a buh liever" (Herr 10).

○ **Benefits (bennies).** There were bennies for everyone-carrots, orange juice, C-rats, lettuce, tomatoes, oranges, water, grape juice, cucumbers, canned hamburgers, three sacks of mail,"— usually dropped by helicopter in parachutes to grunts in the field (Anderson *The Grunts* 139, see also 110).

Goody Drop
by Randy Cribbs

Morning,
After a night
Passed with outcry and
Much uproar,
It descends
From the heavens,
Hesitant, then quickly drops
Into our hell.

Briefly outlined against the pale
Daybreak and then
Gone again;
From its bowels
For us fell,
Happiness
In cans of hot chow
And great bags of mail. (39)

*A supplies drop of bennies
(benefits).*

○ **B-52.** Could drop bombs of 500-, 750-, and 1000-pound bombs from 30,000 feet, silent and invisible from the ground; units in the field could always call for air support. They didn't let a Newbie/FNG give the co-ordinates just in case he couldn't read a map.

A campaign by the North to over-run the US in the air much like they over-ran France at Dien Bien Phu in 1954. That's a B-52 on the left.

○ **Berm.** Perimeter above ground, often overgrown, surrounding a fortification.

○ **Berm Line.** A built-up, foliated area used to divide wet places.

○ **Best Friends.** Both sides of the war recognized the special ones who came along when most needed. "But for Hoa [guide who died trying to protect others] and countless other loved comrades, nameless ordinary soldiers, those who sacrificed for others . . . creating a spiritual beauty in the horrors of conflict, the war would have been another brutal, sadistic exercise" (Ninh 192).

Black Bart
by Randy Cribbs

He could sleep
Anywhere, anytime,
And did.

Humorous with little effort,
Without awareness,
Easy, natural, contagious.
Stress caused calm somehow;
Whether through relentless
Caper or a simple look.

Dirty or tired,
Equally at ease.
Not a leader—more.
Preserving sanity;
His, ours.

Black Bart.
Every unit had one,
Different name,
Same result;
Helping a bad
Situation seem less so;
Without even knowing it.

Black Bart I love you,
Wherever you are. (60)

○ *Betel Nut.* Local nut chewed by men and women. Frequent use turned teeth dark brown; sometimes chewed with tobacco.

○ *Be there for the next guy.* You take care of somebody, and believe that somebody will take of you when you need it. Essential in making a platoon function. "It all comes back to you—ya get what ya give" (Anthony 49).

○ *Big Red One.* 1st Infantry Division. From a vet: If you've gotta be one, be a Big Red One (2009).

○ *Bird aircraft, usually helicopter.* After the war, CBS reporter Morley Safer asked Col. Hoa, a Vietnamese officer, about Americans' air power. "I was jealous every day especially of the C-130s, the big transport planes, and the Chinook helicopters. The Americans could move more supplies and men in an hour than I could in a month." But then he added, "But you see it made no difference in the end. I think we understood our limitations better than you understood your advantages" (Safer 87).

○ *Bird Dog.* A Cessna observation plane. For reconnaissance.

○ *Black Market.* You could buy anything. Weapons, C-rations, ammo, jeep parts—all sold by Americans to Vietnamese to sell back to us (Al, Vet Program 02/04/73).

○ *Bloods.* Black grunts, as they called themselves after about 1969. Of the total deaths reported in Vietnam, 7273 blacks died; that number represented 12.36% of the total deaths reported. That percentage is about the percentage of blacks in the United States. Even though many bloods believed they were fighting "whitey's war," they knew they had to fight together, the blacks and the whites. Blacks knew their real struggle lay ahead in the World where their most respected leader, Martin Luther King, Jr. had been assassinated in Memphis in1968.

"[U]nique experience of the black Vietnam veteran. He fought at a time

A Blood.

when his sisters and brothers were fighting and dying at home for equal rights and greater opportunities, for a color-blind nation promised to him in the Constitution he swore to defend. He fought at a time when some of his leaders chastised him for waging war against a people of color and when his Communist foe appealed to him to take up arms instead against the forces of racism in America. The loyalty of the black Vietnam War veteran stood a greater test on the battleground than did the loyalty of any other American soldier in Vietnam; his patriotism begs a special salute at home" (Terry xv-xvi).

○ **Body bags (also called Glad bags).** Plastic bags used for retrieval of dead bodies on the battlefields. Some troops stuck in a long operation without their normal equipment used these bags as sleeping bags. Since the bags were labeled "Pouch, Human Remains," a lot chose not to (Dunnigan and Nofi 96).

Every grunt carried a body bag; it was part of the regular equipment. Bob, a Vietnam vet from Virginia, saw his pal "Lucky" hit by a sniper. Bob said, "One shot and he's goner. At first I thought he fell, but I knew better. Nineteen, got a wife and a baby on the way. He was already writing to that little baby just in case. One shot.

"The Lt. zipped [not a zipper but snaps] him up in a green body bag. Then a shit bird wrote a note and stuck it in. The Lt. and I reached it about the same time: 'Thank you for the loan of your boy's body. So sorry we couldn't return it in the same condition we received it in.'

"There it is. That's the 'Nam. You don't know who you are anymore." The LT and I brought him in. (Idea from Anderson *Grunts* 75)

Michael Herr, a keen observer and reporter/participant, noticed "Men on the crews would say that once you'd carried a dead person he would always be there, riding with you. Like all combat people they were incredibly superstitious and invariably self-dramatic, but it was (I knew) unbearably true that close exposure to the dead sensitized you to the force of their presence and made for long reverberations; long. Some people were so delicate that one look was enough to wipe them away, but even bone-dumb grunts seemed to feel that something weird and extra was happening to them" (9). Bao Ninh, once in the Youth Brigade, and Adrien Cronauer, the American DJ, have something in common; they both believe that everyone, for every unknown soldier, there was a story.

This story is from Bao Ninh. A half-buried coffin showed up in high water. "Inside the coffin was a thick plastic bag, similar to those the Americans used for their dead, but this one was clear plastic. The soldier seemed to be still breathing, as though in a deep sleep. He looked so alive . . . .

"Then before [the men's] eyes the plastic bag discolored, whitening as though suddenly filled with smoke. The bag glowed and something seemed to escape from it, causing the bag to deflate. When the smoke cleared, only a yellowish ash remained. They fell to their knees around it, raising their hands to heaven praying for a safe flight for the departed soul" (91).

○ **Body counts.** The numbers killed, reported to MACV (Military Assistance Command Vietnam, pronounced MacVee).

"In a war where capturing territory was not as important as eliminating enemy troops, the success or failure of an operation was often difficult to determine. The army initially would merely report that 'enemy casualties were heavy' or 'medium' or 'light' as seemed appropriate and left it at that. But folks back home, namely politicians, and journalists, demanded something more. So the army came to evaluate operations on the basis of something called the 'kill ratio,' that is, the number of enemy troops killed for each friendly soldier lost in action. Thus was born the notorious 'body count.' As the war went on, the Americans back home became more and more sensitive to battlefield losses. Thus there was not only pressure to end the war, either by killing the Communist troops or negotiating, but also to minimize American casualties. In addition, the 'kill ratio' was seen as an excellent way to evaluate combat unit commanders" (Dunnigan and Nofi 75-76).

Although MACV set up regulations about whom to count—dead armed people, soldiers or not, to be counted on the ground, pilots and/or observers had to determine kills "beyond a reasonable doubt" (Ebert 339).

"The body count was quickly corrupted. Since an impressive body count was clearly a career-enhancing event, and the bodies were counted out in the bush by low-ranking troops who might be dead the next day, there was ample opportunity to adjust the numbers as they passed from the infantry platoon level to the White House. Even with all the padding, it was still publicly acknowledged that Communist troops were not being 'killed fast enough,' and could not be without the addition of many more American troops and an invasion of North Vietnam. The troops in the field were not very enthusiastic about the body-count process, as they were sometimes ordered to go counting while the enemy was still shooting. This situation did not do much for accuracy in the count. But then, accuracy was never a major factor in the body-count department" (Dunnigan and Nofi 76).

"We may have enhanced the killing ability of the average soldier through training (that is, conditioning), but at what price? The ultimate cost of our body counts in Vietnam has been, and continues to be, much more than dollars and lives. We can, and have, conditioned soldiers to kill—they are eager and willing and trust our judgment. But in doing so we have not made them capable of handling the moral and social burdens of these acts, and we have a moral responsibility to consider the long-term effects of our commands. Moral direction and philosophical guidance, based on a firm understanding of the processes involved, must come with the combat training and deployment of our soldiers" (Grossman 291-292).

One black grunt said with a straight face—"And (in fact,) they had a habit of exaggerating a body count. If we killed 7, by the time it would get back to base camp, it would have gotten to 28. Then by the time it got down to [General] Westmoreland's office in Saigon, it done went up to 54. And by the time it left from Saigon going to Washington, it had went up to about 125. To prove we were really out there doing our jobs, doing, really, more than what we were doing" (Terry 21). To reporter Michael Herr, a Special Forces captain told him all about body count. "I went out and killed one VC and liberated a prisoner. Next day the major called me in and told me that I'd killed fourteen VC and liberated six prisoners. You want to see the medal?" (172).

"The numbers often seemed so ridiculous that more than one veteran commented sarcastically that American soldiers apparently killed the whole country" (Ebert 343). One of Lifton's Vietnam vets said, "If it's dead, it's VC. Because it's dead. If it's dead it *had* to be VC. And of course a corpse couldn't defend itself anyhow" (64).

"These idiots in the back would say they want a body count. Go back out there and find the bodies. After we found the body count, then we had to bury them. Geneva Convention says we have to bury 'em. And I said, 'What the hell y'all talkin' 'bout the Geneva Convention? We're not in a war'" (Terry 42).

"The American practice of 'body-counting' enemy casualties in the Vietnam War was mindless in innocently assuming that these deaths had a bearing on North Vietnamese capabilities and willpower" (Seabury and Codevilla 121). The military was stuck: with no territory to capture and hold, with no prisoners to take, the only strategy was to kill and kill some more.

○ **Booby traps.** Those bamboo sticks were also called punji stakes. Sharpened to a point, they were often buried point up slightly above ground level and camouflaged with dirt. They penetrated G.I.s' combat boots and caused infections since the stakes were smeared with feces or a poisonous material. According to Dunnigan and Nofi, the "punji stakes [booby trap] caused only about 2 percent of American casualties and virtually no deaths" (70).

"Vietnam was an enemy seldom seen but always watchful. And so, American soldiers, to varying degrees, found themselves plagued by booby traps, harassed by snipers, pummeled by rocket and mortar fire, and surprised by ambushes . . . Explosive booby traps were more common then *punji* pits, especially in the latter stages of the war, and they came in a variety of shapes and sizes: Toe poppers—small explosive charges set in bamboo tubes, hand grenades placed in empty cans or in clay mudballs, or in coconuts strewn along the ground" (Ebert 227-8, 237). As Ebert notes, "Kicking things was a habit common to Americans that the enemy used to his advantage" (238).

"Mines and booby traps were used extensively in Vietnam, by both sides. Some 7 percent—perhaps 11 percent, of US casualties in the war were from mines (*not* 65 percent, as has been alleged by some anti-mine activists), as were about 75 percent of tank and other armored vehicle losses. This was a much higher percentage than in previous American experience, since the introduction of mines in the Civil War" (Dunnigan and Nofi 67).

Marine Lewis Puller, Jr., author of the Pulitzer-Prize winning autobiography *Fortunate Son* in 1992, describes a booby trap and sets himself a reminder to be more diligent. "The following dawn, as we prepared to break camp, one of the men discovered a booby trap at the vertex of the draw, where two hills came together. The device consisted of a C ration can holding a grenade with its pin removed so that the grenade's spoon was held in place by the side of the can. The can was rigged about knee high and located just to the side of the trail with a trip wire crossing the trail to an anchor on the other side. It was the first booby trap I had seen since coming in country, and though rigged crudely, it was fully as lethal as a more sophisticated device. If we had proceeded through the draw in the previous day's twilight rather than stopped to make camp, my point man and perhaps several others would probably have been maimed or killed. I reminded myself that the platoon had to become more disciplined at using probe sticks and staying off trails. I had our demolition man rig a time charge to blow the booby trap in place as we exited the draw" (128).

Booby trap.
A Sticking trap near Cu Chi Tunnels probably covered with vegetation.

"After we finished our meal, I buried the cans and cardboard containers in which the rations had been packaged . . . We knew that the Vietcong could make booby traps out of our refuse . . ." (Puller 133-134).

○ **Boom Boom.** Sex. The 1ˢᵗ Cav built what we called "Sin City" outside An Khe. It even had "soul bars" with bars that played the Temps, the Supremes—any soul music. "The women were much more friendly there. We had heard that it was because they thought of the black man as bein' more stronger, more powerful, because Buddha was black. Take a good look at Buddha. You'll see that he has thick lips and has a very broad nose and very kinky hair. But I didn't know that until I got in country" (Terry 25).

○ **Boom-boom girl.** A prostitute. On his way to Vietnam, LT Puller avoided the prostitutes in Okinawa that, according to one of his friends, "had elevated prostitution to an art form" (75). Wherever the bases or airports with soldiers travelling, there were prostitutes. Near "Sin City" (see above), soldiers could buy "two half-gallons of Gilby's [sic] gin for a $1.65 each. We take a bottle to papa san. Buy a girl for $5 or $10. Whatever came by, or whatever I liked. And still have a half a gallon of gin. We would have to leave the area at six o'clock. Light Bulb Bryant swears the girls were clean because medical personnel would come check them out and get shots if they needed (Terry 26). "You could find plenty of women out in the field, too. We would set up our perimeter, and all of a sudden a little Coke girl would show up with Coca-Cola.

A young girl, probably a prostitute, getting penicillin shot.

And also some broads would show. We would set up lean-tos, or we'd put up bunkers. A guy would go outside the wire, take the broad through the wire to the bunker and knock her off, and take her back outside the wire. Normally, those kinds of deals were a C-ration deal. Or a couple of dollars. We would give a girl a C-ration meal. Ham and lima beans [known as ham and motherfuckers], 'cause nobody in the squad would want to eat ham and lima beans. You'd never give up spaghetti and meatballs" (Terry 26-27).

○ **Boom Boom House.** A whorehouse.

○ **Boondocks.** "Any remote rugged area, from the Philippine Tagalog word bundok (mountain)" (Rottman FUBAR 28).

○ **Boon-Doggle.** Mission considered absurd or useless by grunts. The order for "dig-in" was especially frustrating. Dig-in meant to dig a foxhole. "Digging a hole three or more feet down was a project costly in strength and patience, but at its completion the distant headquarters might call back and direct still another move before nightfall. Whatever explanation offered the troops was insufficient—they considered the dig-in directive no more than unnecessary harassment, a make-work project whose only purpose was to prevent their taking a much-deserved rest" (Anderson *The Grunts* 216-217).

○ **Boonies.** From "the boondocks." In country. In the bush. In the 'Nam, out in the field, away from the firebase or base camp. Roving reporter Michael Herr describes the boonies as a place "where [the grunts] were deprived of all information except what they'd gathered for themselves on either side of the tree line, they'd look around like someone was watching and say, 'I dunno, Charlie's up to something. Slick, slick, that fucker's *so* slick. Watch!'" (47).

○ **Boonie hat.** Slang for the soft camouflage hat worn in the war. Many soldiers put peace buttons and their slang names on them; generally scrunched, out of shape.

○ **Boonie-rat.** A grunt with some experience in the war. Vietnam was distinctly different from any war we have fought before or since, in that it was a war of individuals. With very few exceptions, every combatant arrived in Vietnam as an individual replacement on a twelve-month tour—thirteen months for the US Marines.

"The average soldier had only to survive his year in hell and thus, for the first time, had a clear-cut way out of combat other than as a physical or psychological casualty. In this environment it was far more possible, even natural, that many soldiers would remain aloof, and their bonding would never develop into the full, mature, lifelong relationships of previous wars. This policy (combined with the use of drugs, maintenance of proximity to the combat zone, and establishment of an expectancy of returning to combat) resulted in an all-time-record low number of psychiatric casualties *in Vietnam*" (Grossman 268-269).

According to Marine Lewis Puller, Jr., "fewer than one in ten [draft-age men] ever served in Vietnam" (338).

○ **Boot Camp.** "As soon as I hit boot camp in Fort Jackson, South Carolina, they tried to change your total personality. Transform you out of that civilian mentality to a military mind. Right away they told us not to call them Vietnamese. Call everybody gooks, dinks. Then they told us when you go over in Vietnam, you gonna be face to face with Charlie, the Viet Cong. They were like animals, or something other than human. They ain't have no regard for life. They'd blow up little babies just to kill one GI. They wouldn't allow you to talk about them as if they were people. They told us they're not to be treated with any type of mercy or apprehension that's what they engraved into you. That killer instinct. Just go away and do destruction" (Terry 90).

○ *Bouncing Betty.* The booby trap feared the most. It was trip-wired, with a 3-pronged primer. When the plunger depressed, "Bouncing Betty" would bounce up about three feet and explode (Anderson *The Grunts* 165). Bouncing Betty—bouncing bitch, the castrator; French *soldat silencieux* (or "silent soldier") (Rottman *FUBAR* 28).

"The 'Bouncing Betty' anti-personnel mine is one of the more brutal products of American military technology [actually first created by Germans during WWII]. When triggered, it doesn't explode in the ground and take feet off legs. It springs up four feet before it goes off, and separates heads and arms from bodies and perforates lungs, stomachs, and intestines. Lance Corporal Epps' Bouncing Betty picked him up and, while he flew through the air, ripped off his clothes, legs, hands, and all of his head but the lower jaw, then dumped him on his back—stumps of thighs and arms raised in supplication to a garish sun. The first man on the scene told a corpsman that he thought he saw a pink mist hanging over the corpse for a few seconds" (Anderson *The Grunts* 165).

Light Bulb aka Spec 5 Harold Bryant saved a grunt stuck because he knew he'd stepped on a plunger. "The white dude knew he couldn't move because doing so would destroy him and me since I was so close. After poking around, I knew he was stuck on the three-prong primer of the Bouncing Betty. But I got an idea. We first tried getting his foot out of the boot while I kept pressure by holding the plunger down with the boot.

"Then I got an idea. I knew when the plunger would depress, the Bouncin' Betty would bounce up about 3 feet and then explode. So I got the other members of his team together, and I tied a rope around his waist. And everybody, including me, moved off about 20 yards from the mine and him. And when I counted to three, everyone would pull on the rope and snatch him about 15 feet off the mine. And it would bounce up its 3 feet and then explode. And it did that. And the only damage that he received was the heel of his jungle boot was blown off. No damage to him.

"This was somethin' that they never taught us in school" (Terry 20).

○ *Break squelch.* Break radio silence when in danger. Pushing the "talk" button sent out a *click-hiss* to anyone on that wave length. Sometimes used to ask for help or simply to identify a position. No talk: 1 = enemy near; 2 = all clear (Dunnigan and Nofi 346-7).

○ **Brigade.** Commanded by a colonel. Military structure:

Platoons	approx. 40 each
Companies	approx 80-200 each
Battalions	approx. 1000-1250 each
Brigades	approx. 3500 each

○ **Bring smoke.** Hit'em hard; do it now. Call for air support.

Calling for air Support.

○ **Bro.** Black soldier. Also called a blood.

○ **Bronze Candy.** VC for bullets. In Bao Ninh's *The Sorrow of War,* Kien and his scouts captured four commandos who killed three young girls. Kien made them dig their own graves. Then the commandos wanted a last cigarette. One of Kien's men said, "Why string it out? Give them some bronze candy!" (37). (Note: this euphemism allows the speaker to refrain from saying *kill them.*)

○ **Bronze star.** US Military decoration for heroism.

○ **Brother.** Fellow black Marine.

○ **BS.** Short for border surveillance; short for bull shit.

○ **The Buff.** The Big Ugly Fat Fucker. The nickname for the Air Force B-52 super bomber. It dropped about seven and a half million tons of bombs during the Vietnam War (Reinberg 30, 20-21).

○ **Bug Juice.** Slang for G.I.-issued insecticide that didn't work.

○ **Bummer.** Bad luck, also used sarcastically.

○ **Bunker.** "We went by the grimy admin buildings and bunkers . . . . The Seabee bunker was just a little farther along the road. It was not like the other bunkers. It was the deepest, safest, cleanest place in Khe Sanh, with six feet of timbers, steel and sandbags overhead, and inside it was brightly lit. The grunts called it the Alamo Hilton and thought it was candy-assed" (Herr 123-124).

Bunker
by Randy Cribbs

A bunker.

So loud the rain.

But in my room
Of sand and wood,
Secure, blissful refrain.

Flares through a
Continual mist
Floating, lost,
Hazy,
Like falling stars,
Now like a cross.

White, red, green,
A rainbow in the
Wet sky, burning
In defiance
Of monsoon,
Burning for me,
Secure

In my room . . . (15)

It wasn't always like that. Herr was once in a bunker full of rats. "During those brief moments when the ground all around you was not rumbling, when there were no airstrikes on the hills, no incoming or outgoing or firing from the perimeter, you could sit inside and listen to the rats running across the bunker floor. A lot of them had been poisoned, shot, caught in traps or killed by the lucky toss of a combat boot, and they were here in the bunker too. There was the smell of urine, of old, old sweat, C-ration decay, moldy canvas and private crud, and that mixing up of other smells that were special to combat zones. A lot of us believed that exhaustion and fear could be smelled and that certain dreams gave off an odor . . . . This bunker was at least as bad as any I'd ever been in, and I gagged in there once, the first time. Because there was almost no light, you had to imagine most of what you smelled, and that became something like a pastime" (128-129).

○ *Bunnies.* A white man. Usually said by black men. One of the black veterans interviewed for the book, *Bloods,* Light Bulb Bryant (see *Bouncing Betty* above) learned "that white people weren't as tough, weren't the number one race and all

Stay off the trail. Patrol in the bush.

Stay off the trail. Be safe.

them other perceptions that they had tried to ingrain in my head. I found out they got scared like I did. I found out a lot of them were a lot more cowardly than I expected. I found out some of them were more animalistic than any black people I knew. I found out that they really didn't have their shit together" (Terry 23).

○ **Bush.** Infantry term for field or boonies. Away from a firebase or basecamp. In Country. In Vietnam. In the triple-canopy jungle that attacked the human body: sunburn, dehydration, 106° temperature in the morning, exhaustion, diarrhea, cramps, elephant grass that cut the skin, jungle rot, sprained ankles, yet another hill to climb, and hunger. Water, never enough. Al said that the CDC [Center for Disease Control] couldn't even identify some diseases we came home with (Vet Program 2/4/93).

Then the bush was home to poisonous snakes, monkeys, an elephant or two, giant insects, quicksand, and tigers.

"The next morning, three rifles shots woke me up. Men running. A shout. Voices. I lifted lid of the coffin [where I was sleeping] and sat up. Bien was already awake. The day had just begun to break, but we still couldn't make out faces. 'What is it?' I asked.

'A tiger. It got one of the men.'

'Who?'

"Bien pointed in the direction of the camp. 'San. He had a bad case of dysentery. Huc put him in charge of guarding the camp. I don't know how he could have gotten caught like that. This morning a guy from the lumberjack group went off to pee in the jungle. He saw the tiger drag him off. The guy shouted. Then the guard fired three shots into the air. Then they went in after him . . ." (Duong Thu Huong 189).

In order for soldiers to survive in the bush, the army published a Field Manual first commissioned to train its special forces. This reprint in 1991 states that this reprint is meant for anyone who works outside or for someone who enjoys the challenges of outdoors. But in this reprint there remain many references to Army survival skills—"If you are in a combat situation, find a place where you can conceal yourself from the enemy—remember, security takes priority (1-7).

The following list of "enemies of survival" is nothing if not absurd if these were included in the original field manual as they were in the reprint:

1. **Pain** (better to think of other things to make pain go away)
2. **Cold** (get warm)
3. **Heat** (can get accustomed to it; wear a hat; avoid being out in the hottest part of the day)
4. **Thirst** (drink water if available, particularly with meals since food requires extra water)
5. **Hunger** (eat whatever is available)
6. **Fatigue** (rest; sometimes fatigue is caused by your mental attitude, so change your activity)

7. **Boredom** (keep your goal of survival first; do tasks you must perform)
8. **Loneliness** (learn to become self-sufficient) (1-1 to 1-5)
  (Note: I have greatly simplified the answers to the enemies of survival,
  but the essence is here.)

○ ***Butter-bar.*** Indication of rank. A first lieutenant wore one brass bar; a second lieutenant wore two. The brass quickly turned to black or brown. Many lieutenants were new to the field. Spec 4 Charles Strong got stuck with a dumb LT. "He was literally the word 'stupid,' because he couldn't read a map. And he would say, 'You don't tell me what to do, because they sent me to officers' training school.' When we got one or two sniper fire, he would stop right there and call in artillery to saturate the whole area before you could take another step" (Terry 55).

Carrying wounded soldier unsure if US or NVA.

CHARLIE (C)

"This is not a jungle war, but a struggle for
freedom on every front of human activity."
—Lyndon B. Johnson (1964)

○ *C-1* Hot rations; *C-2* Need individual equipment; *C-3* Need fuel; *C-4* Plastic putty carried by soldiers and also an explosive in Claymore mines which could be opened and extracted for heating. A weapon, but also little pieces pulled away and lit by a Zippo made a nice heater for food, such as spiced beef; *C-5* Need Ammo; *C-6* Need booze; *C-7* Need bennies (benefits) such as Coke, snacks, and cigarettes; *C-8* Need medical supplies; *C-9* Need a spare. C refers to the class of supplies (*A Distant Challenge* 387).

○ *Call for fire support.* Get the artillery in to provide air support. Call for help—in any situation. Don't wait too late and be sure you can read a map. You don't want to send in air support to bomb your own troops.

○ *CAP.* Short for Civic Action Platoon. CAP was all Marines, no Vietnamese participants, although at least one Marine was fluent in Vietnamese—usually 14 Marines volunteered for CAP and one Navy corpsman. "All team members had civilian work experience that could be applied directly to the agricultural economy of the rural Vietnamese village, things like farming, live-stock breeding, construction, and small engine repair. When CAP went to vills to the west and south of Da Nang, an area which had a population of about 260 thousand with an estimated 30 thousand Viet Cong, during 1967-68 the VC recruited

Calling for fire Support. Radio Operator is relaying Coordinates.

only 170 men. Then the villagers there began withholding rice from the Viet Cong and even telling their CAP teams when to expect a VC attack (Anderson *Other War* 69). CAP was inexpensive—cheaper than keeping these men in the field. They served another purpose. They stayed overnight. The Marines were armed, providing an amount of protection for the villagers.

CAP did have a major problem, however. Officials in Vietnam (US Agency for International Development or USAID) with recommendations from military advisors in the field decided "what was needed for South Vietnamese Development: "food, grain, medicines, and construction materials, and equipment" (Anderson *Other War* 69). Once ordered (remember WHAM—"Winning Hearts and Minds"), everything went to a safe port, unloaded by Vietnamese, "then distributed through the Vietnam bureaucracy, down the organization chart from province chief to district chief to village chief and finally to the hamlet chief, who would see that the people who needed the goods got them (Anderson *Other War* 69-70). USAID ended up putting ordered goods into the hands of corrupt Vietnamese who stole from warehouses and ports and sold everything to the black market, but how could the United States claim its host country was corrupt?

∘ **Carbine.** Short-barreled, light weight automatic.

∘ **Chaplains (also called Sky Pilots).** In 1968, there were about 300 chaplains in Vietnam. A platoon waited for a chopper to take out some of the heat casualties. "When the chopper touched down it discharged the last person in the whole division the grunts expected to see—the battalion Chaplain. Chaplains are considered by most Marines to be largely useless appendages on the *corpus militaris*. They're always acting a little too friendly to be for real, and when the bullets start flying what good is some guy babbling about the *Twenty-Third Psalm*? This day, however, the grunts would change their minds about chaplains, for not only had this one bothered to leave his air-conditioned chapel to come out and try to cheer them up a little, but this member of the general's 'God Squad' was actually going to hump with them, share the merciless heat with them" (Anderson *The Grunts* 53).

Al Davis, Vietnam vet, said he never saw a chaplain (Vet program 02/04/93). Grunts had little respect for them. They thought there was something wrong with a chaplain "blessing the troops, their mission, their guns, their killing. As one of the men put it, 'Whatever we were doing . . . murder . . . atrocities . . . God was *always* on our side'" (Lifton 163). The grunts were quick to note the hypocrisy of blessing men who were going out to kill.

From another vet: "Even the chaplains would turn the thing around in the Ten Commandments. They'd say, 'Thou shall not murder,' instead of 'Thou shall not kill.' Basically, you had a right to kill, to take and seize territory, or to protect lives of each other. Our conscience was not to bother us once we engaged in that kind of killing. As long as we didn't murder, it was like the chaplain would give you his blessings. But you knew all of that was murder anyway" (Terry 91).

Man of God
by Larry Rottmann

> The chaplain of the 25th Aviation Battalion
> at Cu Chi
> Prays for the souls of the enemy
> On Sunday mornings
> And earns flight pay as a helicopter door gunner
> during the rest of the week. (Rottmann 24)

Herr understood. A shy Indian boy from Arizona asked him where he could find a chaplain. He'd just volunteered for a "suicide squad, two jeeps that were going to drive across the airstrip with mortars and a recoilless rifle. It looked bad . . . . It might be bad. He just had a feeling about it, he'd seen what always happened to guys whenever they got that feeling, at least he *thought* it was that feeling, a bad one, the worst he'd ever had" (183) . . . ."Listen, though. If it happens . . . I think it's going to . . . will you make sure the colonel tells my folks I was looking for a chaplain anyway?

"I promised, and the jeeps loaded and drove off" (183).

The next morning, Herr learned there had been a small firefight. And that the Indian boy was A-okay. "He wouldn't look at me [at breakfast]. But at noon he came over and squeezed my arm and smiled, his eyes fixed somewhere just to the right of my own" (184), embarrassed, maybe that he'd been wrong or that he needed a chaplain. Herr never knew.

Fear of losing his own life is not what always drew a military person to a chaplain. Rabbi Arnold Resnicoff, a retired Navy Captain, told a story about a Colonel in Bosnia. "'Chaplain,' he said, 'the Army trains me to kill people and break things. Your job, Chaplain, is to keep me from ever getting to a point where I like doing it'" (Sherman 119).

And Then There Were None
by Stan Platke

Men bled
Many dead
A world safe for democracy
But not for life
Rather funny
In an unfunny sort of way

And the Bible said
That when He came
Everyone was dead
No one left to claim

Men bled
Many dead

Yea as I walk through the valley of death
I shall fear no evil
For the valleys are gone
And only death awaits

And I am the evil. (Rottmann 101)

Chaplains had to be willing to assist any person in need of spiritual help, no matter what the person's religion was. Each chaplain was issued a GI kit with religious items most soldiers could relate to. Rabbi Mark Goldman shares a picture of his GI kit from the war.

*Captain Rabbi Mark Goldman's
G.I. Issued Chaplain kit.*

Note: Nearly a dozen chaplains were killed in action and more than a hundred wounded during the war. Three were recipients of the Medal of Honor, two posthumously: LT. J.G, Vincent R. Capodanno and USN, MAJ Charles J. Watters, USA. The survivor to receive the Medal of Honor was CPT Charles J. Litkey. All three of these chaplains were Catholic (Dunnigan and Nofi 164).

○ ***Charlie.*** Singular and plural; refers to a Vietnamese man or the enemy. "It was ghost country, and Charlie Cong was the main ghost. The way he came out at night. How you never really saw him, just thought you did. Almost magical—appearing, disappearing. He could blend with the land, changing form, becoming trees and grass. He could levitate. He could fly. He could pass through barbed wire and melt away like ice and creep up on you without sound or footsteps. He was scary. In the daylight, maybe, you didn't believe in this stuff. You laughed it off. You made jokes. But at night you turned into a believer; no skeptics in foxholes" (O'Brien *The Things They Carried* 229).

○ **Check it out.** Be careful. Be more careful than you've ever been. Look and actually *see*. Not everything is as it seems. Also a request or order to investigate a sound, a smell, a glimpse of something. It's a new way of thinking: an innocent pot of rice could be hiding an entrance to a spider hole where the VC hid their weapons and ammo (Anthony 14).

○ **Cherry.** A new guy to Vietnam; also called an **FNG** "Fucking New Guy"; not especially a welcome addition because the new guy's training has not prepared him for what this war is; will need experience; others afraid the new guy will make a mistake that will kill them all. Johnny Phillips in a talk on January 28, 1993, said, "When I went to Vietnam, I was dumber than dirt. I had to learn real fast."

Students
by Randy Cribbs

We lived by listening,
Watching, being lucky.

From old soldiers like Manny
We learned how to survive,
To let pain take care
Of our body while fear
Kept us alive.
Respect pain but push
Through it when you must,
Manny said;
But always listen to the fear;
Listen closely or be dead.

We existed under
His watchful eye;
He was our pattern
To live and die.

Looking back,
Manny did know best;
Those who understood
And were lucky, survived;
Then there were the rest. (77)

○ **Chieu Hoi.** (Choo Hoy) Vietnamese for "Open Arms." The program's purpose was to get the enemy to give up their arms [desert] and come over to [the ARVN]. A soldier would descend in a helicopter and broadcast these instructions in Vietnamese or drop leaflets after a battle (Terry 79-80).

The bearer of this leaflet is trying to report a mine or boobytrap. He is to be rewarded. Take him to your commanding officer.

Chieu Hoi, Propaganda leaflet.

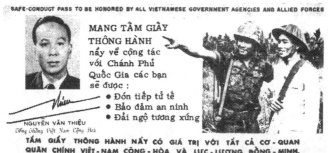

Chieu Hui Program Surrender Safe-Conduct pass.

◦ *Chinook.* Supply and transport helicopter.

◦ *Chop-chop*. Vietnamese slang for food; also means to hurry.

◦ *Chopper*. Helicopter. If a grunt heard its *whump whump whump*, he didn't have to worry. It was a friendly.

◦ *Chuck.* Charlie. Also Mr. Charles. The enemy.

◦ *CIB.* Combat Infantry Badge is the US Army combat service recognition decoration awarded to soldiers—enlisted men and officers (commissioned and warrant) holding *colonel* rank, and lower, who *personally* fought in active ground combat.

◦ *Clacker.* Detonator for Claymore mine. Small hand-held firing device for a Claymore. Squeeze handle made a clacking sound.

◦ *The clap.* Soldiers were told about "black syphilis" a disease so devastating that it killed. This was, of course, a story cooked up by someone in the Army attempting to control troops' contact with prostitutes (Johnny, Vet Program 03/04/93).

◦ *Claymore.* An antipersonnel mine which, when detonated, propelled small steel cubes in a 60-degree fan-shaped pattern to a maximum distance of 100 meters. Lieutenant General John H. Hay, Jr., writing for the Department of the Army explains its importance. "The claymore mine, which was developed by the US Army before the war, was introduced into combat in Vietnam. The mine weighs 3.5 pounds and has a casualty area the height of a man out to fifty meters. More importantly, it can be aimed to cover a specific area. In fixed positions claymore mines were used in depth, with overlapping kill zones . . . . The claymore mine was particularly effective to open an ambush because the extensive, instantaneous kill zone that it generated did not disclose the location of the ambush patrol" (53).

◦ *Clemency.* After President Ford announced a clemency program on September 16, 1974, Marine Lewis Puller, Jr., badly wounded in the war and highly decorated, asked for a place on the Committee making decisions on clemency "for Vietnam military deserters and civilian draft evaders" (333). President Ford increased the size of the committee from nine to 18 members; Puller and three others were the only Vietnam veterans. Over the summer of 1975, Puller read about 5,000 case histories. Puller explains, "We read the summaries ahead of time and then met in three-member panels to make case dispositions. If the panel recommendation was not unanimous, the dissenting member could refer the case to the full board . . . . Usually the only issues to be decided were whether the applicant should be granted clemency and, if so, whether a period of alternative service should be required as a condition of receiving clemency. As a result of our deliberations we granted clemency in almost 95 percent of the cases we evaluated . . ." (337).

Puller came to realize that the problems he faced on the committee were "a terribly unfair conscription system and a tragic war that never should have been fought. Out of the general population of draft-age men during the Vietnam era, fewer than one in ten ever served in Vietnam" (338, 342).

"Looking back, I think we may have done some good for the applicants whose cases we heard, but that good was insignificant when weighed against the irreparable harm caused by the four administrations that mired us in Vietnam and then refused to acknowledge any wrongdoing or culpability. To this day I think we, as board members, were in the business of determining the guilt of the wrong people, and it was for me as shattering an experience as the loss of my legs and a dozen good friends in Vietnam to discover face-to-face the arrogance and the blindness that so often passed for leadership during the Vietnam era" (342-343).

○ *Clerks and Jerks.* The support staff at the rear. Also called REMFs (Rear Echelon Mother Fuckers).

○ *CO*. Commanding officer; *co* = company.

○ *CO*. Conscientious Objector. In 1965 the Supreme Court in *United States vs. Seeger* determined that religion did not have to be church-based in order for an individual to object to war. By 1972, huge numbers of men supported by churches and lawyers' groups outnumbered draftees: for every 130 men granted *CO* status, 100 were drafted. The draft was repealed in 1973. In 1974, President Ford began setting up a clemency program (Kutler 148).

"I [Robert Holcomb] considered the conscientious objector status, but I couldn't do that because I was not a religious fanatic. I decided that the best thing for me to do would be to leave the country. I was not interested in being locked into Canada. I was not interested in Cuba, because it had a very pure form of socialism and didn't permit the kinds of freedoms that I was accustomed to here" (Terry 202-203).

○ *Cobra.* The AH-IG helicopter armed with rockets and machine. An attack helicopter.

○ *Code of Conduct.* Military Rules for the US. "Seymour M. Hersh, in his essay concerning bombing attacks on unauthorized targets during the Vietnam War and the cover-up that followed, completes a story that has represented for me both the best and the worst of the conduct of war (*New Yorker*, Comment, March 26, 2007). During 1971-72, I was assigned to the Air Force's 56th Special Operations Wing at *Nakhon Phanom*, Thailand, as an intelligence specialist. With us was Sergeant Lonnie Franks, who was on temporary duty from the air wing at Udorn Royal Thai Air Force Base, from which the strike missions in question were flown. Sergeant Franks, in de-briefing pilots after their missions over Vietnam, realized that they were being instructed to give fabricated information, and was told that he had to support this action by lying in official intelligence reports. Instead, Sergeant Franks wrote to his Senator explaining that he had been ordered to lie in official reports documenting how the war was being fought. His action exemplifies the military's core ideal: when something is wrong, you must do something." Master Sergeant Bob Schrynemakers, United States Air Force retired, Torrance, Calif. (Letter, published in the April 16, 2007 issue of the *New Yorker*, under the title "In the Line of Duty.")

○ *Combat ineffective.* Bureaucracy for wounded (or dead).

○ *Combat pay.* Everyone serving in Vietnam from cook to colonel got combat pay whether seeing actual combat or not. Combat pay was first issued in April 1965 and made retroactive to January 1965 (Reinberg 47).

But another book, *The Vietnam War Diary,* claims that "Not every United States military man in Vietnam gets special combat pay, officials pointed out today [February 1965]. Only about 20 to 25 percent of the 23,000 American military men there receive such pay.

"The extra pay for exposure to hostile fire is $65 a month regardless of grade or rank. The term 'combat pay' is only a colloquialism and is avoided in official terminology because the United States is not regarded as engaged in combat in Vietnam" (16).

○ *Company*. Military unit composed of two or more platoons.

○ *CONUS.* Continental U. S.

○ *Corpsman.* Marine and Navy term for medic.

○ *Corpsman UP.* Marine term: come ASAP.

○ *Counter Insurgency.* Anti-guerilla warfare usually perpetrated by the LRRPSs (US Long Range Reconnaissance Patrols).

○ *Courage.* "Courage isn't about bullets, guns, bombs and blood like I used to think. Courage is a force that pushes you to stand up for you. You don't have to go off and fight for your country, or go get the stars and stripes tattooed on your forehead to be courageous" (Chris, Vet Program 01/28/93).

○ *Cover your ass.* Watch out behind you. Take care of yourself.

○ *CP.* Command Post.

○ *C-Rations or c-rats.* Some of the C-rations were left over from WWII. They included a can of the basic course, can of fruit, packet of dessert, packet of powdered cocoa, small package of cigarettes and two pieces of chewing gum.

Surgeon Holley rates the C-rations and the dining experience in the bush: C-rations are "small freeze-dried packets of different meals, which when reconstituted with water, make a fairly tasty dinner. We just heat up some water with a small, burning chunk of C-4 plastic explosive, which burns like Sterno, and then pour it right into the plastic bag and eat right out of the container. They have beef stew, chicken stew, and spaghetti, which are our three favorites. Some of the others are awful! We have no chairs, stools, or wash bowls, so our steel helmets serve as a lavatory, kitchen sink to wash yourself and your utensils, and a pot to heat up water. They also serve as a makeshift seat when you get tired of sitting on the ground. Lordy, Lordy, will I ever appreciate the luxurious goodies we have back home in the World.

A grunt eating C-ration.

Well, I must run now as our chopper is coming in, and I have to get one of the pilots to take this letter back to Dong Tam and mail it" (122).

One soldier tore the cardboard from his Spiced Beef meal, wrote a letter on the other side, and mailed it. It got there, too.

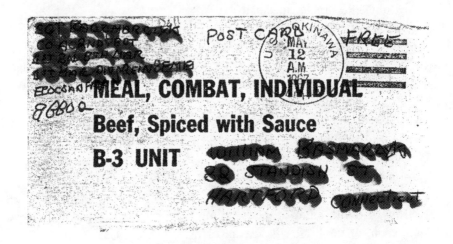

C-Ration cardboard cover used to send mail back to the US.

"During the Vietnam War, the McIlhenny Company sent thousands of copies of the "*Charley Ration Cookbook*"—filled with recipes for spicing up C-rations with Tabasco® Pepper Sauce—wrapped around two-ounce bottles of Tabasco® Pepper Sauce in waterproof canisters. The United States military now packs Tabasco® Pepper Sauce in every ration kit" (Joey Green's *Encyclopedia* 152-153). One such recipe follows:

"FOX HOLE DINNER FOR TWO
("Turkey and Chicken Poulette)

"Two spoons butter or oil or fat
"Two spoons flour
"*One can chicken and noodles
"*One can turkey loaf cut up into pieces
"Three dashes TABASCO® pepper sauce
"*Salt and pepper to taste
"*One can cheese spread
"*12 spoons milk
"*Crackers from one C-Ration can, crumbled

"*This is from your Basic C-Ration.

"No one likes to dine alone, and this recipe is ideal to combine a variety of C-Ration units.

"Melt butter or oil or fat, add flour and stir until smooth. Add milk and continue to cook until sauce begins to thicken. Add cheese spread and cook until cheese melts and sauce is even. Empty cans of turkey loaf and chicken noodles into the cheese sauce. Season with TABASCO®, salt and pepper to taste. Cover poulette with crumbled crackers and serve piping hot" (*The Charlie Ration Cookbook* 3).

For a prank, grunts sometimes stuffed the chemical heating pouch for the C-ration in a bottle. They added water and closed the cap. The bottle eventually expands and explodes. The favorite place to leave it was in a porta-john.

The North Vietnamese supply lines provided Duong Thu Huong and her compatriots with "rice, canned meat, fish, lard, Hai—Chau candies, dehydrated food BA70, and dried patties of shrimp sauce. And the height of luxury, there was concentrated milk from the Soviet Union and powdered eggs from China" (210).

○ *Crispy critters*. Burn victims.

○ *CS & CN*. Riot control hand grenades that burn eyes. Available to control demonstrations and riots if approved by MACV (Military Assistant Command Vietnam). Used to clear out tunnels and caves before any soldiers went in. Later in the war, CS was dropped from helicopters onto enemy base camps or suspected routes or rest areas (Hay 36-38).

○ **Cumshaw.** Chinese for tip or bribe; US for theft or corruption. Then there's Standard Operating Procedure. Cumshaw methods worked by getting food and some equipment—bartering with somebody who knows somebody who knows somebody. Commanding Officers rely on SOP—the right form (which may have been the wrong form yesterday) filled out in triplicate, black ink only, and turned over to the appropriate person. In two months you would be notified that the part you requested is no longer available; use part # f2948750923875 instead. Six weeks later, you might be told that the part had gotten lost. Try again. "Possibly before your tour in Vietnam was half over, the needed piece of equipment would finally come through. According to some people sitting in offices back in Washington, that system was efficient" (Anderson *Other War* 120-121). One resourceful man, Senior Chief Petty Officer B. G. Feddersen, was known as the king of cumshaw. According to a story in *Time*, Feddersen unclogged a harbor loaded with cargoes and airstrips crammed with traffic. "Within 23 days of Feddersen's arrival, he had shaken loose 2,600 lbs. of spare parts for failing trucks and bulldozers, procured vitally needed aluminum sections for the airstrip's 8,000 ft. jet runway, and made MCB 10 (Mobile Construction Battalion 10) the only outfit on the base with a perpetual supply of beer, steaks, lettuce, tomatoes and lumber" (*Vietnam War Diary* 61).

○ **Cut me some slack.** Don't hassle me. I'm doing the best I can.

O'Neal's Living Quarters—My sleeping bag behind me with Net.

DELTA (D)

○ ***Daily Dailys.*** Yellow malaria pills (Chloroquine) and pink salt tablets (Dapson). A doctor in 'Nam explains: "By ordering the pills' consumption, small unit leaders were helping keep their units combat efficient, they were taking care of their men. As far as the troops were concerned, however, both pills only made life in the bush more miserable—the former caused diarrhea and the latter nausea, and besides, everybody had a buddy who took both but still became a heat casualty one day and was medevaced with malaria the next" (Anderson *The Grunts* 216).

Nurses instructing men in daily-dailies.

A grunt knows the humping can be so hard that salt tablets are useless. "Our New Guy sweats and stumbles and looks like he could get lost looking for a place to shit. A heat casualty for sure. The New Guy eats pink salt tablets like a kid eating jelly beans, then gulps hot Kool-Aid from his canteen" (Hasford 151).

○ ***Dap.*** Elaborate ritual. Slaps, hand-shaking, snapping fingers.

○ ***DC-3s (also called "Puff the Magic Dragon)*** called in for air support by a unit. It's dark, but the grunts that have climbed up on a bunker can still see the red tracers. A Vietnam Vet can never forget what he calls the "incongruous"—"With a cold beer, listening to the newest music on a transistor radio, they are two miles away from the action 'where men worked and die to the accompaniment of sounds which at that very moment were provoking bodies to the boogaloo back in Frisco and Denver, Philly and Dallas'" (Anderson *The Grunts* 46).

○ **DD 214.** Discharge papers. Two copies: one is a full copy called an "undeleted copy"; it contains the type of discharge (honorable/dishonorable), lost time, re-up code, and any other essential information; the other is a "deleted copy," much abbreviated, and will not contain all the information above. Above all, do not lose your DD 214. The VA (Veteran's Administration) determines your benefits based on your DD 214: VA home loans, retirement, unemployment, educational opportunities. Deals on cars, apartments, apartments are often available to members of the service, but you will need your DD 214.

    If you lose your DD 214, you can order copies through the National Archives. Note: information obtained through <*http://201file.com/dd214.php*>.

○ **Dear John.** The dreaded letter from home from a girlfriend, fiancée, or wife writing to say that the relationship is over; letters from loved ones were the most valuable connection to the World; the Dear John was the most devastating because that close connection was gone at the worst time of a grunt's life. Charlie Plumb who spent six years as a POW said that the VC withheld mail from them except they didn't waste any time delivering a "Dear John" to one of the POWs (160). With that connection broken, comes isolation; it's not the grunt's fault that a controversial war led to "an increase in Dear John letters. As the war became more and more unpopular back home, it became increasingly common for girlfriends, fiancées, and even wives to dump the soldiers who depended upon them. Their letters were an umbilical cord to the sanity and decency that they believed they were fighting for" (Grossman 277).

○ **Death Notification.** The news is usually delivered by a uniformed officer. Although the family has the right to see the body of its loved one, many were discouraged from doing so. At Grave Registration in country, the body had already been embalmed. Death by a mine or booby trap is not what the military wants anyone to see.

○ **Debriefing.** As most of the men came back one at a time, there was little to no debriefing, no preparing them to reenter the world of civilians. There were also no parades which is why most Vietnam veterans felt that they have not yet been welcomed home. Many wives reported that they could not touch their husbands while they were sleeping for fear of being attacked. Many veterans still carry weapons on their person and many hide when they hear thunder, fearing incoming missiles. The Fourth of July can be hell for some vets.

○ **Dee-dee.** Also *dee-dee mahhh.* Go. Go quickly. Beat it. One of the Vietnamese words grunts used.

○ **Deferments.** College students granted deferments could avoid induction into the military. Issued in July 1965, a Selective Service document, "Channeling," wasn't published until 1967 in *New Left Notes* (Zaroulis and Sullivan 105). "For the first time, students could see how the 'club of induction' [joining the military] was used to control their lives: certain occupations, deemed important by the government, were to be allowed deferments. Thus without directly ordering young men to become, say, engineers, the government was able to assure that an adequate supply of engineers would be available by granting deferments to students enrolled in that discipline" (Zaroulis and Sullivan 105).

College students, however, had to be in good standing. "Many college freshmen were suddenly faced with the pressures of an 'A, B, C, D, Nam' grading system, which only increased the pressure on students who had trouble enough adjusting to the rigors of academic life and social responsibility. The rule, of course, was well understood. Once a deferment was lost, it was gone for good" (Ebert 25). "Deferments also ran out after graduation" (Ebert 26).

○ **DEMOS**. Also called **MOS**. Military Occupation Specialty. (Not necessarily your real specialty. You might go over assigned to drive a truck but end up a cook.)

○ **DEROS.** "Dee-ros." **D**ate of **E**xpected **R**eturn from **O**verseas; rotated out of service. According to psychologist James Goodwin, "DEROS did its job: For those who had been struggling with a psychological breakdown due to the stresses of combat, the DEROS fantasy served as a major prophylactic to actual overt symptoms of acute combat reaction. For these veterans, it was a hard-fought struggle to hold on until their time came" (Ebert 397).

○ **Deserters.** "The formal definition of 'deserter' is someone absent without leave for thirty days or more, without extenuating circumstances" (Dunnigan and Nofi 338) or "being absent with the intention to remain away permanently" (Kutler 157). The first definition is easier to apply; an authority can determine if the "extenuating circumstances" were reasonable. The second definition, however, is nearly impossible. How is one to determine another's "intent" to do anything?

"During the Vietnam War, desertion rates reached an all-time high of 73.5 out of 1,000 soldiers in 1971, a 400 percent increase over the 1966 rate of desertion" (Kutler 158). Johnny explained in one of the Vet programs why some Americans deserted. "If caught, what could they do? Court martial you and send you home?" (1/25/03). Desertion, in combination with AWOL incidents, cost the army approximately 550,000, of whom approximately "92,000 were declared deserters" (Dunnigan and Nofi 339).

○ **Desertion.** According to Master-Sergeant Duncan, the number of VC desertions cannot be trusted. "In an effort to show waning popularity for the Viet Cong [South Vietnamese Communist sympathizers], great emphasis was placed on figures of Viet Cong defections. Even if the unlikely possibility of the correctness of these figures is accepted, they are worthless when compared to ARVN [Army of the Republic of Vietnam] desertions. The admitted desertion rate and incidents of draft dodging, although deflated, was staggering. Usually, only those caught are reported. Reading [Operational Summaries] and newspapers while in Vietnam, I repeatedly saw reference made to hundreds of ARVN listed as missing after the major battles. The reader is supposed to conclude that these hundreds, which by now total thousands, are prisoners of the Viet Cong. They are definitely not listed as deserters. If this were true, half of the Viet Cong would be tied down as guards in POW compounds—which, of course, is ridiculous" (Duncan 92-93).

Desertion was a universal problem. "Desertion was rife throughout the regiment at that time, as though soldiers were being vomited out, emptying the insides of whole platoons. The authorities seemed unable to prevent desertions" (Ninh 23). "Between 1965 and 1972, The Republic of Vietnam Armed Force (RVNAF) lost about 120,000 servicemen annually to desertion. The ARVN sustained the greatest losses with soldiers deserting at 2.5 times the overall RVNAF rate . . . . Desertion rates—officially considered defections—from the NLF and NVA were significantly lower than those for the RVNAF, averaging about 20,000 per year between 1967 and 1971 . . . . Scholars attribute the difference in desertion rates . . . to the greater commitment and offensive, guerilla fighting style of the North" (Kutler 158).

○ **Det cord.** A detonation cord, fuse for demolition. Burns as fast as 2500 feet per second.

○ **Deuce and a half.** A 2.5 ton truck.

○ *Dew, dew-like.* Marijuana. Plentiful and cheap in Vietnam. Two and a half pounds cost as little as five dollars (*Vietnam War Diary* 170). Heroin was available for $2 a "fix"; it was nearly pure (*Vietnam War Diary* 203).

○ *Dien Bien Phu.* A fifty-five day fight from March 13, 1954 to May 7, 1954 over control of Vietnam. Probably the grunts knew only a little of Vietnam's recent past, but they did know that a DMZ had been established at the 17th parallel. And that a North Vietnam and a South Vietnam were two countries of sorts. The North supporting Southerners in South Vietnam (the VC, a guerilla force) to take over the South, and reunify the country, South Vietnam attempting to repel dissidents (VC) and troops from North Vietnam to remain its own country. Then there were the Vietminh (Cambodian Communists) and the Montagnards (indigenous mountain people, anti-Communist). Then the United States to keep South Vietnam from going Communist sent in military advisors and Special Forces; by May of 1962, the United States had 5000 troops in Vietnam; 3000 Marines were on the way.

Vietnam and the countries around it had been seen as a buffer between two much larger countries: India and China, hence the name of the region called "Indochina." It would be March 29, 1973 before the last American troops leave (Bowman 210-211).

Dien Bien Phu Campaign Victory Pin issued after French defeated in 1954.

○ *Dig in.* Dig foxhole for shelter in case of attack; most soldiers considered this to be make-work project since they were likely to be ordered to advance, thereby leaving their foxholes for someone else to use. (See Boondoggle above.) Marines, apparently, *never* dug in. Herr reports on the situation at Khe Sanh near the DMZ where Marines have been shelled for 45 days, with no resupplies or evacuations possible. Peter Braestrup of the *Washington Post* asked, "General, why haven't those Marines *dug in*? The room was quiet. Braestrup had a fierce smile on his face as he sat down. When the question had begun, the colonel had jerked suddenly to one side of his chair, as though he'd been shot. Now, he was trying to get his face in front of the general's so that he could give out the look that would say, 'See, General? See the kinds of peckerheads I have to work with every day?'" (150-152).

Home is where you dig it.   *Digging in before assault on Hill 875.*

DIG
by Raymond Bolton
(Marine who served at Khe Sanh during the siege)

What do you see?
I see nothing! A mute night
as thick as death.
It must be death.
Dig deeper!
I cannot penetrate the darkness
and the aloneness.
Dig deeper!
What do you see?
Ideas and dreams, hope and
fantasies and innocence.
Dig deeper!
What do you see?
Young men and birds,
water and the blue sky.
Dig deeper!
I hear voices and weeping.
I hear the flutter of wings
on the other shore.
Don't weep! Don't weep!
They are not on the other
shore. The voices, the
weeping and the wings are
your own heart. (Eichler 17)

○ *Dime.* The number 10. A good number.

○ *Dinki dow.* Crazy. For when nothing made sense, when you knew it was all wrong. Another Vietnamese phrase grunts used to describe the war. Sometimes you just gotta expect it. Like when one of your men does something you can't explain away. "[Taylor] would keep saying he couldn't take it no more. He was always singing old hymns. I had him carrying 200 pounds of ammo once, and when I got to the hill to set up for the night, I said, 'Taylor, where's my ammo?' he said, 'Man, you know that song about loose my shackles and set me free? I had to get free about a mile down the road. I got rid of that stuff in that stream. Them chains of slavery'" (Terry 47).

○ *Dinks, slopes.* More derogatory words for any Vietnamese. Derogatory names made the Vietnamese seem less human and made them into objects (Randy Cribbs, Jan 29, 2008). Also, *Chink.*

Offensive words, Herr noted, dehumanized the enemy. "Well you know what we do to animals . . . kill 'em and hurt 'em and beat on 'em so's we can train 'em. Shit, we don't treat the Dinks no different than that" (219).

Safer asked "[General] Westmoreland about the dreadful losses the South Vietnamese army was suffering. 'Oh, yes,' he said. 'But you must understand that they are Asians, and they don't really think about death the way we do. They accept it very fatalistically.'

"This was a widely held attitude among many Americans in Vietnam . . . . It was partly racism—'they're only gooks'—and partly that ancient defense mechanism of war, which is to reduce the enemy to a subspecies" (35). Claude Anshin Thomas, a Vietnam veteran (now a Buddhist monk), sees a more dangerous aspect to basic training—the creation of the Other. "The enemy was everyone unlike me, everyone who was not an American soldier. This conditioning is an essential ingredient in the creation of a good soldier. Soldiers are trained to see anything other as dangerous, threatening, and potentially deadly. You dehumanize the enemy. You dehumanize yourself" (7).

This attitude shared about the Asians' different way of thinking about death served the purpose of the Army, even though it wasn't necessarily true. A North Vietnamese member of a clean-up squad (called MIA) after a battle, Kien talks of death. He had once read, "There is no terrible hell in death . . . . Death is another life, a different kind than we know here. Inside death one finds calm, tranquility, and real freedom . . ." [Ninh's ellipsis]. "To Kien dead soldiers were more shadowy yet sometimes more significant than the living. They were lonely, tranquil, and hopeful, like illusions. Sometimes the dead manifested

themselves as sounds rather than shadows . . . ." The head of the MIA team (similar
to the United States' **Grave Registration**—see below) told his group, "'If you can't
identify [the dead bodies] by name we'll be burdened by their deaths for the rest
of our lives . . . He used to describe his work as though it were a sacred oath, and
ask others to swear their dedication. An oath was hardly necessary for Kien or the
others in the MIA team. They'd emerged from the war full of respect and mourning
for the unfortunate dead, named and nameless alike'" (Ninh 90-92).

○ **Ditti Bop.** Be cool. Be happy. Do it in style. Walking carelessly. "First was a style
of walking called the ditty bop. A direct expression of the new 'I-am-somebody'
pride among minority personnel, the ditty bop was accomplished by
exaggerating the normal roll and swing of hips, shoulders, and arms, and
locking one knee" (Anderson *Other War* 150).

○ **Ditt mow.** Move fast. Now.

○ **Division.** Three brigades.

○ **DMZ (or Z) De-militarized Zone.** Five mile-wide-strip separating North
Vietnam from South Vietnam. The Geneva Convention that established the
DMZ in 1954 also determined that there would be no firing through the **DMZ**
or over it. "It was dismissed, and our forward observer said that in school they
had told him that the Geneva convention says you can't fire white phosphorus
at troops; so you call it in on their equipment" (Grossman 203). The young
artilleryman's logic was "if we're gonna find ways around the Geneva convention,
what do you think the enemy is gonna do?" (Grossman 203).

   "Throughout its existence, the DMZ has come to mean different things to
different people. To the diplomats who drew it, the line represented a face-saving
truce to a problem whose solution was too deeply tied up with personal vanity
and national honor to be dealt with realistically, a truce which saved but little
western face and few Vietnamese lives. To the Vietnamese living south of it, the
line meant a flimsy guarantee that rice could be planted and harvested in peace,
that a governing group could have its sovereignty recognized the world over.
To the Vietnamese living north of it, the line was a constant and humiliating
reminder that the reunification of a homeland and a way of life, ravaged by
westerners for more than a century, was still unfinished . . . . To the young
grunts . . . the DMZ meant other things still . . . The Z was the reason the grunts
were in Vietnam; if it had never been violated, the grunts would not be in
Vietnam" (Anderson *The Grunts* 124).

○ **Doc. Medic** (Army); **Corpsman** (Navy) A respectful term for an enlisted medical assistant.

○ **Doctors and Surgeons.** Dr. Holley wrote home about the impact of the environment on grunts' health One poor sufferer, Charles Strong, took his immersion foot (jungle rot) home with him. "My feet was all scriggled up. My skin was raw and coming off. I still carry an infection on my feet right now that I have to visit the VA hospital on a regular basis to take treatment for. Then I started to take drugs to stop the pain in my feet" (Terry 56).

○ **Dog and Pony Show.** Visitors and/or VIPs in camp. Herr's reporting of VIPs' conversations makes it clear why he resisted joining the Command in the field. ("Where are you from, son?" "Macon, Georgia, Sir." "Real fine. Are you getting your mail okay, plenty of hot meals?" "Yes, Sir." "That's find, where you from son?" "Oh, I don't know, God, I don't know, *I don't know!*" "That's fine, real fine, where you from, son?" (216).

○ **Dog Tags.** Each G.I. was given two. (But a lot of grunts had as many as four or five, thinking of them as lucky charms.) Grunts in the bush often put one on an ankle, one around the neck in case killed in action . . . in hopes they could be identified. "Dog tags were two oval or rectangular (with rounded ends) tags worn by servicemen on a

President Johnson greetings nurses. Oct 27, 1966.

chain. Stamped data varied between services and period, but typically included name, serial number, blood type, and religion. Examples of other entries were tetanus inoculation dates and home address. If a soldier were killed one tag was left with the body and the other turned in. One tag had a notch in one end and it was rumored that this was to be inserted between the teeth of the dead man. This is a myth; it was a positioning notch for a stamping machine" (Rottman *FUBAR* 41). (See also Appendix E, the government's report on dog tags found in SE Asia.)

○ **Do it right or don't do it.** If you don't do something the right way, you could get killed and get others killed. You might not be able to learn from experience because you might never get a second chance. As a new LT, Lewis Puller gets an invaluable lesson. Most of the company had eaten when it was still light and heated their food with little pieces of C-4 (a plastic explosive); Puller had neglected to bring any rations, so he thankfully took a can of beans and franks from a member of another platoon. "They're better hot," he was told. But then he got his "first lesson in field comfort. Food can be eaten hot only during the daylight hours since the light from the heat tabs and plastique can be spotted by the enemy. I would remember next time, but hungry as I was and as newly acquainted to C rations, even cold, the grub tasted delicious" (88-89).

○ **Domino Theory.** President Eisenhower explains the Domino Theory, the underpinning of the Vietnam War: "You have a row of dominoes set up, and you knock over the first one and what will happen to the last one is the certainty that it will go over very quickly. So you have the beginning of a disintegration that will have the most profound influences" (*Vietnam War Almanac* 35). Based on containing Communism, the Domino Theory was the same policy behind the fight in Korea (Kutler 177). Staff Sergeant Browne knew all about the Domino Theory—"you know, the Communists taking South Vietnam and then the Philippines and marching across the Pacific to Hawaii and then on to the shores of California" (Terry 156).

"Americans were always talking about freedom from Communism, whereas the freedom that the mass of Vietnamese wanted was freedom from the exploiters, both the French and the indigenous. The assumption that humanity at large shared the democratic Western idea of freedom was an American delusion" (Tuchman 256).

"I was not unique among my contemporaries in knowing most of these things ['that the Vietnamese people are anti-Saigon or pro Viet Cong']. However, when anybody questioned our being in Vietnam—in light of the facts—the old rationale was always presented: 'we have to stop the spread of communism somewhere . . . if we pull out, the rest of Asia will go Red . . . . these are uneducated people who have been duped; they don't understand the difference between democracy and communism'" (Duncan 93).

"This [domino] theory quite simply reduces a hodgepodge of peoples, each possessing its own lengthy, confused and emotionally charged history and cultural patterns into so many abstract names—neat black dominoes all ready to fall . . . . The thesis is a simple one. The devil is China, obsessed with a desire to conquer the free and independent nations of Southeast Asia. The Chinese have created a pattern of successful subversion first in North Vietnam and now South Vietnam. If they are allowed to attain victory there, it will create a momentum that will cause all of Southeast Asia to fall" (Scheer 37).

Robert McNamara says about the domino theory: "'Nineteen sixty-five is when American combat troops were sent to Vietnam. They were sent to deny victory to the hated and deeply feared Communists, to save some fantasized Southeast Asian dominoes from tumbling'" (Hendrickson 123).

Michael Herr, reporter, offers one reason why United States' troops were in Vietnam. "Not that you didn't hear some overripe bullshit about it: Hearts and Minds, Peoples of the Republic, tumbling dominoes, maintaining the equilibrium of the Dingdong by containing the ever encroaching Doodah; you could also hear the other, some young soldier speaking in all bloody innocence, saying, 'All that's just a *load*, man. We're here to kill gooks. Period'" (20).

○ ***Don't bunch up.*** Don't walk too close to the grunt just ahead. Ten feet. Follow ten feet behind. Take care of others by doing the right thing yourself. All bunched up, and a sniper could take out a bunch in a hurry. Ten feet and the guy ahead steps on a booby trap—you might be okay.

○ ***Don't choke.*** Do what you know is right. It might be what you've been trained to do. It might be instinct. Don't hesitate.

○ ***Don't think.*** Don't even think about it. Use your training.

○ ***Donut Dolly.*** A Red Cross volunteer, a "round eye" (Western woman).
   "'Round-eyed women' were viewed as part mother figure, part inaccessible movie goddess. The nurses were also, of course, officers and therefore doubly untouchable. Donut Dollies, the Red Cross volunteers who also visited China Beach, were held in somewhat less awe" (Safer 177).

○ ***Do's and don'ts in South Vietnam.***

        Do be courteous, respectful, and friendly;
        Don't be overly familiar with the Vietnamese.

        Do learn and respect Vietnamese customs;
        Don't forget you are the foreigner.

        Do be patient with the Vietnamese attitude toward time;
        Don't expect absolute punctuality.

        Do appreciate what the South Vietnamese have endured;
        Don't give the impression the US is running the war.

Do learn some useful Vietnamese phrases;
Don't expect all Vietnamese to understand English.

Do be helpful when you can;
Don't insist on the Vietnamese doing things your way.

Do learn what the South Vietnamese have to teach;
Don't think Americans know everything.

(From "*A Pocket Guide to Vietnam*" by the Armed Forces Information and Education & the Department of Defense, 5 April 1966, 94.)

NINE RULES
Assistance Command, Vietnam
For Personnel of US Military

The Vietnamese have paid a heavy price in suffering for their long fight against the Communists. We military men are in Vietnam now because their government has asked us to help its soldiers and people in winning their struggle. The Viet Cong will attempt to turn the Vietnamese people against you. You can defeat them at every turn by the strength, understanding, and generosity you display with the people. Here are the nine simple rules.

"Remember we are special guests here; we make no demands and seek no special treatment.

"Join with the people! Understand their life, use phrases from their language, and honor their Customs and Laws.

"Treat women with politeness and respect.

"Make personal friends among the soldiers and common people.

"Always give the Vietnamese the right of way.

"Be alert to security and ready to react with your military skill.

"Don't attract attention by loud, rude, or unusual behavior.

"Avoid separating yourself from the people by a display of wealth or privilege.

"Above all else you are members of the U. S. military forces on a difficult mission, responsible for all your official and personal actions.

"Reflect honor upon yourself and the United States of America."

(Armed Forces Information and Education. Department of Defense. *Vietnam*, iii).

Guidelines for American Vietnamese Rapport
Religions of South Vietnamese in Faith and Facts
US Navy, Bureau of Naval Personnel, Chaplains Division (1967)
at sacred-texts.com

"Be prepared for difference in thought, behavior, customs, etc.

"Be patient, persistent, consistent, acceptable, and accepting.

"Be interested in people as individuals.

"Be alert to areas of agreement rather than disagreement.

"Be aware of possible long-range consequences of gifts, actions, and reactions.

"Be adaptable when moral principles are not involved.

"Be prepared to treat Vietnamese as you would desire to be treated.

"Be aware of your attitudes. Your actions will produce good or bad for you, your buddies, and those who follow you.

"Be understanding, compassionate, and concerned.

"Determine to be the best American example possible."

◦ ***Draft.*** In 1968, defense officials announced that 302,000 men face draft—this is still lower than 1966, but these men are needed to replace men with completed tours. In a few cases, a judge volunteered a young man, offering him jail or the Army. It was mandatory to register with Selective Service at age eighteen and carry the draft card at all times. Used for the Vietnam War, the first time since 1942. The draft in December 1969 actually became a lottery. On December 1, 1969 when troops were badly needed overseas, every birth date minus the year: January 12, March 9, November 21, April 17, February 13, etc. was pulled out one-by-one. The first date chosen would be #1—it was September 14—and any young man at least eighteen born on September 14 knew he was first to be considered. All dates were chosen one-by-one and numbered accordingly. Those young men whose birth dates were low numbers knew they were at risk of being drafted. A good number, the best number, was 365. Chances were

*Selective Service System Notice
of Classification.*

you'd be waving a friend goodbye. Because many young men Uncle Sam wanted had the same numbers, the letters of the alphabet became the second determiner.

Five young men with the same number were then considered in alphabetical order by last name: Bickerstaff, Ford, Johnson, Pike, and Welch. The draft/lottery ended in 1973.

In WWII, 66% of American military personnel were draftees. In Vietnam, only 25% (or 648,500) were draftees. These draftees accounted for 30.4% (or 17,725) of combat deaths in Vietnam (Government Report in Appendix D for totals by every war Americans have participated in; casualties and deaths by branch and rank).

"The draft in the Vietnam era was full of inequities. Applicable standards for deferments and exemptions varied from place to place, depending in part on whether a local board was having trouble meeting its quota. Reserve and National Guard units became safe havens—for those with the right connections or who happened to be at the right place at the right time" (*Roanoke Times*, 21 September 1992, A10). "The student draft deferments, along with the decision not to ask for a declaration of war and not to mobilize our reserve forces, were part of a deliberate Presidential policy not to arouse the passions of the American people" (Summers *On Strategy* 22).

The draft policy had even wider implications. "Draft policy during the war exempted from military service those men who either were students or held certain jobs, such as teaching, that required a university degree. Since the proportion of minority members in universities during the 1960s were far below the minority proportion for the general population, the draft policy amounted to a form of discrimination" (Anderson *Other War* 149).

With a draft in place, young men found themselves in a waiting game. "I really didn't have an opinion of the war at first. I was praying that the war would bypass me. I chose not to evade the draft but to conform to it. I figured it was better to spend two years in the service than five years in prison. And I figured that for nineteen years I had enjoyed a whole lot of fruits of this society. I knew that you didn't get anything for free" (Terry 55).

Johnny was 19 when drafted "cause I couldn't afford no college. So when I went to Vietnam, I was dumber than dirt" (Vietnam Program 1/28/93). Al thought there should never be a draft unless we were in all-out war (Vet Program 2/4/93).

In a letter that appeared in *The Roanoke Times and World News*, 3 December 1990, Owen Schultz said, "In 1969, the Smithtown, N.Y. draft board granted me classification 1-H following a hearing about my conscientious-objector status. This meant I awaited induction and assignment to alternative, humanitarian service in lieu of military duty. It also meant that I would not go to Vietnam, or to federal penitentiary for five years, or pay a $10,000 fine. I don't remember who got the money, but dissent had a clear price tag against which you could weigh your choices."

Vietnam
by James Griffin

We are men who stand alone,
12,000 miles, away from home.
Our Hearts are emptied, all but blood
Our bodies are covered with sweat and mud.
This is the life we choose to live
A year of lifetime is what we give . . .
You never know what it's like to be here,
You, with your party girls and beer.
Over there, you aren't even trying,
While over here our men are dying.
March at dawn, and plant your signs on the White
House lawn.
Shout out, ban the bomb, and there is no war in Viet
Nam . . . .
Pop some pills, and roll in the sun,
Simply refuse to carry a gun.
There's nothing else for you to do?
And I am supposed to die for you?
Stand fast prepare for a blow,
I'll tell you something you do not know.
It's not for you and me this war goes on,
It's for the people of South Vietnam,
All they want to do is live and be free,
And to live in human dignity.
There is another thing I want you to know,
And that's where I think you should go.
We are already here and we are here to stay.
We'll be here tomorrow,
If we make it through today. (Eichler 53-54)

○ **Draft Dodging.** Willard Gaylin, MD, in an article that appeared in the *LA Times*, Thursday, October 29, 1992 (B7) said, "I worried about what might happen to these young men [draft dodgers] . . . in Federal prison.

"We needn't have worried. In 1967, when I began what turned out to be three years of research, there were all of 70 imprisoned political war resisters in the entire country.

"Where were all the rest? They were utilizing the loopholes and dodges that were built into the Selective Service Act to protect the children of the middle class. Even when most middle-aged influential men supported the war, they were making sure that their sons did not serve. As late as 1969, I did not have one friend, one colleague or patient who had a child serving unwillingly in Vietnam. How did they get out? They wriggled through the loopholes that had been designed for them.

"It is not difficult, therefore, to see why Bill Clinton squirmed through procedures made available to him by an Establishment that did not want to send educated white boys to war. Nor is it difficult to understand why the wealthier, better-connected Dan Quayle had to do less squirming to get himself leapfrogged into a choice position in the National Guard. Neither young man had to be ashamed of the action he took; they were expected to take such action. Republicans and Democrats, pro—and anti-war, we protected our children" (Gaylin B7).

"In North Vietnam, it was more difficult to 'dodge the draft' . . . North Vietnam had a very practical attitude towards reluctant soldiers. If a soldier in the north deserted, or refused to show up for military duty, some soldiers were sent to the man's village or city or neighborhood and spoke with his family. Avoiding military service was shameful" (Dunnigan and Nofi 272-3).

○ **Drugs.** Spec.4 Richard J. Ford III watches a friend, Davis, who didn't make it as a LRRP (Long Range Reconnaissance Patrol), so he turned to trouble. "First chance we go to town, he go get some cash. 'cause he stayed high all the time. Smokin' marijuana, hashish . . . And some guys used to play this game. They would smoke this opium. They'd put a plastic bag over their head. Smoke all this smoke. See how long you could hold it. Lot of guys would pass out.

"In the field most of the guys stayed high. Lot of them couldn't face it. In a sense, if you was high, it seemed like a game you was in. You didn't take it serious. It stopped a lot of nervous breakdown.

"See, the thing about the field that was so bad was this. If I'm working on the job with you stateside and you're my best friend, if you get killed, there's compassion. My boss say, well, you better take a couple of days off. Get yourself together. But in the field, we can be the best of friends and you get blown away. They put a poncho around you and send you back. They tell 'em to keep moving.

"We had a medic that give us a shot of morphine anytime you want one. I'm not talkin' about for the wounded. I'm talkin' about when you want to get high. So you can face it" (Terry 37-38).

Late in his tour, Spec.4 Robert Holcomb writes: "people started getting very hostile towards each other, because it was getting late in the war. And there were a lot of drugs around. And a lot of people were taking them. The Communists were making sure the American soldiers got them. And others were making sure drugs were available, because they could make a lot of money. Drugs took a great toll on all soldiers.

"Some guys were choked to death in their sleep, because they drank too much alcohol or were taking drugs. Some ODed. They were mainly not really smoking grass so much anymore, but taking 'number tens,' which are something like Quaaludes, and speed. And that was devastating, taken together. Of course, there was the scag. And whether you smoked it or snorted it, you really got fucked up" (Terry 211-212).

○ **Dust-off.** Med evacuation by helicopter; also called Medevac. "Dust Off" was an unused call word until the United States was fighting in a country sometimes dry and dusty. This gave a formal name to Medical Evacuations. "Because of the bravery and devotion to duty of these helicopter pilots and crews, many lives were saved. Often Dust-off choppers landed under heavy enemy fire to pick up wounded soldiers or hovered dangerously above the battlefield as an injured man was hoisted up to the helicopter. The seriously wounded were taken directly from the field to a hospital . . . [saving] many lives and greatly improving the soldiers' morale" (Hay 39). A Dust Off chopper could also carry non-wounded under the condition that the chopper might have to abandon them if called to evacuate wounded soldiers (Dorland & Nanney 30-31).

This job carried many risks: crashes, unsafe landing sites, vulnerable while hovering. "Statistics also confirm the impression that the air ambulance pilots and crewmen stood a high chance of being injured, wounded, or killed in their one-year tour. About 1,400 Army commissioned and warrant officers served as air ambulance pilots in the war. About one-third of them ended up as casualties—to hostile fire, nonhostile crashes as a result of weather and night flights. Helicopter losses on medical missions were 3.3 times that of all other forms of helicopter missions in the Vietnam War" (Dorland & Nanney 117).

Night Dust-Off
by Basil Paquet

A sound like hundreds of barbers
stropping furiously, increases;
suddenly the night lights,
flashing blades thin bodies
into red strips
hunched against the wind
of a settling slickship.

Litters clatter open,
hands reaching
into the dark belly of the ship
touch toward moans,
they are thrust into a privy,
feeling into wounds,
the dark belly all wound,
all wet screams riven limbs
moving in the beaten night. (Rottmann 18)

(Note: Basil Paquet was drafted into the U. S. Army as a conscientious objector and served from 1966-1968 as a medic, including service in Vietnam, 1967-68 with the 24th Evacuation Hospital. During his service, he refused to carry a gun. A slickship is a helicopter troopship. During his tour, he realized he couldn't be one-half CO. What was he doing in a war?)

ECHO (E)

"We are not about to send American boys nine or
ten thousand miles away from home to do what
Asian boys ought to be doing for themselves."
—Lyndon Johnson, 1964

○ *E-1.* Recruit. Monthly pay, Vietnam $115.28.

○ *E-2.* Private. Monthly pay, Vietnam $127.80.

○ *E-3.* Private First Class, Monthly pay, Vietnam $155.10.

○ *Early-Outs.* Leaving your unit before your term of service. Drop or reduction in time of service. Soldiers with 150 days or less. After DEROSed out, the Army term was ETS or estimated time of service. A number of Purple Hearts could get you an Early-Out, but not because you wanted to go to college. Soldier Steve Frederick had calculated two plans to get out of the field. He wrote his dad about the plans: (1) get him enrolled in college, any college and get him registered for 12 credit hours; that would knock 60 days off his tour; (2) if that didn't work because his company commander really liked what he was doing temporarily in the rear—well, he was torn. "I couldn't [stay in this job in the rear] because I have too much pride in myself. And besides, I feel I should stay with my men and do the best job I can in keeping them alive. Don't get me wrong, if I can get a rear job, I'll take it, but I could never have it said that I was in the rear because I was a dud or was scared" (Ebert 404).

○ *Eat the Apple and Fuck the Corps.* Marines talking about the Marine Corps.

○ *Elephant grass.* Tall, razor-sharp tropical plant. Because it is razor-sharp, it is nearly impenetrable. "Forget the Cong, the *trees* would kill you, the elephant grass grew up homicidal, the ground you were walking over possessed malignant intelligence, your whole environment was a bath" (Herr 66).

∘ *EM.* Enlisted man. In a rank below warrant officer or commissioned officer.

∘ *EM Club.* The enlisted man's club.

Entertainment at an enlisted man's club.

∘ *Entrenching tool.* Carried by the infantry. It was a multi-purpose device—a shovel and a pick. Mainly a shovel for digging in.

∘ *EOD.* Explosive Ordnance Disposal. Usually a team is sent to disarm explosive devices.

∘ *Extraction.* Withdrawal of troops by helicopter.

FOXTROT (F)

"You can kill ten of my men for every one I kill of yours,
but even at those odds, you will lose and I will win."
—Ho Chi Minh to the French (late 1940s)

○ *Fatigues.* Standard combat uniform. Early in the war, the Army issued what it already had. Some of what soldiers wore was not suitable for the ground and weather in Vietnam. With 100 percent humidity, nothing stayed dry. Soldiers were always requesting socks from home since theirs rotted. "Fatigue uniforms were equally deplorable; the constant dampness rotted the seams and weakened the threads and the jungle constantly clenched and tore at the clothing, making short work of the hardiest material" (Ebert 198). Because of the fungus that caused immersion foot (and other parts of the body), many soldiers chose to skip underwear because it stayed damp all the time—just as their feet did. So with fatigues rotting and falling apart, some soldiers were left "with their asses hanging out" (Ebert 198).

Danny Phillips dressed in fatigues.

◦ *F-4.* Phantom jet fighter–bomber.

◦ *FIGMO.* Acronym for "Fuck it, I got my orders!" used by GIs to indicate that they had received their orders telling them they were going home (Ebert 417).

◦ *Firebase or FB.* Home place for artillery and grunts. "The smaller bases were firebases, where artillery or mortars were set up to provide fire support for nearby infantry. Firebases were often temporary, set up for a particular mission and then abandoned. Firebases often contained some infantry to help out with defending the places against Communist attack. There were not a lot of troops operating from firebases; the emphasis was on protecting the big guns. Firebases were often put in hard to reach places, like the tops of hills. This made them easier to defend and gave the guns an easier shot at targets below" (Dunnigan and Nofi 154-155).

Setting up firebase.

Aerial View of Firebase.

○ **Firing Rate.** "There is a profound resistance to killing one's fellow man. In World War II, 75-80 percent of riflemen did not fire their weapons at an exposed enemy, even to save their lives and the lives of their friends. In previous wars non-firing rates were similar.

"In Vietnam the non-firing rate was close to 5 percent [or a firing rate around 90-95%].

"The ability to increase this firing rate, though, comes with a hidden cost. Severe psychological trauma becomes a distinct possibility when psychological safeguards of such magnitude are overridden. Psychological conditioning was applied en masse to a body of soldiers, who, in previous wars, were shown to be unwilling or unable to engage in killing activities . . . . The triad of methods used to achieve this remarkable increase in killing [from 25% to 95%] are desensitization, conditioning, and denial defense mechanisms" (Grossman 250-251).

○ **Five O' Clock Follies.** The daily press briefings, colloquially known as Five O'Clock Follies, held by the US Information Agency. More of a public relations exercise. The US continued to head to victory with charts of body counts of the enemy to show success. Herr refers to these briefings as "an Orwellian grope through the day's events as seen by the Mission" (99).

"Wooden-headedness, the 'Don't-confuse-me-with-the-facts' habit, is a universal folly never more conspicuous than at upper levels of Washington with respect to Vietnam. Its grossest fault was under-estimation of North Vietnam's commitment to its goal" (Tuchman 375-376).

George Orwell, writing about the Spanish Civil War, almost 25 years before the Vietnamese War, said "Political language . . . [is designed to make lies sound truthful and murder respectable] (139). Defenseless villages are bombarded from the air. The inhabitants [were] driven out into the countryside. The cattle machine-gunned, the huts set on fire with incendiary bullets: this is called pacification. Millions of peasants are robbed of their farms and sent trudging along the roads with no more than they can carry: this is called transfer of population" (139, 136).

Linguist Peter Farb lists a few of the deceptive words from the Vietnam War: *air raid*—routine limited duration protective device; *defoliation*—a resources control program; *a condolence award*—the $34 given to South Vietnamese families who lost a family member by our mistake; one way for a poor South Vietnamese adult to get money was to pretend to be hit by a passing Jeep or other military vehicle; reparations varied, depending on the acting skills of the so-called injured man; *our bombing errors*—navigational misdirections; a *new life hamlet* became a refugee camp; we upgraded a destroyed straw hut into a *structure*; *sinking a dugout* became the sinking of a vessel; logs thrown across a stream was turned into the *destruction of a bridge*; a hastily-built bomb shelter blown up was really a *bunker or maybe even a network of tunnels*. Farb calls this language "*ornate euphemism*" meant to hide or soften the death and destruction of war (155-156).

Herr noticed another problem with language: repetition. Watching television news night after night, year after year, a news anchor or reporter would "say that American casualties for the week had reached a six-week low, only eighty GI's had died in combat, and you'd feel like you'd just gotten a bargain" (215).

○ *Flack jacket.* Heavy vest (12 pounds) worn for protection against shrapnel, not bullets; most didn't wear it because they were already humping at least 40 pounds. First jackets were fiber-glass filled; later ones were ceramic.

○ *Flare.* Any illumination projectile either hand or weapon-fired. Frequently used at a landing zone to alert the pilot of the conditions: red=hot, enemy near; yellow=careful; green=safe to land.

○ *Flower Power.* A counter-culture that started in San Francisco and moved east. Woodstock, psychedelic music, Make Love Not War.

Americal Division
By Sgt. Dudley Farquhar

Was it really that long ago?
They called us the Flower Generation,
Children of the '60's, the Beatles,
Hula Hoops and Woo-Woo Ginsburg,
But along came Vietnam
They sent us to Basic Training,
To learn about "Mr. Charles."
We were young, and it seemed exciting,
But why don't the faces go away?
We left our American Bandstand world,
But America wasn't behind us.
We fought the gallant fight,
But weren't allowed to win.
Some of us were lucky: we came back
The POW/MIAs can't say the same.
The media did a job on us,
A portrayal that wasn't fair.
The drug addicts and baby killers came home,
And we lived with Calley's mistake.
For years we hid in our closet world,
And hoped America would come around.
We watch the "Hot Spots" with vivid reality,
Knowing it could happen, once again.
The war is over, but the battle lingers on,
So Washington erected "THE WALL."
Names on top of names,
But one meant so much to me
        DAWSON
To most everyone, just a name among the thousands,
But to his platoon, he was the best.
He gave his life for his men.
Six letters on a wall, no thank you.
Words don't tell the story.
        VIETNAM
The Hurt Lives On.

Dedicated to the memory of SSGT ROBERT C. DAWSON, KILLED IN ACTION 18 JUNE, 1970, CHU LAI, VIETNAM. Some people come into our lives and quickly go. Some stay for a while and leave memories on our hearts and we are never, ever the same. Bob Dawson was more than a soldier in a strange land—he was my friend. (Written in 1982 after attending the dedication of the Vietnam Veterans Memorial in Washington, D.C.)

○ **Flying lesson.** Disposing of a prisoner; i.e., tossing him or her out of an airplane. "This brother and the squad leader, a white dude, for some reason they felt they could interrogate this man. This man wasn't speaking any English. They did not speak any Vietnamese. I could not understand that at all. But they hollerin', 'where you come from? How many you?' And they callin' him everything. Dink. Good. Mother-fucker. He couldn't say anything He was scared.

"The next thing I knew, the man was out of the helicopter.

"I turned around and I asked the folks what happened to him.

"They told me he jumped out.

"I said, 'naw, man. The man ain't jumped out.'

"The brother said, 'yes he did. He one of those tough VC'" (Terry 94-95).

○ **FNG.** Fucking New Guy. Because of the Army's system of rotation replacements, troops constantly had a new soldier in a squad whose inexperience and incompetence could put others in harm. A Marine coming in new remembered hostile looks. "He interpreted the veterans' glances to be a silent but subtle warning: Hey, you better get your act together quick" (Ebert 131). In a few months, that soldier would have the experience he needed, but because others are rotating in and out, his goal was to complete his term, to think more about how much time he had left to serve (to become a short-timer with fewer and fewer days left to serve). "The trouble was, especially for combat soldiers, there weren't a lot of people willing or eager to show the FNG (fucking new guy) the ropes. With the exception of that few percent of returning troops who had been in combat before, the guys who had been in the bush for six months or so, and survived the process, were leery of getting too close to an FNG. New troops did not know how to move, they made mistakes, and often those mistakes got the FNG killed, as well as anyone standing close to him. Walking into booby traps, minefields, and ambushes were common FNG mistakes. What was the effect of all this?" (Dunnigan and Nofi 77-78). No unity, no bonding, no cohesiveness; even the best of units experienced the endless comings and goings; destruction of traditional support found in other wars through lack of training.

All of the senses were assaulted when a new grunt landed in South Vietnam. "My impressions weren't unique for a new arrival in Saigon. I was appalled by the heat and humidity which made my worsted uniform feel like a fur coat.

Smells, Exhaust fumes from the hundreds of blue and white Renault taxis and military vehicles. Human excrement; the foul stagnant, black mud and water as we passed over the river on Cong Ly Street; and overriding all the others, the very pungent and rancid smell of what I later found out was *nuoc mam*, a sauce made much in the same manner as sauerkraut with fish substituted for cabbage. No Vietnamese meal is complete without it. People—masses of them! The smallest children, with the dirty faces of all children of their age, standing on the sidewalk unshod and with no clothing other than a shirtwaist that never quite reached the navel on the protruding belly. Those a little older wearing overall-type trousers with the crotch seam torn out—a practical alteration that eliminates the need for diapers" (Duncan 78-79).

∘ **FO.** Forward Observer. A person attached to a field unit to coordinate the placement of direct or indirect fire from ground, air or naval forces.

∘ **Follies.** The daily report on the war to journalists covering it. Example: the United States announces an "incursion into Cambodia," which is a joke because soldiers had been fighting in Cambodia long before. One vet in a Vet Program told about dragging a buddy back into Vietnam from Laos. "We weren't supposed to be there, either," Bobby said. "He was dead but we couldn't put down where he got dead."

∘ **Foo gas.** A mixture of explosives and napalm usually set in a fifty gallon drum.

∘ **Fours.** F-4's. Jet fighter-bomber.

∘ **Four F.** Not qualified for the armed services for medical and/or psychiatric reasons by the Selective Service Board. Four F is the final determination. If the draft board gave you a 1-Y, you could be recalled later to see if you were now fit to serve.

∘ **Frag.** Fragmentation grenade.

∘ **Fragging.** Killing a higher-ranked man considered to be dangerous to a squad or other unit; an assassination, usually by a grenade that could be easily tossed. "[Fragging] has always been an uncommon occurrence, particularly in the US armed forces. However, beginning in 1969, fragging incidents began to rise, a matter that soon came to the attention of the media. From 1969-1972, there were 96-126 incidents with 37-39 deaths; 290 incidents with 34 deaths; 333-335 incidents with 12 deaths; 37-59 incidents with 1-4 deaths" (Dunnigan and Nofi 221).

"Every soldier, marine, sailor or airman who fragged a unit leader believed at the time of the incident that he acted with more than ample justification. Such a view may sound incredible now, but anyone who has seen combat and perceived what it does to one's thinking processes can appreciate the extreme difficulty, perhaps even the folly of making value judgments on the thoughts and actions of men in a combat environment from a haven now made safe by both time and distance" (Anderson *The Grunts* 217-218).

One incident occurred when a captain, checking on the perimeter, found everybody on guard asleep. I just decided enough was enough, and at the last bunker, I woke the men up and took their names . . . . . 'I'm gonna kill you, you mother f . . . . .'

"I heard him pull the pin, and I went down fast into a ditch. The frag sailed right past me and sent off a few feet away. As soon as the dust cleared, I was right back on top of that bunker, and I really whaled on that guy. I think I would have killed him, but people pulled me off. He's in the stockade now. I hope he stays there" (*Newsweek* qtd. in *Vietnam War Diary* 194).

"Explanations offered for the fragging of unit leaders, indicated a belief that one's survival was threatened. Two specific and one general type of incident provoked nearly all such assumptions. First, two dates were always in the minds of Americans in Vietnam: R & R and Tour Rotation, one's last day in the 'Nam. The last thing a trooper wanted to hear was that either of those dates had been changed. In his anxiety to leave the war, he could see no real justification for either of those two dates being 'messed with by some paper-shuffling lifer in the rear.' Yet these important dates were sometimes changed often with no explanation to the grunt.

"The occurrence of a fragging is even more understandable, though no more justifiable, in the light of a second incident. Normal, though unofficial, practice among field units was to relieve men of patrol responsibilities within a few days of their rotation. Both troops and leaders were aware of the practice and the former naturally looked forward to the few days they could pass out water, C-Rations and mail instead of stalking VC or NVA. Occasionally, however, the combat situation dictated that such a policy be set aside. In such cases the troops affected were convinced there was someone around who 'didn't like me and wanted to screw me out of some slack time and even get me zapped.'

"The general variety of incident can be labeled 'unnecessary harassment.' With their different training, duties and outlook, leaders and troops held as completely different interpretations of unnecessary harassment as they held of the *take care* concept. [Examples of unnecessary harassment are nearly infinite in number, but the most frequently and loudly bitched about included making troops: cut their hair, salute and shine their boots in rear echelon areas; collect and bury all refuse from C-Ration meals in the field . . . plus the standard three mind blowers in the bush, malaria and salt pills, flak jackets and helmets, and the constant word changes" (Anderson *The Grunts* 218-219).]

○ **Freak.** Radio frequency; also a junkie or doper.

○ **Freedom Bird.** The plane that takes you home again. Sixteen hours home with little or no debriefing, no information about how you might be received, nothing about what had changed: your wife running the household, your wife with a job, a baby born while you were in 'Nam.

"From life and death to snooty bitches and a pile of rubber, steel, grease and vinyl from Detroit called 'Something to Believe in' was too great a distance for the veterans to cover in sixteen hours, or even sixteen days. It could be done physically but not mentally. Few could quickly assimilate that stark dichotomy, few could quickly move away from it and formulate those things their parents call career goals" (Anderson *The Grunts* 181).

LRRP Ford couldn't absorb the fact that he was leaving: "I should have felt happy I was goin' home when I got on that plane in Cam Ranh Bay to leave. But I didn't exactly. I felt—I felt—I felt very insecure 'cause I didn't have a weapon. I had one of them long knives, like a big hacksaw knife. I had that. And had my cane. And I had a couple of grenades in my bag. They took them from me when I got to Washington, right? And I felt insecure. I just felt real bad" (Terry 31).

Surgeon Byron Holley almost missed his flight. His friend, Hack, took him out the night before for one last dinner and a few beers. Much later, about 5 a.m., Hack and Holley managed to get back to the 229th Dispensary where Holley had worked as CO. He set his alarm for 6:30 a.m. and crashed. "The next thing I knew it was twelve noon! *'Damn it to hell! I've missed my flight!'* I hollered, as I stumbled out of bed and went next door to look for Hack. His bed was empty, neatly made up, with a note on the spread. 'Doc, tried to wake you up, but you were like a wild man. See Abella, and he will get you on the next flight out. Keep in touch! Hack'" (197-198). I had such mixed feelings. "I found I was irritated at myself for missing my flight after waiting for 365 days and now at feeling so poorly on a day I had thought about for so long. But the wild and crazy night with Troy and Hack had been worth it, and would laugh about it later—me being the klutz who slept through his DEROS flight!" (198).

At the beginning of his tour, Holley said, "I thank God every day for America and I vow to kiss her good earth the minute I get off that big freedom bird 358 days hence! We have the finest country in the world, and anybody who doubts it should come to Nam for a spell as a grunt" (24). He kept his promise when his tour was over. When his Freedom Bird landed at Travis Air Force Base, he got off, dropped down, and kissed the grimy surface. "I had promised myself I would kiss the good old ground if God would just let me return home" (199).

In 'Nam, the name of the plane, "Freedom Bird," spoke volumes about what going home meant. But *Freedom Bird* hit a raw nerve with the CBS Bureau's Vietnamese staff. It found the name too casual, "[A]s if their tragedy, their national hemorrhage was nothing more than a stop on a Disney tour" (Safer 318).

Back to the World.

○ *Free strike zone* or *Free fire zone.* Fire at will. An area where everyone was deemed hostile and a legitimate target by US forces. No permission needed.

○ *French Fort.* A distinctive triangular structure built by the hundreds by the French when Vietnam was its colony.

○ *Freq.* Radio frequency.

○ *Friendly Fire.* A mistake that causes one side to fire on its own forces. An air strike might be called for help but given the wrong co-ordinates; bombs might be dropped on the wrong hill. Any deaths were added to the body count, as well as any dead animals. Relatives of any soldiers killed by friendly fire were told only that their beloved soldier died in battle. The Department of Defense called it a misadventure. In WWII, it was referred to as "own fire."

○ *Fuck.* Used so frequently that it became just an ordinary word: non-sexual, not to shock.

"Oh, how the grunts could swear. The four-letter words came out of the young faces as smoothly as they flowed from a forty-year-old whore's mouth in a Singapore alley. It lost its profanity, even started to sound a little beautiful against the absurdities of the day" (Anderson *The Grunts* 60). Michael Herr "saw that language like this was appropriate for the story of the Vietnam War, that its coarseness, ugliness, shockingness—whatever term you choose—was a just analogy for the ugliness of the war itself" (Hynes 205).

"Members of a community are defined not only by their proximity to one another but by their ability to recognize situations that determine language.... A speech community is not simply a group of people who have a language in common: it is also a community of people in daily interaction and who therefore share rules for the exact conditions under which different kinds of speech will be used" (Farb 18).

When Lynda Van Devanter returned to the World, she said, "Mary, pass the fucking salt" at a dinner the first day home. But she really wasn't home yet. Her mother scolded her in the kitchen: "around this house that word is not to be spoken" (256).

Lynda was still in the war. "Freud theorized that obscene speech in general serves as a substitute for aggression—as, for example, the hostility of the expletive '*Fuck you!*' The non-sexual use of the word in its many forms and combinations shows that it is always employed in speech situations that call for an aggressive vocabulary" (Farb 104). Doc Holley realized even before he left the 'Nam that he would have to think before he spoke. He writes to his girlfriend: "We have been talking about how we've all turned into crude animals—I know I can tell it from my language. Well, Baby, I now cuss like a sailor. It's a survival factor. It seems like the more you cuss, the less chance you have of going batty or nuts over here. I'm still the same old Byron, but I've aged a little, I'm sure. I'll just have to work on cleaning up my act when I see you again" (121-122).

○ *Fucked Up.* Messed-up. In one context: wounded terribly, maybe terminally; loss of body parts, third degree burns. In another, being stupid, high or drunk.

○ *Fuckin' A.* That's right. It's the best. "We should all have an affirmation and be able to shout it out. Sometimes we just got to tell the world we're feeling good. Fuckin' A! Right on! It means what it means—and it keeps it simple" (Anthony 82).

○ *Fugazi.* Shortened form of expression, "where the fuck are we." Fucked up or screwed up.

○ *FULRO.* United Front for the struggle of Oppressed Races. Resistance organization in the highlands of Vietnam made up of Montagnards, Cham, and ethnic Khmer. FULRO is still conducting resistance against Communist operations to subjugate the indigenous tribal peoples (Reinberg 90).

○ *Funny papers.* Topographical maps.

A Memphis Memorial to those from Shelby County who died in Vietnam.

GOLF (G)

"Tell the Vietnamese they've got to draw in their horns or we're
going to bomb them back into the Stone Age."
—Gen. Curtis LeMay (May 1964)

○ *Garbage.* Even when encamped in fairly remote firebases or while patrolling
in the bush, American troops maintained a rather high standard of living.
And they generated a lot of trash. Of course, one man's trash is another man's
treasure. What passed for garbage among Americans was often immensely
valuable to some poverty stricken Asian.

"In Vietnam the enemy often made use of American trash. Things like
broken boxes, old pallets, empty ration tins, and so forth, could be turned into
raw materials. Lots of reparable items were often found, such as broken radios,
damaged tools, worn clothing, and so forth, and the enemy seems to have had
workshops devoted to repairing damaged items of this sort. American troops
were often careless about policing up spent ammunition cases, which provided
a useful supply of brass for the enemy. And sometimes 'dud' ammunition was
left behind, rather than being destroyed, to be recovered and repaired by the
enemy. Worst of all, perhaps, Americans were careless of paper.

"It takes a lot of paper to run a modern army. Officially all paperwork likely
to be of use to the enemy is supposed to be destroyed. But this was not always
done efficiently. Things like preliminary drafts of reports or other official papers
were sometimes not treated with the respect the final versions received.

"So whenever they had the chance, the enemy pawed through American
garbage" (Dunnigan and Nofi 63).

Policing the area to clean up all garbage.

Tin Trap
by Randy Cribbs

That peanut butter tin
Became a must keepsake,
Not left for the
Surprise Charlie could make.
Never eat it,
Caused too much thirst,
There in the boonies
Nothing worse.
But with it
Those C's you could heat,
By mixing slowly with
A squirt of OD Deet.*
Hot chow for
The whole team;
Important then,
Silly as that
May seem;
And
Better to keep
It now than to
Feel it later in our lap,
Among the innards
Of Charlie's booby trap. (41)

*OD=olive drab; Deet = insect repellant

"In Vietnam, our soldiers were a major part of the enemy's supply system.
[emphasis added]. The US soldier, by nature, was rather wasteful, a trait that
carried over from his civilian life. He tended to discard anything he considered
extra and the idea of policing the battlefield was distasteful to him . . . . The
enemy by contrast was a scavenger. He made use of practically everything he
found on the battlefield and his scavenging teams habitually searched our old
campsites. The amount of US equipment found on enemy dead and prisoners
could be startling" (*Distant Challenge* 83).

An analysis by US Army Higher-highers determined that the grunts
were contributing to their enemy's main source of supplies. The enemy was

a scavenger. From weapons, C-ration cans, and ammunition. "Almost every enemy soldier killed or captured by our battalion during a four-month period [in 1967] carried a bottle of US Army insect repellent" (*Distant Challenge* 83).

But the Higher-highers ordered a policing action called Operation Baker (April 19 to September 20, 1967). Found: 174 US grenades recaptured—probably because the US soldiers just left them; 172 booby traps—of these, 35 were found the hard way, 32 men KIA and 70 WIA—and 24 were made from discarded C-ration cans, 35 from captured US hand grenades, four from US claymores—and others from gun shells, mortar rounds, and naval gun shells (*Distant Challenge* 84).

"Policing the immediate battlefield and campsite was not enough. [Our battalion] found a large number of dud bombs and artillery shells in our areas of operation . . . and we located and destroyed seventy-six 250-pound bombs, and 189 artillery and mortar shells, all of which could be turned into booby traps" (*Distant Challenge* 84).

Marine Lewis Puller, Jr. "buried the cans and cardboard containers in which the rations had been packaged, and Leslie checked the squads to make certain that the men had done likewise. We knew that the Vietcong could make booby traps out of our refuse, and there was no point in making their job easier for them" (133-134).

Duong Thu Huong, one of three survivors of her volunteer group of twenty, also took care "to preserve our strength, to prepare rations for the final battle. We had always planned our movements so as not to leave a single trace. Like cats, we erased all signs of our presence. Cooking fires were carefully covered over, our footprints meticulously swept away, our excrement buried. The previous year the enemy had detected an entire unit just because instead of pissing into the bushes one guy had done it into a wildflower that camouflaged an American sensor" (229).

○ **Geneva Convention.** Rules of engagement; rules governing the conduct of war. "An international agreement . . . made in 1864 in Geneva, Switzerland and followed by the US, Great Britain and other nations, establishing rules for humane treatment of prisoners of war, and of the sick, the wounded, and the dead in battle" (*Webster's Encyclopedic Unabridged Dictionary*).

"Finally we were given a copy of the rules of engagement and made to sign a statement saying we had read them and agreed to abide by them. The document was fairly voluminous and outlined various Geneva conventions for the conduct of war. I read it out of curiosity but realized that the clerk who handed us our copies was simply following regulations and did not expect us to take it seriously. It seemed odd to me that warring countries would expect their troops to kill each other in a gentlemanly and humane manner, and odder still that the Marine Corps would require its junior officers to undertake such an exercise in hypocrisy" (Puller 78).

○ *Get some; get me some.* Sleep, that is. Whenever you could. The average hours of sleep per night was about four hours (Ebert 192).

Whenever you could, it was important to get some sleep.

Sleeping
by Jim Gray

I never got used to sleeping all night
Waiting for the siren's wail.
Somebody still needs the Cav.

Waiting

Not quite sleeping, partly resting
Mostly suffering.

Waiting

There are ghosts in the night
Who still have fantasies to tell.

Waiting

Maybe forever. (9)

○ *GI.* Government Issue. Just a plain ordinary person. In World War II, grunts were called GIs; in World War I, doughboys.

○ **Gooks.** Derogatory word for the North Vietnamese; also "dink" and "slope." "Black people seemed to get along better with the Vietnamese, even though they fought the Communists harder than the white GIs. Two or three of the NVAs I interrogated told me they knew when black soldiers were in action, because they would throw everything they could get their hands on—grenades, tear gas, anything. They feared the black soldier more than the white soldier, because the black soldier fought more fiercely, with more abandonment" (Terry 83).

Sculpture of WWI doughboy from Memphis, Veterans of War Plaza.

"Most of the language used in Parris Island [Marine Training Center] to describe the joys of killing people is bloodthirsty but meaningless hyperbole, and the recruits

Typical GIs of the Vietnamese conflict.

realize that even as they enjoy it. Nevertheless, it does help to *desensitize* them to the suffering of an 'enemy,' and at the same time they are being indoctrinated in the most explicit fashion (as previous generations were not) with the notion that their purpose is not just to be brave or to fight well: it is to kill people" (Grossman 252).

"As soon as I hit the boot camp in Fort Jackson, South Carolina, they tried to change your total personality. Transform you out of the civilian mentality to a military mind.

"Right away they told us not to call them Vietnamese. Call everybody gooks, dinks" (Terry 90).

Another problem was that the "only civilians many Americans met were pimps, whores, draft-dodgers, black marketers, informers for the VC or starving street urchins trying to steal the watches off their arms. For many, the logical conclusion was that since Vietnam was full of such types, the 'gooks' really were worthless, deserving of hatred and abuse" (Anderson *The Grunts* 211-212).

○ **Go slow.** Go too fast, and you miss what's important. In war, go too fast and you miss the trip wire that's connected to the mine that's got your name on it.

○ **Got nothin' to lose.** Nonchalance is another coping strategy. Of course, you do have something to lose—a limb, your buddy, your life.

○ **Go to hell rag.** Often a white towel worn around grunts' necks; for wiping perspiration, cleaning weapons; an important piece of equipment. In pictures you often see these small once-white towels.

○ **Gotta have eyes in the back of your head.** Watch out. Everything is dangerous. Not just booby traps: poisonous snakes, leeches, mosquitoes, tigers, monkeys. Spec 5 Emmanuel J. Holloman took this lesson he learned when he was in boot camp with him to the World. "I keep reverting back to Vietnam, when I had to watch all the time. I stayed over there so long if a rocket would fire 10 miles away, I'd be up and out of there and out of reach when the rocket hit because I could hear 10 miles away. I've conditioned myself. I see stuff that other people don't see, so I'm always looking for something. I'm always on guard" (Terry 88).

○ **Gotta laugh.** When you are powerless, you might as well laugh, even if it makes no sense. "Once in some thick jungle corner with some grunts standing around, a correspondent said, 'Gee, you must really see some beautiful sunsets in here,' and they almost pissed themselves laughing" (Herr 10).

Johnny at one of the Vet Programs confessed that in a secure area, he fired his weapon, everyone landed in the mud, and then he said, "Sorry, my weapon misfired" (2/4/93).

"Genuine humor served to take some of the sting out of life in the field. Every unit had its clowns who somehow made the worst bearable and helped everyone endure beyond their limits. Such men were worth their weight in gold in helping to maintain a unit's morale" (Ebert 289).

Doc Holley and his ambulance crew were fired on. Before returning, Doc called for some help because the only way to return was by the same road they took before. Even with the escort of a deuce-and-a-half (two-and-a-half-ton truck) with a machine gun mounted on the top, five shots passed over their heads. "You could actually hear them whiz over the top of our jeep, and Mitch swerved wildly and sped up. He looked over at me, grinning, and said, 'That wasn't even close, Doc. Besides, you never hear the one that kills you anyway!' We all burst out laughing. It's really amazing how humor plays along with fear" (46).

○ *GP*. General Purpose. Anything that could be used for routine purposes.

○ *GR point.* Graves Registration on military base where identification and embalming take place. The Quarter master was in charge of embalming processing. It was quite different for the Vietnamese. A female soldier who led a Communist Youth Brigade writes about a woman living in a wooden shelter. The woman, covered in blood, explains: "What about it? I'm in charge of N22 Cemetery. My job is to gather corpses in these parts. All the unidentified ones are behind the hill. They're all combatants. Just like the three who were killed by this morning's bombing. I pass them along to the army when they come through" (Duong Thu Huong 40-41).

○ *Greased.* Killed. Zapped. Blasted. Cut down. Mowed down. Scorched. Dinged. Hosed down.

○ *Green machine.* The Marine Corp.

Just Another Marine
by Robert Hall

Seek me where the fight was thickest,
Where the issue was in doubt
But apart from thee
I shall show my love for things,
Never meant to be.
Where my blood and bone in battle
Stayed the line and stopped the rout.

Seek me where the triple jungle
Formed a cauldron for our host,
Or out where the frozen mountains
Barred our pathway to the coast.

Seek me in the ruined village
Where our cause was sorely tried
Or upon the waste of desert
Where we turned the bitter tide.

Seek me where the fight was thickest,
Where they pressed the issue keen,
Gently sleeping, slain in battle,
Lies another dead Marine. (Eichler 57-58)

○ **Ground Pounder.** A grunt whether Army or Marine.

Then
by Terry Crosby

Boy Scouts, was Great!
Pup tents, tying knots, camping,
Ya know, Man stuff.
Boyscout, not Cubscout,
I was a man.
Not enough, more complicated
knots required. Thoughts.
Thoughts of my father, he was
in the War, they WON ya know! He
was a real man, fought a war, and won.

The Marine Corps needed a few
good men, I was 17. I joined,
I was a confirmed man, a Marine!
My dad went to War-and won.

I went to Vietnam, a police
action. I was a man, in a
police action, and Lost!

I could tie real good knots, I
could put up a tent pretty good too.
But, I, I had never ya know,
killed anybody, but I was a man,
a Marine.
I, killed, I cried, I died, soulfully, mentally, on my
honor
to do my best, to do my duty to
God and country.
DIED! Sometimes I wish I had.
Boy Scouts, was great.
I was a boy, then. (*Eichler* 33-34)

○ **Grunt** The lowest-ranked soldier in service in Vietnam. Fighting with 40-60 pounds on the back, too little mail, too little food, too little understanding of a plan. He also wore a Durolon flak jacket that weighs 12 pounds; camouflaged helmets that weigh three pounds; and weapons that weigh six pounds. A Marine says, "Our real enemy is the jungle. God made this jungle for Marines. God has a hard-on for Marines because we kill everything we see" (Hasford 150).

Picture taken in 2011. Some never forget.

The grunts learned early on that they "were no longer in a geographical place named Vietnam. They were in a box of adversity and suffering, all the things one could think of to complete the old phrase, 'anything but that.' But this box had no limits—they would walk but they would never reach the other side, the end . . . . They were now the young newly-made old; bodies carrying their own corpses of youth" (Anderson *The Grunts* 49-50). Soldiers were fighting while trying to adjust to the heat and not enough drinkable water. Heat exhaustion was common, even at 9 am when the temperature would reach 104° (Anderson *The Grunts* 112). Soldiers were also fighting wearing boots and socks constantly wet from the rivers and jungle, with foot fungus common. Another medical problem was a fungus called jungle rot, which caused cracks and craters in the skin that oozed pus and rotted. Soldiers asked for baby powder and socks from home to keep their feet dry and protected.

"To the dirt-eating grunt, Vietnam was an endless succession of bummers. Besides, the never-ending fear of death, we had to endure a host of miseries: merciless humps through a sun-scorched landscape packing eighty pregnant pounds, brain-boiling heat, hot house humidity, dehydration, heat exhaustion, sunburn, red dust, torrential rains, boot-sucking mud, blood-sucking leeches, steaming jungles, malaria, dysentery, razor-sharp elephant grass, bush sores, jungle rot, moaning and groaning, meals in green cans, armies of insects, fire ants, poisonous centipedes, mosquitoes, flies, bush snakes, vipers, scorpions, rats, boredom, incoming fire, body bags, and a thousand more discomforts. Despite all this the grunt did his job well" <http://www.vwam.com/thewaryears.html>.

Because dysentery was a problem due to unclean water, soldiers requested Kool-Aid and Jell-O gelatin from home to disguise the taste of water that had been treated with chlorine or iodine.

"Something about war was becoming very clear now. It was not the drama of one side named US against the other side, called the Enemy. There was more to it than that. War in the middle of the twentieth century in Vietnam was a constant fight to survive against heat, thirst, poisonous centipedes, endless HUMPS, spreading jungle rot, sunburn, chapped and cracked lips and noses, twisted ankles, dehydration, intricate and constant patterns of pain from joints and muscles, unimagined extremes of boredom and exhaustion, stupid rumors about mad tigers that pounce on inattentive Americans at night, too few letters, too little food and booze and women, too much diarrhea, and too much despair that all this shit would never end, that home would never be seen again" (Anderson *The Grunts* 55-56).

SGT. Danny Phillips and Army buddy.

Grunts on patrol.

G-R-U-N-T The sound a soldier usually makes when lifting his 50-pound rucksack. "The vocalized grunt was a point of pride, earthy and indicative of the life the soldiers lived. Grunting the load onto their backs also signified a readiness or acquiescence to spend another day as an infantry soldier" (Ebert 206).

Ode to the Grunt
by Bill Person

The thickly growth snarls in withering heat,
And reddish mud clings at my plodding feet,
I labor on through smells that suit me not,
Scarcely inhale this jungle's breath so hot.
Have we gone only a mile or several more?
Does lofty MAC-V really know the score?

The pack straps knife through my quaking flesh
Soaked and caked red, no longer OD mesh.
Sweat rolls down fast to sting my eye,
My fluids drain, but my mouth is dry.
My canteen tastes of iodine bitter,
The rain pours down, a depressing pitter.

My pulse, I feel it in my temples throb,
Steel helmet weighs down my strength to rob.
M-16 in hand on "rock n roll."
Ready to reap a deathly toll.
Short breaths, I take in tiny swallows
I search for death in the bushy hollows.

A World War I Grunt, also known as a doughboy.

Then calm is breached with stabs of flame
The grim reaper springs his horrid game,
My throat grips fast to my warning shout.
Not a whisper from my lips gets out
Midst screams of pain, men drop to the ground
Charlies' fatal slugs have their target found

The ambush is answered in blistering volley,
A doubtful hit, tis all in folly.
We're zapped but good, now Charlie's gone
He's slipped back into his safety zone,
We've not but our dead to carry back,
All bagged and tagged in a body sack.

The fallens' tour is done, they're homeward bound
For loved ones there to inter in hallowed ground.
Whilst we suffer on to serve in anguished pain,
Soaked to the soul by monsoon rain.
Two enemies to fight, one real, one fear
The truth be known? I'll know this year! (Eichler 92-3)

Later in the war, grunts, whether Army or Marine, faced feeling unimportant. "No matter how many patrols they went on, how many air strikes they called, how many rounds they fired at sounds in the night, and no matter how much money they gave to build schools and hospitals, nothing ever got any better. Vietnam stayed as backward and screwed up as it was at the beginning of everyone's tour. The war then became an apolitical and personal project—the struggle to survive it. The only thing the grunts found to win in Vietnam was 365 consecutive days of life" (Anderson *The Grunts* 232).

"[That grunt] hadn't been anything but tired and scared for six months and he'd lost a lot, mostly people, and seen far too much, but he was breathing in and breathing out, some kind of choice all by itself" (Herr 16).

Experienced grunts looked at everything around them everywhere they went; they prayed; they carried a good-luck charm. They had to go through 'trial by fire' before they knew how they would react to war. Most grunts thought they themselves weren't heroes, just guys doing their job. Claude Anshin Thomas, Vietnam Vet and Buddhist monk, said this about the war: "My job in Vietnam was to kill people. By the time I was first injured in combat (two or three months into my tour), I had already been directly responsible for the deaths of several hundred people. And today, each day, I can still see many of their faces" (20).

This Last Time
by Basil T. Paquet

This last time
the sun dries his lips
and bakes dry his earth,
he sees green rice rows
wander towards a white temple,
tin roofs shake their heat at the sun,
water buffalo wander
near a temple.

This last time sun fevers his head
black mynas cry a warning,
fire breaks from shadows
of a tree line.

This last time sun bursts his eyes
he sees darkly the fall of sparrows
against a shaken sky. (Rottmann 19)

○ **Guerilla War.** The definition of guerilla war is a small war. Vietnam remained a Conflict instead of a War, even a guerilla war, in hopes of avoiding a nuclear war and keeping China out of the way. But the United States never determined why it was fighting this war; if it was indeed a war; it needed the support of the American people who had to be willing to shoulder the burdens that would come their way. Was it a civil war, with one part (the South) wanting people's control *versus* the North wanting a Communist leadership? Was the American public ready to take a stand against Communism 17,000 miles away? Close by the United States, Castro was taking over Cuba. Was this a **war of counter-insurgency** (a supposed "new war" against South Vietnamese insurgents—the Viet Cong—demanding new tactics, new strategies, even new weapons? Or was this a **war of aggression** when the NVA (North Vietnam Regular Army) invaded the South? The United States decided to fight a **war of containment.** That meant, according to a Colonel in the Army of the Republic of South Vietnam, "The Americans had designed a purely defensive strategy for Vietnam. It was a strategy that was based on the attrition of the enemy through a prolonged defense and made no allowance for decisive offensive action" (Summers 71).

Michael Herr sees guerilla war and what it means to US forces. "The ground was always in play, always being swept. Under the ground was his, above it was ours. We had the air, we could get up in it but not disappear in*to* it, we could run but we couldn't hide, and he [the Viet Cong] could do each so well that sometimes it looked like he was doing them both at once, while our finder just went limp. All the same, one place or another it was always going on, rock around the clock, we had the days and he had the nights" (14).

Surgeon Holley also sees what has to happen. "Lieutenant Tahler and Hack have devised this real neat tactic for hunting Charlie at night, which heretofore has been his time to come out and play . . . . Last night, I was on one of the machine guns and spotted five sampans, and before they could fire at us, I plastered them with tracer fire, and then watched as the Cobras dropped down and rained death and destruction on them. Larry estimated the body count at thirty VC dead to zero GIs killed or wounded. That's the kind of odds we need to keep up to ever win this damn war. Hack is ecstatic about the early success of the program. We are finally outguerillaing the guerilla—shortened to 'out-G the G' as our new slogan has become known around the **AO** [area of operations]" (150).

○ *Gulf of Tonkin.* "The specific incident that triggered the [American] bombing of North Vietnam was the encounter of the two American warships *C. Turner Joy* and *Maddox* with North Vietnamese PT boats in the Gulf of Tonkin" (Stoessinger 126). The Gulf of Tonkin lies near what was then North Vietnam, close to Haiphong, southeast of Hanoi. President Johnson ordered a response, and the military bombed North Vietnamese PT boats and an oil refinery. "The US had directly entered the Vietnam war without declaration at 11 am, 5 August 1964" (Maclear 190).

The evening of 5 August 1964 (Vietnamese time) a young North Vietnamese member of a Youth Brigade, Bao Ninh, attended a vacation camp for the sixteen-year old members at Do Son, on the Tonkin Gulf. The teenagers pitched their tents and lit a bonfire. Around the fire they sang and drank beer and wine. At night, when most of the teenagers were sleeping, the bonfire was still burning—and a sailor with a rifle came up and kicked sand in the fire to put it out. Those still awake asked why.

"'Don't ask why. We got orders tonight. No fires on the beach. No lights. They order it, we carry it out. We aren't allowed to ask why, it's a military order.'

Gulf of Tonkin, 1966.

"'Is singing banned, too?' asked Phuong, feigning innocence.

"The sailor lowered his gun, softened his stance, and sat down with them. 'No. Don't stop singing. That's got to go on at all costs. Sing us a song now,' he invited.

"Two others from the shore patrol returned . . . .

"'Sing all the same, sister,' [the sailor] said sadly. 'Sing a farewell song to us. I'll tell you a secret; you'll know tomorrow anyway. It's war. America has entered the war. We're fighting the Americans.'"

Phuong's Song

The winds, they are a-changin'.
The harsh winds blow in the world from tonight,
No longer the peace
We were hoping for.
Our loved ones will grieve for those who'll be lost.
No longer in peace
Our children will live.
From this moment on,
The winds, they are a-changin'. (Ninh 175)

Bao Ninh was one of ten who survived out of a Youth Brigade of 500, but he was at Do Son, a sixteen-year-old who shouted "War! War! The sea roared out the message in the small hours of 5 August 1964. A small storm began far out across the Tonkin Gulf and the group looked on as distant forked lightning seemed to signal the start of the war" (175).

◦ *Gulf of Tonkin Resolution.* Approved August 10, 1964. This resolution permits "the President, as Commander in Chief, to take all necessary measures to repel any armed attack against the forces of the United States and to prevent further aggression" (Kutler 655). This resolution gives Congressional approval and support to the President (Kutler 655). "Subsequent studies have cast serious doubts upon this official version [of the events that took place on the Gulf of Tonkin] .... [T]he President misled Congress and the people, and through that deception was able to obtain congressional authorization for a war that he had decided on months before while promising the voters peace" (Stoessinger 126).

◦ *Gung-ho.* Super-enthusiastic. Like John Wayne. Or Rambo for a newer generation.

◦ *Gunships.* Cobra Helicopters (Hueys), equipped with rockets, 40 cannons and mini-guns.

◦ *GVN.* The government of South Vietnam. Under attack by VC who want a change in leadership in South Vietnam; by the NVA, the North Vietnamese Army who want a Communist South Vietnam or a united Communist country.

HOTEL (H)

"We should declare war on North Vietnam . . . .
We could pave the whole country
and put parking strips on it, and still be home by Christmas."
—Ronald Reagan (1965)

○ *Hamlet.* A small group of buildings; villages (or vills) usually contained several hamlets.

○ *Hanoi Hannah/also called Helen.* The Vietnamese counterpart to Axis Sally in World War II. [She was also known as "Berlin Betty" and "Berlin Bitch." Axis Sally was American; worked for Berlitz School of Language; then radio, then began broadcasting propaganda to American soldiers along with popular American music. She was returned to US in 1948; she was tried for treason, and spent the years 1949-1961 in prison. She died in 1988. Her real name was Mildred E. Sink. She and Tokyo Rose broadcast propaganda to troops in WWII (Rottman *FUBAR 20).*]

A LRRP was singled out once by Hanoi Hannah. She read a letter to him that had been in a mail drop from a chopper that crashed. It was all about how much his wife missed him (Terry 39). But what really got to them was what she said after Martin Luther King, Jr. was assassinated: "Soul Brothers, go home. Whitey raping your mothers and your daughters, burning down your homes. What you over here for? This is not your war. The war is a trick of the Capitalist empire to get rid of the blacks" (Terry 39). LRRP Richard J. Ford III was bothered. "I really thought—I really started believing it, because it was too many blacks than there should be in infantry" (Terry 39).

Hanoi Hannah
by Yusef Komunyakaa

Ray Charles! His voice
calls from waist-high grass,
& we duck behind gray sandbags.
"Hello, Soul Brothers. Yeah,
Georgia's also on my mind."
Flares bloom over the trees.
"Here's Hannah again.
Let's see if we can't
light her goddamn fuse
this time." Artillery
shells carve a white arc
against dusk. Her voice rises
from a hedgerow on our left
"It's Saturday night in the States.
Guess what your woman's doing tonight.
I think I'll let Tina Turner
tell you, you homesick GIs."
Howitzers buck like a herd
of horses behind concertina.
"You know you're dead men,
don't you? You're dead
as King today in Memphis.
Boys, you're surrounded by
General Tran Do's division."
Her knife-edge song cuts
deep as a sniper's bullet.
"Soul Brothers, what you dying for?"
We lay down a white-klieg
trail of tracers. Phantom jets
fan out over the trees.
Artillery fire zeros in.
Her voice grows flesh
& we can see her falling
into words, a bleeding flower
no one knows the true name for.
"You're lousy shots, GIs."
Her laughter floats up
as though the airways are
buried under our feet. (141)

○ *Hanoi Hilton.* A prison for prisoners of war; actual name, Hoa Lo. It was built by the French when Vietnam was its colony. At this time, it is a museum.

John McCain's white flight uniform is in a glass case, and full-sized figures crafted in what looks like clay are spread around the various rooms. There are still chains on some of the doors, and cots are small. A visitor has no sense of how many were housed in any one room. At the site now is a six-story building; a company planning to build a hotel there backed out for good reason.

Aerial view of Hanoi Hilton. Hoa Lo Prison.

POWs communicated through a system of tapping; propaganda pictures sometimes made their way to the United States, such as a picture taken at Christmas time with a Christmas tree. Many POWs refused to participate in any propaganda effort much to the detriment of their health, which was already poor if not worse.

"The yellow, high-walled Hanoi Hilton . . . was about to be torn down. Giving mute testimony to its past and present use as a city prison, the rooftop bristled with jagged glass and electrified barbed wire, and the few windows were heavily barred" (Brownmiller 32). Brownmiller's guide told her that "he was familiar with the inside of the Hanoi Hilton. While a student, he was encouraged to practice his English with those POWs who welcomed the harmless diversion" (34).

Prison Cell in Hanoi Hilton.

The Hoa Lo was not supposed to hold prisoners. Instead it was built for political internees not subject to the Geneva Conventions. Between 1964-1973, Hoa Lo held over 700 POWs (Kutler 219).

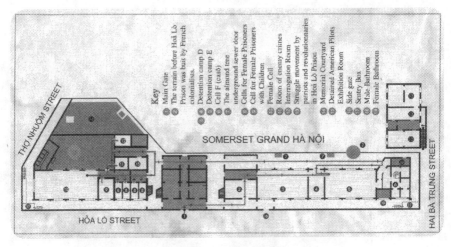

Map of prison. Hanoi Hilton.

○ **Hate.** "It is obvious that the Vietnamese resent us as well. We are making many of the same mistakes that the French did, and in some instances our mistakes are worse. Arrogance, disrespect, rudeness, prejudice, and our own special brand of ignorance, are not designed to win friends. This resentment runs all the way from stiff politeness to obvious hatred. It is so common that if a Vietnamese working with or for Americans is found to be sincerely cooperative, energetic, conscientious, and honest, it automatically makes him suspect as a Viet Cong agent" (Duncan 80).

> "I Wanna Go To Viet-Nam
> I Wanna Kill A Viet-Cong.
>
> With A Knife Or With A Gun
> Either Way Will Be Good Fun
>
> Stomp 'Em, Beat'Em, Kick 'Em In The Ass
> Hide Their Bodies in The Grass
>
> Airborne, Ranger, C.I.B.*
> Nobody's Gonna Fuck With Me
>
> But If I Die In The Combat Zone
> Box Me Up And Ship Me Home

Fold My Arms Across My Chest
Tell My Folks I Done My Best

Place A Bible In My Hand
For My Trip To The Promised Land"
—Army Marching Cadence
(*C.I.B. =Combat Infantry Badge;
given only to those who fought in combat)

○ **Haul ass.** "Tank unit procedure, as seen from the infantryman's embittered perspective—bypass resistance, advance fast, let the infantry mop up" (Rottman *FUBAR* 32).

○ **Hawk versus dove.** Symbols of debate in the United States about the Vietnam War. Doves wanted Peace. Hawks wanted Victory. At first the split wasn't obvious, but as the war dragged on, both sides became more vocal, factions showed in Congress and in the White House as well. At first, Johnson was concerned about the Hawks (Republicans and conservative Democrats) who wanted to win the war. The Hawks in Congress subscribed to the "Domino Theory" while the Doves questioned how Vietnam was of value to us. The increased bombing ordered under President Nixon in 1972 seemed to be the last straw. Doves eventually forced Congress to reconsider our involvement. Even though Nixon vetoed the bill, Congress passed the War Powers Act in 1973. Unlike the blank check given to LBJ to run the war in Vietnam through the Gulf of Tonkin Resolution, the War Powers Act took the checks back. Now a current president could not wage a war without Congressional approval (Kutler 221-222).

○ **Hearts and Minds.** The United States' philosophy in the Vietnam War: win citizens' hearts and minds. According to Olson's Dictionary, this phrase was taken from John Adams' explanation of the American Revolution by Lyndon Johnson in 1965 when he was president. From John Adams: "The Revolution was effected before the war commenced. The Revolution was in the hearts and minds of the people" (194). From LBJ: "So we must be ready to fight in Vietnam, but the ultimate victory will depend on the hearts and minds of the people who actually live out there" (194-195).

This proved more difficult in Vietnam than in the colonies that formed the United States. According to Marine Lewis Puller, Jr.: "Because of our previous losses in the area, the platoon was in no mood to waste time winning hearts and minds, and when the villagers realized that we were going to be in their midst for several hours, they became inhospitable" (138).

Morley Safer describes the waste after the war: "Nothing of us remains, except the decay of this colossal wreck, boundless and bare . . . . Which desk held the treasures of that safari-suited Foreign Service officer who mouthed on about hearts and minds and was thinking R and R. Which one belonged to the moronic colonel who hired Vietnamese craftsmen to carve into mahogany for him conversation pieces like 'Take them firmly by the balls and their hearts and minds will follow' and 'Join the Marines! Travel to exotic lands . . . meet exciting people . . . and kill them'" (189).

The *Time* cover story of May 11, 1962, had some prescient observations. The United States was into Vietnam, Mohr wrote, for the duration "even if it takes a decade—as well it may. For the first time he[Mohr] used the phrase that would mark and damn the war, the need 'to win the hearts and minds of the people'" (Prochnau 66).

"The Mission was to pacify the village, conduct a thorough search, root out the Viet Cong infrastructure, gather intelligence, and 'win the hearts and minds of the people'" (*Vietnam Studies* 137-138). Over and over, the stated goal was to protect the South Vietnamese from Communist infiltration; to allow the South Vietnamese to live free.

Later in the war, in 1971, "The Pentagon Papers" were secretly copied and given to Neil Sheehan of the *New York Times*. The so-called "papers" were 47-volumes and 7000 pages detailing the United States' involvement in Vietnam from 1945-1968 (Kutler 428). Embedded in those pages was a memo to Secretary of Defense Robert McNamara from the Assistant Secretary of Defense that "set forth American goals in South Vietnam in terms of the following priorities:

"70 per cent—To avoid a humiliating US defeat
"20 per cent—To keep South Vietnamese territory from Chinese hands
"10 per cent—To permit the people of South Vietnam to enjoy a better, freer way of life."

(Note: These priorities can be found in *"The Pentagon Papers"* published by Quadrangle Books, 263.)

Thus, the official reason that was given to the American people for the intervention in Vietnam with air power and ground troops made up only one-tenth of the real reason (Stoessinger125-126). Sometimes, winning hearts and minds came to be called WHAM.

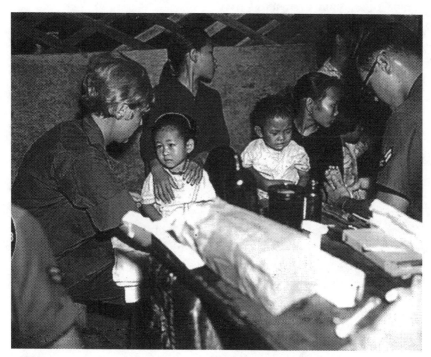

Winning Hearts and Minds Operation MEDCAP.

○ ***Heat, Heat Stroke.*** Tropical climate, heavy rains between May and October; extreme heat between February and April. The South is consistently warm and humid with frequent downpours during the rainy season.

"Everything went smoothly, quietly until about eight thirty when Doc Richards told Andrew he had a heat casualty. 'What do you mean a heat casualty? It ain't even nine o'clock yet!'

"Temperature of a hundred and four. I noticed he looked real weak after we got off the hill, then a little later he just fell over in the water" (Anderson *The Grunts* 112).

"Ecroyd was sent out on the next chopper for his psychiatric evaluation. The grunts debated the next day whether Ecroyd had staged a scene like the Dennis Moy incident of two and a half weeks before just to get out of the bush or whether he really had, like Moy, cracked in the heat. They decided it probably was the real thing when they learned later they had humped through a 118° afternoon" (Anderson *The Grunts* 127).

○ *Hero.* "Courage, and even heroism were possible in Vietnam; even the bitterest of the war-hating narrators have their stories of brave men. But the courage that is reported in the narratives is not usually demonstrated in acts against the enemy; stories of killing VCs are often terrible, sometimes murderous, and are told without positive moral weighting. It's the protective acts—recovering one's own wounded, or the dead, or covering withdrawal—that carry moral and emotional weight. Courage and heroism were possible in Vietnam narratives; the *ideal* of courage, the Heroic Man of the war tradition, wasn't" (Hynes 214).

○ *Higher-higher.* Command or commanders.

○ *Hippies.* The time of do your own thing, be your own person, say what you think, believe that you know best. The usual rules don't apply. The stereotypical hippies wore their hair long, wore flared jeans, love beads, bracelets, sandals or bare feet, leather fringed belts, vests, or jackets. Grass was shared freely; they sometimes travelled in vans and cars painted with peace symbols and were considered anti-establishment.

Thomas Aloysius Meade
by Patrick J. Fitch

"Hippiecrits" he called them.
Students in the World
Did they know? Did they care?

His name was Thomas
Apostle of Doubt
Penultimate Aloysius
Surname Meade

The rocket; round
Directly taken
"Chest high, No Cry"

He had a name, and it wasn't Corporal
Left a twin brother
And a father who asked:
"How did he die?"

But the letter was a lie
No body bag need apply
A backpack sufficed
For the arm and the watch
We tagged remains

Just another stat
Body count ours
On a damp little mesa

Just a faded memory of the 26th Marines
in a place called Khe Sanh

His death was obscene. (Eichler 40-41)

○ *Hmong*. They are the Montagnards of Laos, an indigenous people, anti-Communist, living in the northern mountains. They made up the bulk of the Laotian Royal Army. After 1973, a number immigrated to the United States;

many others were slaughtered by the North Vietnamese (Dunnigan and Nofi 184-185).

○ *Ho Chi Minh.* Leader of the revolution against the French and later against the Americans in an attempt to reunify Vietnam. "We will be like the elephant and the tiger. When the elephant is strong and rested and near his base we will retreat. And if the tiger ever pauses the elephant will impale him on his mighty tusks. But the tiger will not pause and the elephant will die of exhaustion and loss of blood" (Ho Chi Minh).

Sculpture of Ho Chi Minh.

○ *Ho Chi Minh slippers.* Sandals with soles made from tire tread, straps from inner tubes of tires; sometimes a sign in the US Army that soldier had made a kill.

○ *Ho Chi Minh Trail.* The trail was first set up in 1959. In 1961, it was little more than a jungle track. Americans gave this trail its name. The North Vietnamese called it the Troung Son Route because it cut through the Truong Son Mountains which formed a natural boundary along the border between Laos and North/South Vietnam. Troops who had to walk all the way called it the ten thousand mile route, probably because it took over a month of walking to get down the trail (Dunnigan and Nofi 296-297). Troops moved at night, stopping to pick up weapons discarded by the French who left in 1954. The United States knew early on that a trail was there, but it and North Vietnam had signed an agreement not to involve Laos or Cambodia in any war. One major worry for the United States throughout the war was that China would overtly become a North Vietnamese ally; covertly, China was providing weapons and other materiel, but the US was powerless to stop it.

According to an early advisor to MACV (Mac-vee, the headquarters for all forces in Vietnam), Col. Everett Smith said Vietnam had over 1,000 miles of border—that includes its northern, and northeastern border with China. There was no way, he said, to safeguard that 1,000 miles. "What we needed to do was isolate South Vietnam and draw the guerillas' attention to show our sympathy for their dislike of the South Vietnamese government and to offer them land. But we had never been able to isolate the South because of the Ho Chi Minh Trail" (Smith).

"We had agreed in the early 60s that no war would make its way into Laos or Cambodia" (Dunnigan and Nofi 170-171); the United States certainly didn't want a nuclear war, nor did it want one of the other super-powers to jump in (Smith). One of Gen. Westmoreland's first plans, Col. Smith said, was to invade Laos to control the Ho Chi Minh Trail and cut off troops and supplies carried by porters to aid the guerillas in South Vietnam, members of the NLF (National Liberation Front or the VC).

For many reasons, the Vietnam War (never declared a "War") was unconventional when compared to the first and second World Wars. There was no front line to advance (Smith said—use firepower and advance), no territory to take and hold, and prisoners were taken and shut away, yet the United States had fought a similar "unconventional war" just twelve years earlier in Korea. But politics played a major role in discussions about the Vietnam War; if it were "unconventional," then the idea was planted that we would win, as we had in Korea. Also, if it were unconventional, then the military would surely get as many troops, weapons, and money as it requested. According to Smith, we could never isolate South Vietnam from outside influences. "The enemy was like ghosts. They just disappeared. We were going to have to change some military minds to think about small fighting units—squads, platoons, companies, and supporting troops—a complex situation" (Smith). During this discussion, one general had some sort of breakdown and had to be carried away in a strait jacket (Smith).

Col. Smith said the plans for the war included using guerillas (our Special Forces—LRRPs, SEALs) to counter guerillas (see also Dunnigan and Nofi 168). But one problem that had no solution was the weather. Monsoons affected both sides; to make it more difficult, the monsoons struck during different months in North and South Vietnam, Laos, and Cambodia.

| September to January | North Vietnam |
| May to September | South Vietnam, southern Cambodia, and Laos |

The North Vietnamese couldn't move troops who were walking in mud, so this hampered getting supplies and troops to Laos and Cambodia in order to mount assaults across the border into South Vietnam. The Americans were not supposed to fire across the borders, but we had been conducting a secret war in Laos for some time [announced to the public in August, 1967] according to the *Vietnam War Diary* (89). The main objective was bombing the Ho Chi Minh Trail. During monsoons, our main offensive weapon, the helicopter, was not efficient. Helicopters had to fly more slowly, there was no convenient place to hover and to disperse troops so there was less conflict, and if the weather was especially bad (sometimes the rain came down the size of hail) the helicopters weren't flying. Both sides had to wait for the dry weather that was good for them.

The first attempts to break up the Trail were to drop anti-vehicular mines onto the trail. The ordnance used was the Claymore, but set up, not covered up, to be detonated by trip wire or by timer. The Claymore spread hundreds of steel balls in a conical area to shred what was there. Workers were always improving the trail. It eventually became a truck route (Dunnigan and Nofi 114-115), so the North Vietnamese set up heavy guns anticipating helicopters coming over the trail.

If the Ho Chi Minh Trail had been a straight line, it would have been 300 miles long; but because it crossed mountains, it was about 600 miles. And it was not one trail. It split into three separate routes into Laos; a fourth trail went through the DMZ—Americans were not supposed to fire across the DMZ—and a trail through the DMZ was a clear violation of a UN mandate. There were also "many parallel trails that weaved back and forth and branched into South Vietnam every dozen or so miles" (Dunnigan and Nofi 296). The United States could shut one or two down, but the North Vietnamese would simply go to another route. The trail was actually **ten to thirty miles** wide [emphasis added] to accommodate vehicles, as well as 300 miles long. Except the interlocking and parallel trails added twelve thousand miles spread over some seventeen hundred square miles, about the size of the state of Rhode Island.

Map of major routes along Ho Chi Minh Trail.

The Trail was so valuable that it was constantly improved, as well as any bomb craters from US aircraft filled in. By 1964, the United States estimated 6,000 people moved down the trail. By 1965, it was the main supply route for trucks coming from China and Russia with aid for guerilla forces and regular North Vietnamese Army forces. Over the years of improvement 100,000 (mostly women) labored on the trail; local Laotians and Yards were often forced to work as porters bringing supplies down from North Vietnam. Before trucks came, porters loaded bicycles with heavy equipment or ammo and pushed the bike down the trail. By 1967 about 69,000 troops came down the trail making sneak attacks across the Cambodian and Laotian border.

At its peak, in good weather, the North Vietnamese were able to move *each month* 10,000 troops, over 1,700 tons of food, almost 7,000 weapons, 800 tons of ammunition, and tons of other supplies. These men and porters were supported by 40,000 troops stationed at or along the Laotian border with the assistance of 60,000 Laotians, porters and laborers who built and maintained the trail. It was so well thought-out that there were 50 bases along the way for a rest, and thousands of trenches and bunkers there for protection from bombing once the trucks came. They were much easier to spot than green-clad troops among the mountains and swamps and jungle (summarized from Dunnigan and Nofi 296-297).

○ **Homosexuality.** In one Vet Program, this issue came up. Johnny said he treated 'em like a brother, but not too close. Al noted that everyone had a rifle, so there were no arguments in the bush (2/4/93).

○ **Hooch or Hootch.** Primitive hut for military or civilians. Some were one-story, wooden, sheet metal roof. Much longer than wide and lifted off the ground for protection during the rainy seasons. The plywood sides reached only halfway up, the rest was screened in hopes of getting air. The Vietnamese considered

A Vietnamese Hooch.

the hooches luxurious; the Americans considered the hooches backwoods shelters (Anderson *Other War* 31). Rural people lived in thatched bamboo homes easily burned in Zippo raids. (See Zippo Raids below.)

○ **Horn.** A radio.

○ **Hot LZ.** A landing zone under enemy fire; marked by soldiers with red flares for the helicopter. It was safe to land with a green flare; warning with a yellow flare. Medevac choppers often landed in dangerous zones to pick up casualties despite risks to their own safety.

○ **Hotel.** Sometimes used sarcastically to indicate a prison; a place where POWs might be kept. The Hanoi Hilton was the infamous place known to house POWs.

○ **House Mouse.** A small tunnel rat; a soldier small enough to get into one of the VC tunnels. (See Tunnel rat below.)

○ *Howitzer.* A short cannon, medium velocity, high trajectory.

○ *Hueys.* Nickname for the Bell UH (utility helicopter). Heavy use of the helicopter was another innovation necessary in this war. "In a land that favored the easily hidden, lightly loaded foot soldier, the helicopter balanced the odds. Airmobility was a dramatic new dimension, which allowed the precise application of a variety of combat power" (Hay 3). If you heard a Huey, you knew it belonged to the US "Helicopters were the 'army mules' of the Vietnam War. They performed all sorts of missions, seemed capable of going everywhere, and often took incredible amounts of punishment and just kept on flying. An important consequence of the Vietnam War was that it hastened the widespread use of helicopters by the armed forces, a trend that was already in evidence" (Dunnigan and Nofi 109).

Michael Herr, a reporter who hopped helicopters at will, had mixed feelings about a war that was deadly boredom one minute, acute panic the next. "Fear and motion, fear and standstill, no preferred cut there, no way even to be clear about which was really worse, the wait or the delivery. Combat spared far more men than it wasted, but everyone suffered the time between contact, especially when they were going out every day looking for it; bad going on foot, terrible in trucks and APCs [armored personnel carrier], awful in helicopters, the worst, traveling so fast toward something so frightening. I can remember times when I went half dead with my fear of the motion, the speed and direction already fixed and pointed one way" (15).

"Airmobility, dig it, you weren't going anywhere. It made you feel safe, it made you feel Omni, but it was only a stunt, technology. Mobility was just mobility, it saved lives or took them all the time (saved mine I [Herr] don't know how many times, maybe dozens, maybe none), what you really needed was a flexibility far greater than anything the technology could provide, some generous, spontaneous gift for accepting surprises, and I didn't have it. I got to hate surprises, control freak at the crossroads, if you were one of those people who always thought they had to know what was coming next, the war could cream you" (13).

From a North Vietnamese soldier's memoirs: "In my bedroom, on many nights the helicopters attack overhead, the dreaded whump-whump-whump of their rotor blades bringing horror for us in the field. I curl up in defense against the expected vapor streak and the howling of their rockets. But the whump-whump-whump continues without an attack, and the helicopter image dissolves, and I see in its place a ceiling fan. Whump-whump-whump" (Bao Ninh 46).

Escorting prisoners to Hueys.

○ **Hump.** Infantry heading out of camp, usually wearing a 40-pound backpack; used as a verb, as in "We humped over the hill." It usually meant 25 days in the field, a rotation period. Marion Lee ("Sandy") Kempner wrote his parents and a few others about humping. "I spent a three-day 'walk in the sun' (and paddies and fields and mountains and impenetrable jungle and saw grass and ants, and screwed-up radios and no word, and deaf radio operators, and no chow, and too many C-rations, and blisters and torn trousers and jungle rot, and wet socks and sprained ankles and no heels, and, and, and) for a battalion that walked on roads and dikes the whole way and a regiment that didn't even know where the battalion was, finished off by a 14,000-meter forced march on a hard road" (Edelman 36).

Kempner's "walk in the sun"—as he called it—didn't mention everything he carried in his rucksack that hung off the straps or belt or around his neck—all of which weighed about half his weight. What did he carry? Necessities: can openers, pocket knives (or KA-bars), a Zippo, heat tablets, wristwatches, dog tags, duct tape for covering up anything shiny, mosquito repellant, chewing gum, candy, cigarettes, salt tablets (temperature could reach as high as 109° by nine a.m. with 100% humidity), packets of Kool-Aid to add to treated water that tasted of chlorine, lighters, matches, sewing kits, Military Payment Certificates (MPCs, instead of money), C rations for about three days, 2-3 canteens of water. All of this weighed between 15-20 pounds.

Grunts also carried good luck charms (a picture, a silver dollar, a cookie from home, cut-off ears of VC, the small infantrymen's Bible), their M16 assault rifles (7.5 lbs), plus ammo, rifle magazines, fragmentation grenades, a smoke grenade, and they wore a steel helmet (5 lbs., also called a steel pot), jungle boots (2.1 lbs.), jacket (6.7 lbs.), poncho (2 lbs.). So far, the average is about 69 pounds. Depending on your MOS (field specialty) and rank, you could have more to carry to do your job. A medic carried another 20 pounds for field medicine; machine gunners carried an M-60 for another 23 pounds—plus there was the 10-15 pounds of ammo usually criss-crossed around their necks and shoulders. All grunts took their turn at carrying the 28-pound mine detector and the 30-pound scrambler radio. Newbies would stuff non-essentials in their rucksacks.

Platoons had to carry heavy equipment that they took turns carrying.

The hump you were on or had just finished was the worst one you'd ever been on. "There was no sense in thinking about how one got into this activity and how and when one would get out of it. Time no longer figured in the equation. Every grunt, every man everywhere, was born into this mindless trudging in the heat, and every man everywhere would die still involved in it. Dreams were illusions, one's last day in

Grunt wearing several good luck charms and a religious symbol.

Vietnam was an illusion, ambitions and plans to pursue back in the World were illusions, so why make up any more? All the grunts really had out here in the hot green maze was a sense of mutual dependence, of belonging to the next few minutes of each other's lives" (Anderson *The Grunts* 61-62).

○ *Hurry up and Wait.* Lynda Van Devanter reports, "One of the first things they taught us was the meaning of the old army expression 'Hurry up and wait.' There was always a rush to go wherever we were supposed to be, and then a long, boring wait while supply sergeants and administrators took their sweet time" (68).

Hurry up and wait, taken at DUC PHO Aug 31, 1967.

INDIA (I)

"Above all, Vietnam was a war that asked everything of a few
and nothing of most in America."
—Myra MacPherson (1984); author of *Long Time Passing* about Vietnam
and journalist for the *Washington Post*

○ *I and I.* Leave granted to soldiers once a year. Called "I and I" because of the soldiers' two principal activities, intoxication and intercourse. Also known as R and R (rest and relaxation).

○ *I been there.* Mostly said with indifference. You can read about the war, talk to others about it, but you can't know what it was unless you've been there—jungle rot, over 100° every day, mud, and Charlie out there waiting for you to pass. "And a lot of things that might scare a lot of other people in terms of danger, I can just walk right on through without backing away, shying away, or making compromises that really should not be made. I've been there" (Terry 142).

○ *IC.* Innocent Civilians. "Much of the war in Vietnam was conducted against an insurgent force. Against men, women, and children who were often defending their own homes and who were dressed in civilian clothing. This resulted in a deterioration of traditional conventions and an increase in civilian casualties, atrocities, and resultant trauma. Neither the ideological reasons for the war, nor the target population, was the same as that associated with previous wars" (Grossman 267).

An innocent civilian.

Michael Herr, reporter, tells a much-heard story: "[S]ome reporters asked a door gunner, 'how can you

141

shoot women and children?' and he'd answered, 'it's easy, you just don't lead 'em so much'" (37).

○ *ID Cards.* "All Vietnamese—strictly speaking, `all Vietnamese under the rule of the 'government side' are supposed to have such Identification Cards [ID Cards]" (Honda 17).

"Two women came out. One of them was an old woman, and another was middle-aged. Each was holding up reverently a slip of paper with both her hands, and joined her palms in prayer facing the gun muzzles of the approaching American soldiers. . . . The slips of paper they came holding out were their identification cards . . . . It is true, however, that ID Cards are being sold and bought . . . They are particularly coveted by deserters from the Government troops and by those who are trying to escape from conscription" (Honda 16-17).

○ *Immersion Foot.* A serious fungal infection due to constantly wet feet. A common problem for several reasons: the lack of appropriate footwear for the environment (see Fatigues above) and too much time in the bush and too many funguses (see Medic below). Puller writes about a medical doctor who didn't understand where missions put him and his men. In one visit to the Seabees compound with air-conditioning, USO shows, ice cream, showers, and cheap beer (Seabees = CBs, for Construction Battalions of the Navy), "a medical doctor in standard utilities stopped me to complain that several of my men had the beginning symptoms of immersion foot and that I should see to it that they kept their feet dry. He was a well-meaning sort who I am certain took his Hippocratic oath seriously, but he seemingly had no sense of life outside the wire. I knew that it would be pointless to explain to him that some of us involved in the war lived in the mud, bled in the mud, and would escape our fates only by surviving it or dying in the mud. I left him scratching his head as I excused myself without responding to his concerns and headed back to the bush, toting a case of warm beer" (159).

○ *In-coming.* Bombarded by mortars or rockets; enemy fire. "But once in a while you'd hear something fresh and a couple of times you'd even hear something high, like the corpsman at Khe Sanh who said, 'If it ain't the fucking incoming, it's the fucking outgoing. Only difference is who gets the fucking grease and that ain't no fucking difference at all'" (Herr 30).

○ *In country.* In Vietnam. In the 'Nam. In the bush. Or maybe in the craziness, you weren't sure where you were. In-coming, out-going, in-coming, in-coming.

"Tell me *you* ain' scared shit!"

"You'll never see *me* scared, motherfucker."

"Oh no. Three night ago you was callin' out for your *momma* while them fuckers was hittin' our wire."

"Boo-sheeit! I ain't never getting hit in Vietnam."

"Oh no? Okay, mothafucker, why not?"

"'cause," Mayhew said, "it don't exist." It was an old joke, but this time he wasn't laughing (Herr 125).

○ *Insert, insertion.* To be dropped by helicopter into hostile territory.

Grunts in country.

Grunts being inserted into enemy territory.

○ *Indirect Fire.* Artillery fired at an unseen target.

○ *Intel.* Military intelligence. TV reporter, Morley Safer had little respect for what he saw of Intel. "American intelligence was so awful it seemed that no one bothered to read even the travelers' tales, dating back to the eighteenth century and repeated into the twentieth, describing the honeycomb of caves in the mountains. All through the war it struck me that enlisted men had a better understanding of the place than did the officers and civilians commanding them. Battalion commanders would complain that the Vietcong would not stand up and fight, as if they expected them to play by some book prepared at West Point or Annapolis" (176).

○ *Iron Triangle.* A 40-square mile jungle dominating land and river routes into Saigon, the capital of South Vietnam. It was controlled by ARVN (Army of the Republic of Vietnam) by day, but the Vietcong by night. The Iron Triangle contained Cu Chi, the largest Vietcong base, only 24 miles from Saigon. Underneath the area were many tunnels because the area is close to Saigon.

"When they moved us from Cu Chi to Dau Tieng, that's when the shit got bad. The Iron Triangle. Oh, man. That place is not fit for God, let alone man. That was a tough assignment. After we got pinned down, that's when I began to rebel" (Terry 177).

"Then one day the entire company is working in that Iron Triangle. In very tall weeds. The darn man must have hit us from behind. We had to figure now how the hell we going to get out. If Charlie had been up high, he could have just picked us off. Apparently, he was down on ground level, and they would fire every once in a while to let you know they're still there" (Terry 178).

○ *It don't mean nothin'.* Being callous, or unfeeling, or indifferent can be protective. RTO (radio telephone operator) Krehbiel numbed himself to the question about why he was in Vietnam and to all other questions. "It doesn't matter. Get home. It's okay. You just numbed out" (Ebert 288). Tony Anthony, a sergeant in the infantry, covered operations, including secret ones, as a correspondent for the 198th Light Infantry Brigade. He's not worried on patrol. He cuts his own trail. He does everything right. He feels ready to help anyone who needs it. "A shot rings out in the jungle up ahead. The point man's in trouble. I rush ahead to help him. He's hit. He's down. I reach out to cover his wound and suddenly I'm hit in the shoulder. *It don't mean nothin*" (90-91). A mantra of acceptance, resignation, and self-preservation.

Don't Mean Nuttin'
by Randy Cribbs

It don't mean nuttin',
Or so we said,
But 'it' was there,
Somewhere in our head.

All that stuff,
Tucked way in the back,
To preserve sanity;
Added to the stack.

We wished it away
And moved on
To confront another
Time, alone.

It don't mean nuttin'.
Death was not real,
Filed away in a place
We could not feel.
To survive
Was the chore.
To live.
Nothing more.

No room for
Remorse or pain;
Everything to lose
And nothing to gain.

It don't mean nuttin'.
But we knew it did,
And now, often,
It creeps from
Under the lid

To remind us
That we are here,
Alive
With nothing more to fear

Except all that stuff,
In there,

Year after year. (74-75)

A Visit
by Basil Paquet

"You don't look bitter,"
           she said.
           He thought,
"Bitter is a taste,"
           feeling her words
           scrape across
           memory's slow healing
           like a slow knife.
           Did she think she could see
           how he felt?
"It don't matter,"
           he said, and heard
           outside—voices
           In the wind
           In humming tires
           voices running against
           the windows in a heavy rain. (Rottmann 110)

○ **It's gonna be too late then.** Listen and learn from those who have been in the war. If you don't, then it will be too late for anyone to help you.

Rest and relaxation at China Beach.

JULIET (J)

> "You have my full assurance that we will respond with full force
> should the settlement be violated by North Vietnam."
> —Richard Nixon in a letter to President Thieu (January 1973)

○ *Jane Fonda.* Also known as Hanoi Jane. She was and still is reviled by the grunts for her outspoken support of North Vietnam during the Vietnam War. She travelled to North Vietnam during the war to demonstrate her support. In Hanoi, "she actually sat in an antiaircraft facility which had been used to shoot down American aircraft during the conflict" (Daugherty and Mattson 449). In the 1990s when I was teaching courses on the Vietnam War with the help of Vietnam veterans, I showed the movie "Coming Home" about a grunt (played by Jon Voight) that returns to the World a paraplegic. In the movie, Jane Fonda is the wife of a soldier (Bruce Dern) just off for his tour in Vietnam. For several reasons, the vets refused to come to the movie. First, it starred Jane Fonda whom they thought should have been arrested for treason upon her return to the US Secondly, Fonda betrays her husband in the movie. Jon Voight becomes a Jody, the name given to the man back in the World that steals the love and affection of the girlfriend or wife of a soldier overseas. That the Jody was a vet himself made his actions all the worse; he, too, was a traitor in the movie. He stole the heart of a soldier's wife and chained his wheelchair to the gates of a recruiting center in his own anti-war protest.

Forgive and forget is not part of the grunts' philosophy towards Fonda. Even now, in 2011, after Fonda's years of explanations and apologies for her actions during the war, the veterans and many others forced QVC, a shopping channel, to cancel Fonda's scheduled appearance on the show. They wrote so many letters vilifying Fonda and threatening to boycott the QVC channel if Fonda appeared that ultimately, QVC asked Fonda not to appear on the show. And she didn't.

○ *Jell-O.* Jell-O and Kool-Aid were the two most popular methods for disguising the taste of iodine used to purify the water found in the field. Packets of Jell-O and unsweetened Kool-Aid came in packages from home. Nothing, however, could purify the water sprayed with dioxin or other chemicals.

○ *Jody.* Name for the man back home who steals your girl. Lynda Van Devanter, nurse in training for duty in 'Nam, explains to her friend: "I overheard a drill sergeant say to one of his men, 'Your best friend, Jody, is already pumping your girlfriend, Mary Jane Rottencrotch, asshole. When you walked out the front door, he slipped in the back.' It's supposed to help turn the guys into killers" (68). Jody, according to a slang book, is a black term used in World War II and is probably related to an earlier man named Jody Grinder who was executed for being a fornicator (Chapman 245).

○ *John Wayne bar.* A chocolate and toffee candy bar found in C-rations. Often left in porta-johns as a joke.

○ *John Wayne High School.* Nickname for the home of Studies and Observation Group (SOG) in Fort Bragg, NC. SOG fought against the NVA, especially NVA strongholds in Cambodia and Laos; and even in North Vietnam. SOG groups included Green Berets, locals (such as Montagnards), but no officers. Their missions were so secret that not even the Higher-highers knew all of them (Dunnigan and Nofi 199).

○ *John Wayne Image.* In the Western movies, John Wayne usually played a man of honor, loyalty, and courage. That image, however, doesn't work so well in war. Instead, the John Wayne image became "Violence-prone super-maleness" (Lifton 255). But this war wasn't that kind of war. "For the Vietnam generation, 'John Wayne' was the Hollywood war-in-their-heads, exposed and mocked by the real, bitter thing. It's a sign of how completely the old values had faded that Wayne, the hero of the Westerns and war movies that the Vietnam War generation had grown up on, and the embodiment of what seemed a particularly American kind of independent courage, had become a soldier's joke, an anti-hero, everybody's example of how *not* to fight a war" (Hynes 215).

○ *John Wayne Tactics.* Crazy, risky military tactics designed to glorify the troop leader without concern for the troops. "A lieutenant or platoon sergeant who would want to carry out all kinds of crazy John Wayne tactics, who would use their lives in an effort to win the war single-handedly, win the big medal and get his picture in the hometown paper" (Anderson *The Grunts* 219). The John Wayne mentality was gung-ho, don't let anyone stop you, go it alone and don't worry about it, use whatever weapons are handy, kill the enemy one at a time—guerilla-style. Go after the government if you have to.

"There were people over there that were just putting their time in, and I [James Ebert] was one of them. We did what we had to do but we weren't out to be John Wayne. There were 'John Waynes' who loved what they were doing and would re-up (re-enlist for another term in the field). And then there were some that were there because they had to be there and weren't doing what they had to do.

> ## BOUNTY HUNTER
> "WE AIM TO KILL-FOR A FEW DOLLARS MORE"
> 24 HR. SERVICE   7 DAYS A WEEK
> DELTA'S TOP GUN SPECIALIZING
> IN DEATH AND DESTRUCTION OF
> V. C. & N.V.A.   BUNKERS   SAMPANS
> AUTOMATIC & CREW SERVED WEAPONS
> ROCKET & MORTAR SITES
> WE DEFEND -
> OUTPOSTS, SPECIAL FORCES CAMPS, LOST GRUNTS
> HAMLETS, CONVOYS AND BASE CAMPS
> SPECIAL RATES FOR NIGHT COMBAT ASSAULTS
> "WHEN IT'S BAD ENOUGH TO WARRANT
> THE TOP GUN-WIRE 191ST"

"The ones that thought they were John Wayne would get to you eventually (with their war stories): 'Well Kid, stick close to me and you'll be all right. I'll show you how to survive here.' I don't want to be cynical. There were some who were saying that and really meant it. I met some good people over there. But there were some that were crazy and really loved it and I considered them crazy then and I consider them crazy now" (Ebert 137-138).

"There is much evidence of the currency of Wayne's name in the combat zone as a term identifying all those daring individual acts that succeed in the movies but are only dumb stunts that will get you killed in a real war" (Hynes 215).

∘ *John Wayne.* The Hollywood image didn't fade away. One veteran said in group therapy, "I'm sorry. I don't know why I felt sorry. John Wayne never felt sorry" (Lifton 121).

∘ *Jolly Green Giant.* A long-range Huey (helicopter). A C-47 used to support troops.

A long range Huey, also known as a Jolly Green Giant.

During the end of the Vietnam War, the Air Force operated the Super Jolly Green Giant, a heavy-lift Sikorsky.

◦ *Jungle Boot.* Partly stainless steel with holes to keep the water from staying in the boot. It was supposed to dry out quickly. But the boots had a tendency to stay wet causing jungle rot on feet, also called immersion foot. By the end of a tour, a grunt's boots would be ringed and stained white, a far cry from the spit-shining so important in basic training. Also, according to Olsen's *Dictionary of the Vietnam War*, the jungle boot had "DMS," a Direct Molded Sole (508). Goodyear Tire & Rubber Company was already advertising its part in the jungle boot—when the Marines were arriving in Vietnam without jungle boots and none available. The company was putting into magazines: "Boots with Chemivic synthetic rubber vinyl soling compound outlast old boots by 300 percent in Vietnam" (Ebert 196).

Super Jolly Green Giant used late Vietnam War.
A heavy-lift transport helicopter.

◦ *Jungle Rot & Creeping Crud & Immersion Foot.* When Doc (Byron Holley, M.D.) finishes his stint in basic training and in military medicine, he writes to his girl friend, Sondra (later, his wife) about his duties. "Apparently I will be spending a lot of time out on operations in the field with the troops [in my battalion], treating a variety of skin diseases, leech bites, punji stake wounds, noncritical shrapnel and gunshot wounds. Because of the tremendous level of heat and humidity, something can turn green from mold in a matter of a few days! I can just imagine how quickly infection spreads under these conditions. The environment is a perfect culture medium for fungi and bacteria. Most of the natives have faces marked from smallpox suffered in childhood. Most of the grunts suffer with a condition called immersion foot. It is a peculiar type of cellulitis, which causes a very painful red, scaly, swollen foot, ankle, and lower leg, usually not extending above the knee. It usually begins to occur after five to seven days of continuous exposure to water loaded with bacteria and fungi . . . .

Lots of times the grunts have to urinate and defecate in waist-deep water. To avoid rashes men don't wear undershorts, and they are reluctant to drop their pants in leech-infested waters. So they literally get 'wet-rot' of the feet and legs" (27-28).

Vietnam has monsoons, but it also has its dry spells. All Holley can hope for is a combination of oral and topical antibiotics and antifungals, along with elevation and dry weather. "They are told to wear thongs and cut-off fatigue pants. The informality bothers some of the life officers, but that's too bad. You don't see any of them sloshing around in this crap and getting immersion foot" (28).

Picture of three grunts with memorial wall in background taken at a memorial day celebration.

Capturing Charlie and radioing in.

KILO (K)

"We believe that peace is at hand."
—Henry Kissinger (October 1972)

○ *KA-Bar.* Marine combat knife. "This marine 7in-blade fighting knife was a virtual symbol of the Corps. The Union Cutlery Company offered its heavy-duty model 1217 fighting knife to the Marine Corps in 1942. . . . The marines adopted it and other companies manufactured it as well, but it became known as the KA-Bar. According to the company's own history . . . the name was derived from the pre-WWII testimonial of a satisfied trapper who crudely wrote that his rifle had jammed and he had used his knife to kill a wounded bear attacking him" (Rottman *FUBAR* 67).

○ *Keep your head down.* Watch out. Everything around you is dangerous, even if you think it isn't. War is like that. There's a bullet with your name on it.

Grunts walking 10 feet apart because dikes in rice paddies were often mined.

Please
by Yusef Komunyakaa

Forgive me, soldier
   Forgive my right hand
          for pointing you
       to the flawless
tree line now
   outlined in my brain.
         There was so much
Bloodsky over our heads at daybreak
        in Pleiku, but I won't say
        those infernal guns
        blinded me on that hill.

Mistakes piled up men like clouds
   pushed to the dark side.
    Sometimes I try to retrace
       them, running
         my fingers down the map
           telling less than a woman's body—
we follow the grid coordinates
   in some battalion commander's mind.
        If I could make my mouth
         unsay those orders,
        I'd holler: Don't
          move a muscle.
            Stay put,
& keep your fucking head
down, soldier.

Ambush.
Gunsmoke.
  Last night
    while making love
        I cried out,
        Hit the dirt!
        I've tried to swallow my tongue.

You were a greenhorn, so fearless,
even foolish, & when I said *go*, Henry,
          you went dancing on a red string
of bullets from the tree line
as it moved from a low cloud. (133)

○ *Khe Sanh.* Near the DMZ. Hills of red clay; Marines under siege for 77 days.
No resupply possible.

From part of the poem "**Red Clay**," by David G. Rodgers, assigned to the
13th Marines from August to mid-October 1967 at Khe Sanh.

So the story is told by the hills themselves
As they speak in jargon unfamiliar today
That a Marine came along stalking the "cong"
With his rifle to "search and destroy" his prey
His comrades came, too, to render support
Each finding ruggedness causing them to say
These hill are infested with a potent enemy,
These hills of Khe Sanh made of red clay. (Eichler 110)

Khe Sanh
by Robert Ratkevich

*In years to come some Old Gunny will tell
of this place called Khe Sanh, on the border of Hell.*

*He'll tell some Young Boot bout the "Old Corps Marines,"
The Tough Fighting Men of His Mighty Green Machine.*

*He'll tell of the days when the sky rained hot lead
Of the Padre who knelt and prayed for our dead.*

*In years to come some old Gunny will tell
And he'll cliché the words, War Is Hell*

*But few will remember and less, less will care
Except for some Jar Head Marines, that were there. (Eichler 100)*

○ **Khmer Rouge.** Also known as Red Cambodians, the Communist party in Cambodia. The Khmer are the predominant people of Cambodia and the official language. They were organized by both North and South Vietnamese Communists. The Khmer Rouge fought a guerilla war against the neutral government of Cambodia.

○ **KIA.** Killed In Action. Wasted. Greased. Bought the farm. Serviceman's Group Life Insurance paid the beneficiary (usually the parents if grunt was unmarried) $10,000, which was said to be enough to pay off a farm mortgage. Shortened to "bought it" (Rottmann *FUBAR* 31-32).

○ **Killing zone.** An area where everyone can be killed. No rules of engagement necessary. A zone is usually designated, but it can be changed. Towards the end of the American involvement, the president set up a no-kill zone near the border with China so China would not become involved.

○ **Killing the time.** Waiting Time. The war see-sawed from hours of pure boredom to five minutes of sheer panic. "The rest of Bravo Company's time in the flatlands was filled by just about all the small hour-by-hour activities experienced by all other grunts in all other wars. There were 27 poker games played, 137 weapons cleaned, seven mustaches grown, six night ambushes run, 328 foxholes and 12 mortar pits dug, an uncountable number of bitches uttered, two promotions awarded, 488 malaria pills

Killing Time.

taken, 1220 C-ration meals eaten, 125 cans of Seven-Up drunk, 389 pieces of mail (which included one birth announcement and three dear Johns) received, 93 canteens of Kool-Aid mixed, 18 guards caught sleeping on post ('Must be a bad battery in the radio, Captain'), nine cases of diarrhea suffered, 347 letters written, and an infinite number of sexual conquests dreamed" (Anderson *The Grunts* 121).

An average day for some vets. Bowman remembers the day came, the day left. George Albright, a veteran of three wars, interrogated Vietnamese, translated, passed on information to officers; then he had recon while the information was sent back to the rear. Ward's day was out in the field before daylight after coffee and something to eat. He was a mine sweeper, could pull back, sit there and play cards, get drunk, check radios, guns, and move. Then

he'd go to a base camp, maybe help put up concertina wire around the perimeter, and drink. Then he'd spend two hours on guard, four hours off. Ward said he seldom slept all night. "But it was a job, and it was professional, and I had to do it" (Vet Program 03/04/93).

Killing Time.

SGT. *Danny Phillips*
with two Kit Carson Scouts.

○ **Kit Carson Scouts.** Former VC defectors who worked with the Marines by choice. General Lewis W. Walt, Marine Corps: "we began to accept some of these volunteers, cautiously at first because of the obvious danger both to the volunteer and to our own men. We waited for one of them to turn against us, or lead a Marine unit into an ambush—it didn't happen. Instead, we found no adequate substitute for their knowledge" (Walt 42-44).

○ **Klick.** Short for kilometer (approximately .6214 miles per klick).

○ **Kool-Aid.** Often requested from home; a sugary Kool-Aid made a decent cover-up for local water that had to be purified first.

○ **KP.** Kitchen police, kitchen duty,

Looking for more NVA soldiers.

Surrounding an NVA soldier.

LIMA (L)

"Let us understand: North Vietnam cannot
defeat or humiliate the United States.
Only Americans can do that."
—Richard M. Nixon (1969)

○ **Language.** "In all the language dealing with Vietnam—whether fiction or poetry or film—you will notice the obscenities. Most of the writers and filmmakers argue that this is done on purpose, to reflect the real-life happenings. If this is so, then we are being asked not to condemn the language merely because we are outsiders. If the language is true to the experience, then the language is being defined by the community that shared the Vietnam experience—and we cannot judge it by standards our community shares" (Farb 102, 18).

"Herr . . . used the troops' own vocabulary and made it into a new literary language. Some of the language was army slang—words and phrases by which soldiers separated themselves and their world from the outside world of civilians, a way of expressing their conviction that if you weren't there you can't understand. Some of it was the common obscenities of the American street . . . . [Herr] saw that language [as described above] was appropriate for the story of the Vietnam War" (Hynes 204-205).

"The language of war helps us to deny what war is really about, and in doing so it makes war more palatable" (Grossman 93, see also 92).

○ **LBJ.** Lyndon B. Johnson, president of the US following the assassination of John F. Kennedy on November 22, 1963. President Johnson kept plans to aid South Vietnam; in 1965, two years into his presidency, the infantry arrived in South Vietnam. There has been much speculation about what JFK's actions would have been. LBJ is also the acronym for Long Binh Jail.

○ **Leave.** Approved absence from duty.

○ **Leave it behind.** Let it go. Don't take the bad things home with you.

◦ *Leeches.* In the water wherever the grunts went. They took as many precautions as they could. Tightening laces on their shoes, pulling the web belt tighter. Some grunts even wore condoms to protect themselves. After crossing water, they checked each other to pull off all the leeches. The VC were not magically immune from leeches. A retired colonel from the PAVN [People's Army of Vietnam] explained to Morley Safer that a "man could lose two hundred grams of blood every day from the leeches. The leeches have an anticoagulant . . . many of my men bled to death. Food was a constant worry, especially for the big units. I remember we shot an elephant once, and for five days we had meat. Men drowned; they fell off cliff; they died of malaria and snake bites. I used to look up in the sky and envy you in those helicopters" (32). And any way that a VC could die, an American could, too.

◦ *Licensed.* Combat soldiers were licensed to kill.

◦ *Lifers.* Career Army person. Lynda Van Devanter, nurse, explains: "One of our main targets for frustration was the attitude of the lifers who tried to appear gung ho and who frequently forced us to perform meaningless tasks. It was made more difficult by knowing that they, too, probably questioned the war in private, but would not voice their opinions because their precious career might be damaged" (210).

In Anderson's book about being in the rear echelon, he shows a quite different opinion of the lifers. "Their complete lack of reluctance to hide any of their views made the lifers the easiest group to identify. In blustery voices they made known their version of truth on any and all subjects, whether one wanted to listen or not (Anderson *Other War* 17).

A Vietnam Vet, Dr. Lifton works with many vets. What he found was a chasm between the grunts and the lifers. Whether drafted or enlisted, the newbies brought to Vietnam some of the culture of the 60s: rock music, soldiers who didn't care if their hair grew long, Afros with a special comb to keep the style, pot-smoking, peace signs, and even antiwar literature. In contrast were the lifers, the regular military complete with a "conventional and authoritarian military ethos" (230). The contrast was extreme. Crew cuts, alcohol as their drug of choice, soft music (230). Vietnam then became the site of the same generational war that was happening in many places in the US Lifton speculates that this had a lot to do "with the actual violence of 'fragging' incidents" (231), the complete misunderstanding and non-acceptance of each group for the other.

○ **Little people.** The enemy.

○ **Lit up.** Fired upon.

○ **Lightening.** Making a backpack lighter; carrying all the equipment you were expected to carry weighed from 30-70 pounds. "It was an exercise that had more to do with mental health than weight" (Anderson *The Grunts* 65). The act of lightening usually resulted in leaving only a pound behind—a grenade sacrificed for old letters, a picture of a girl friend, and one of Mom's cookies (Anderson *The Grunts* 65-66, 78). Sometimes, however, they threw away something that might protect them from shrapnel. Some ditched the fiberglass plates in their flak jackets. "Just getting rid of something—anything—made them feel better, made tomorrow look a little more tolerable" (Anderson *The Grunts* 78).

○ **Living room war.** Over a TV dinner the public could watch the day's result of the war: the body count, the helicopters whumping away. The tired faces. Morley Safer, CBS reporter, reflected years later, "In Vietnam, television, most of journalism, merely confirmed to Americans that the entire affair had a certain stench to it. [General] Westmoreland and many others fully believed the stench came from the lies, inexperience, and manipulations of journalists" (134). Herr, another journalist, saw problems with his job. "Conventional journalism could no more reveal this war than conventional firepower could win it, all it could do was take the most profound event of the American decade and turn it into a communications pudding, taking its most obvious, undeniable history and making it into a secret history. And the very best correspondents knew even more than that (218).

Adrian Cronauer called the war the First Electronic War—could show in living room all the horrors of war. The military was unprepared for the American people's reaction, so it tightened up the news. As an example Cronauer said a pilot returning from a raid might be "exhilarated," but bureaucratic censorship changed the word to "gratified."

In Desert Storm-1, there were ground rules for reporters: they had to be escorted and their stories often censored. Michael Herr and other reporters in Vietnam just went wherever and whenever.

○ **Lock and load.** Get ready.

Danny Phillips locking & loading.

○ **Look it in the eye.** Don't blink. Face it head on; it's not going away. "Here it was—bam bam whack! Tough shit, kid. Now it looked like one's Freedom Bird would never come. The whole damn planet and all of life looked like a lie now, there would be no end to this shit. The Freedom Bird and the States were all myths. They would never come true. And the myths were the President's gifts to all good grunts in the World; for Christmas, for New Year's, for birthdays, for all days. Thanks for signing up anyway, kid. We had no way of knowing it would be all this bad, but thanks anyway—we needed the warm body. Carry on . . . above and beyond the call . . . with complete disregard for his own personal safety . . . carry on, kid" (Anderson *The Grunts* 75).

○ *Long green line.* Infantry humping through the bush.

○ *Long Range Patrol.* Generally the baddest of the bad; good at individual work such as scouting or watching "also known as poop and scoop."

○ *Lose your attitude.* Listen and learn. Don't think you're John Wayne.

○ *The look.* Some veterans still in uniform and back in the World noticed how others viewed them. There was "The look"—as combat nurse, Lynda Van Devanter said. "I was a pariah, a nonperson so low that they believed they could squash me underfoot; I was as popular as a disease and as untouchable as a piece of shit" (248). (See also The Thousand Yard Stare.)

○ *LP.* Listening post. Two-to-three-man position set up at night outside perimeter, away from main body of troops as early warning system.

○ *LRRPs (Long Range Reconnaissance Patrol).* An elite team usually comprised of five to seven men who go deep into the jungle to observe the enemy. They dressed tough, acted tough, and took no prisoners. After 1969, they were called Rangers. "Some of them got down and dirty, and looked like animals" (Johnny, Vet Program 02/01/93).

○ *LT or Looey.* Lieutenant. A soldier had to take NCO (Non-Commissioned Officer) course for six months to qualify. Many just out of NCO found themselves in Vietnam heading a platoon relying on them to keep them safe.

○ *Luck.* Karma. Herr watched what grunts held onto: the ritual moves, carry your lucky piece, wear your magic jungle hat . . . ." Five-pound Bibles from home, crosses, St. Christophers, mezuzahs, locks of hair, girlfriends' underwear . . . pictures of John Kennedy, Lyndon Johnson, Martin Luther King, Huey Newton, the Pope, Che Guevara, the Beatles, Jimi Hendrix . . . . an oatmeal cookie . . . wrapped up in foil and plastic and three pairs of socks" (56-57).

Then there would be a magic grunt. Nearly every unit had one. Maybe he stepped on a dud of a mine or had ESP—he just knew where the VC were. "[If] you had special night vision, or great ears, you were magic too" (57).

Thanks
by Yusef Komunyakaa

Thanks for the tree
between me & a sniper's bullet.
I don't know what made the grass
sway seconds before the Viet Cong
raised his soundless rifle.
Some voice always followed,
telling me which foot
to put down first.
Thanks for deflecting the ricochet
Against that anarchy of dusk.
I was back in San Francisco
wrapped up in a woman's wild colors,
causing some dark bird's love call
to be shattered by daylight
when my hands reached up
& pulled a branch away
from my face. Thanks
for the vague white flower
that pointed to the gleaming metal
reflecting how it is to be broken
like mist over the grass,
as we played some deadly
game for blind gods.
What made me spot the monarch
writhing on a single thread
tied to a farmer's gate,
holding the day together
like an unfingered guitar string,
is beyond me. Maybe the hills
grew weary & leaned a little in the heat.
Again, thanks for the dud
hand grenade tossed at my feet
outside Chu Lai. I'm still
falling through its silence.
I don't know why the intrepid
sun touched the bayonet,
but I know that something
stood among those lost trees
& moved only when I moved. (154)

◦ **LZ.** Landing Zone for helicopters. If grunts send up red flares, the LZ is a hot or "dangerous" zone; don't land here. A green flare means safe. A yellow means caution. Sometimes the pilot ignored a hot zone. Doc Holley said his friend Hack was "coming down for the third time to pick up wounded men when his bird took heavy AK-47 fire from the wood line, and he and three others were shot in their legs. They told me he had loaded up his chopper to the point where there wasn't any room for him inside, so he stood on the skids as the chopper slowly labored to lift its heavy load up and out of the hot LZ" (147).

One doctor takes a chopper ride on a search and destroy mission after being persuaded that his life is boring. His men think he's crazy to go out in the bush voluntarily. All is okay until somebody yells from another chopper: Red smoke! Hot LZ! "As we started our descent, I looked out the front window of our bird and saw red smoke rising from the LZ. I remember thinking, Lucky me, my first LZ would have to be a hot one, then I countered with, Well, stupid, nobody made you come out here so go for it" (Holley 105-106).

Hot LZ. Smoke in red to indicate not safe to land.

Safe LZ (landing zone) green smoke means A-okay.

This scene is North of Marble Mountain on ocean.

MIKE (M)

"Some of the critics viewed Vietnam as a morality play in which
the wicked must be punished before the final curtain and
where any attempt to salvage self-respect from the outcome
compounded the wrong. I viewed it as a genuine tragedy.
No one had a monopoly on anguish."
—Henry Kissinger (1979)

○ **M-16.** Automatic or semi-automatic assault weapon. Weighed 7.6 pounds, 20-round cartridge. Range 460 meters. Automatic firing rate is 650-700 rounds per minute. Made a crackling sound when fired. One of the innovations made necessary to fight "in the jungle where visibility was poor, targets were fleeting, and contact was normally at short range" (Hay 51). The M-16 was sent to Vietnam in 1965 after eight years of development. Its ammo was lighter than the M-14 so soldiers didn't need to be resupplied as often (Hay 51).

But grunts didn't trust it. It was being battle-tested, handed to grunts without any real testing. It had a tendency to jam. Back to the field-tested AR-15, new and improved. Only it wasn't improved. After further improvements, the M-16 became "one of the premier infantry rifles of the World. In addition to equipping US troops, nearly one million M-16s were supplied to the South Vietnamese from 1967 onward" (Dunnigan and Nofi 68).

An official statement: *The M-16 rifle you are armed with is the best weapon there is for use here in Vietnam . . ." Captain Paul Von Hoene, Tropic Lightning News, 25th Infantry Division, Cu Chi, Vietnam, July 3, 1967* (Rottmann 11).

Rifle, 5.56MM, XM16E1
by Larry Rottmann

The M-16 sure is a marvelous gun.
    In a god-awful war
    it provides some keen fun.

The bullet it fires appears too small to harm.
    But it makes a big hole
    and can tear off an arm.

Single shot, semi, or full automatic.
    A real awesome weapon,
    though often sporadic.

Listen to Ichord and forget that stuck bolt.
    You aren't as important
    as a kickback from Colt.

So carry your rifle (they don't give a damn).
    Just pray you won't need it
    while you're in Vietnam.

The M-16 is issue, though we all feel trapped.
    More GIs would protest,
    but somehow they got zapped. (Rottmann 11)

LRRP Richard Ford was amazed at the equipment that was handed out without a question. "It was really weird how the old guys would ask you what you want to carry. It wasn't a thing where you get assigned an M-14, M-16. If you want to carry an M-16, they say how many rounds of ammo do you want to carry? If you want to carry 2,000, we got it for you. How many grenades do you want? It was really something. We were so in the spirit that we hurt ourself. Guys would want to look like John Wayne. The dudes would just get in the country and say, 'I want a .45. I want eight grenades. I want a bandolier. I want a thousand rounds of ammo. I want ten clips. I want the works, right?' We never knew what the weight of this ammo is gon' to be'" (Terry 35).

Humping, chopping through grasses, all that stuff got heavy. So every now and then a grunt would toss grenades in the river or under bushes. Then off came the bandoliers. Ford said he once threw away 200 rounds of ammo. 'I'm carrying my C rations, my air mattress, poncho, and five quarts of water, everything you own. The ammo was just too heavy . . . . I said it got lost. The terrain was so terrible, so thick, nobody could question that you lost it" (Terry 35). Once back at the rear, Ford said nobody asked any questions, even if you loaded up with the same stuff the next day (Terry 35).

This attitude about tossing valuable things away is a little like what you read by Lewis Puller and others in Garbage (above). Except in this case, the LRRPs were throwing aside things valuable to *them*. And they knew it. It did take a little time for them to learn that a can from a C-ration box could be as deadly as a grenade.

○ **M-60.** Standard light machine gun. American-made, belt-fed. Often called "The Gun." "The M-60 machine gun was designed to replace both the .30 caliber Browning light machine gun and the .50 caliber heavy machine gun . . . . Mounted on a tripod, the M-60 served as a heavy machine gun, used primarily to defend fixed positions. As a light machine gun, the M-60 used a folding bipod attached to the barrel . . . . The M-60 is the first truly portable machine gun . . . . Capable of being fired from the hip while moving, the M-60 proved well-suited to the type of fighting found in Vietnam" (Olsen 267-268).

○ **M-109.** Fires a 98 pound projectile about 14,600 meters or 9 miles with incredible accuracy. Russian or Chinese 152mm traveled 11 miles.

○ **MACV.** Pronounced "Mac Vee." Military Assistance Command Vietnam.

○ **Mail/Mail Call.** Turn-around time for mail was about two weeks. But for grunts on the move, mail had a hard time catching up with them. When a resupply chopper finally arrived, "the grunts bent all their attention to their mail. They tore it open and studied over and over the words written by feminine, parental, brotherly, sisterly, or wifely hands. The packages full of Hershey bars and canned hot dogs and

Receiving mail.

peaches and apples and peanuts and homemade cookies and cakes were passed around the hill" (Anderson *The Grunts* 58). For most, mail was about the only thing that kept them going. Doc writes to Sondra, "Keep your letters coming. When I don't get one, I hear my men saying, 'Well, Doc's got a case of the ass today. He didn't get a letter from Sondra!' That's their expression for being pissed off. But when I do get one or two from you, my huge grin gives good evidence of how happy I am, and when I'm happy, so are my men. People back in the World have no idea what a morale boost mail call is to those of us over here. If I couldn't get letters from you, I think I'd go crazy, really! I read your letters, and for a few minutes, it's almost as if I'm home with you" (103).

Mail Call
by Randy Cribbs

Easy to tell who did well
    And who appeared
      Under a spell.

Last name called
    And still some linger,
Longing to feel the paper
Between trembling fingers.
Glancing down
    To the ground,
Searching for that
    Not to be found.

Just yesterday, soft
    Words of forever
And now, maybe, her
    Touch again, never.
Seeing her last
    As she turned
And now
    Spurned.

Mail call;
No cookies to share,
    No one to care,
Not even that special one—
    Back there . . . (55)

Writing letters home.

Christmas cards were specially welcomed.

Charlie Plumb, a POW for nearly six years, said "The V never made us wait for 'Dear Johns'" (160). The V did, however, stash mail for POWs undelivered, yet not destroyed. "Once a POW, alone in the room, found a bushel basket filled with letters from the States. He grabbed a couple of them, concealed them under his sleeve, brought them back to the cell, and passed contents through the walls to their overjoyed owners" (161).

Mail was moved by chopper when resupply was called for or if bennies were dropped. Says a chagrined nurse, Lynda Van Devanter, in a letter home (150).

> *Dear Mom and Dad,*
>
> I hang my head. Mail call just brought six letters from you in addition to the nicest care package I've ever seen. Postmarks go back as far as a month. I don't know what the holdup was, but mail call was bright for the first time in a very long time. I'm sorry I misjudged you. It's hard to keep my spirits up when there's no mail to cheer me, the move to An Khe was canceled again. The rumor mill is still buzzing, but this is supposed to be the final word.
>
> *Love,*
>
> *Lynda*

"There was mail service [for North Vietnamese soldiers], although because of the American firepower along the Ho Chi Minh Trail and the need to carry the mail much of the way via courier, a lot of it never arrived or took months to do so if it did" (Dunnigan and Nofi 270-271). This is confirmed by Morley Safer's conversation with a former North Vietnamese soldier. Safer asked, "What about mail . . . messages from home?"

"For us? No, never for us. Some of us brought along with us letters we received from sweethearts before we left for the South. We passed them among ourselves and read them aloud and laughed and teased each other with some of the things girlfriends say to soldiers going off to war" (45).

○ *Mama-san.* Female Vietnamese, usually older, probably raising a family and planting rice. Wears an *ao da,* a shimmery dress with a conical hat.

Mama-San.

Mama-San
by Jim Gray

Yours was a village of a dozen thatched roofs
Surrounded by palm trees and rice paddies.
I guess you were born in that village
Somewhere near Song Mao
Its name escapes me now.

I'd say you were a dark-eyed beauty once
Before the paddy sun faded you.
Raising children and crops
Long before the war
Finally reached your door.

We came to your village not expected or invited,
Impolite teenagers in noisy helicopters.
Not respecting your age
We came with the sun
Before your sleep was done.

We landed by your house, in the garden
You guarded from the village boys.
In a huge flying insect landed
Tearing up the rows
You so neatly hoed.

We saw you in your anger charge
Shuffling down the path to the garden.
Your gray hair back in a bun
Chasing off the boys
Playing with their noisy toys.

We had little to report of that morning mission
Just minor damage to a single helicopter.
A dented right side pilot's door.
You made quite a shot
With your cast-iron cooking pot. (29, 31)

○ **Marines.** "Marines are not allowed to die without permission; we are government property" (Hasford 13). (Note: There is no such thing as an *ex*-Marine. A Marine may retire but he's still a Marine. Their motto is *semper fi*, always faithful.)

> Hey, Marine, have you heard?
> Hey, Marine . . . .
> L. B. J. has passed the word.
> Hey, Marine . . . .
> Say good-bye to Dad and Mom.
> Hey, Marine . . . .
> You're gonna die in Viet Nam.
> Hey, Marine, yeah! (Hasford 25)

"The Marines were well disciplined but were not in very good condition . . . They were also utterly untrained for the assignment. No one seemed to tell them there were 'friendlies' around. The decision to put an elite assault force into static positions in a highly populated area [was a mistake]. In Vietnam they were given the worst assignments and the most outdated equipment" (Safer 162).

○ **MARS.** Military Affiliate Radio System, free for calling home. At a PX. "I have been told there is a radio communications system available to us known as the MARS network. What it amounts to do is this—our shortwave operators in Dong Tam get in touch with a ham operator in the United States, and he in turn makes a long distance call to the party we are trying to reach. Then the party reached only has to pay for the long-distance call from the ham operator's location . . . You have to remember that it is not two-way communication, *i.e.*, you have to say what you want to say and then say 'over,' and then it is my turn" (Holley 28).

"The airtight, guaranteed-to-get-permission excuse was to say you had to go to the MARS station to send a message back to the States. . . . No commander would dare say no to that reason because to do so might cause the offended man to fire off some privileged correspondence to his congressman which would provoke a request-for-clarification from the congressman's office. Letters of complaint from members of Congress were considered definite threats to one's career . . ." (Anderson *Other War* 30).

"I am planning to get up in about four hours and call you on the MARS line. I really need to make these calls while we are in the rear area because when we finish Dong Tam security we will be back to flying all over hell's half acre and I won't have access to the phones" (Holley 84). (Note: These days in a war soldiers carry cell phones.)

○ **Martin Luther King, Jr.** This Civil Rights Leader assassinated in Memphis on April 4, 1968. He became increasingly opposed to the war for several reasons: that the US was doing nothing but provoking violence; and his perception that young black men weren't able to get the college deferments young white men could get.

"In April 1967, the Reverend Dr Martin Luther King, in his 'Declaration of Independence from the War in Vietnam' given at Manhattan's Riverside Church, noted that during the conflict, apart from the usual brutalizing process to which soldiers are exposed in any war, 'we are adding cynicism to the process of death, for our troops must know after a short period that

Martin Luther King, Jr.

none of the things we claim to be fighting for are really involved'" (Ebert 292).

"Considering the rapid change during the 1960s in black Americans' views of themselves and their rightful position in American society, it cannot be surprising that the black grunt on his return found even bigger hypocrisies. The American dream and its documentary accompaniment about all men being created equal and entitled to equal protection under the law seemed more than a joke than ever before suspected. It takes little effort on the part of any member of any race to imagine the deep rage and bitterness a black grunt on patrol in a nameless jungle or sitting in a foxhole must have felt on hearing that thirty-two of his brothers and sisters had been gunned down in the streets of Detroit in 1967, or that in 1968 his most effective leader in the fight against a second class existence in white, 'who-needs-niggers' America—Martin Luther King, Jr.— had been assassinated. At some point in their tours, most blacks came to feel that in Vietnam they were being used to fight 'whitey's war'" (Anderson *The Grunts* 186).

"But [Hanoi Helen] didn't unsettle the brothers as much as when she got on the air after Martin Luther King died, and they was rioting back home. She was saying, 'Soul brothers, go home. Whitey raping your mothers and your daughters, burning down your homes. What you over here for? This is not your war. The war is a trick of the Capitalist empire to get rid of the blacks.' Ford really listened to her words 'I really thought—I really started believing it, because it was too many blacks than there should be in the infantry'" (Terry 39).

This idea is an enduring myth. According to CPT Marshal Hanson, a retired researcher for the US Naval Reserve, "86% who died in Vietnam were Caucasians; 12.5% were black." He quotes from sociologists Charles C. Moskos and John Sibley Butler's new book, *All That We Can Be*: "Black fatalities amounted to 12 percent of all Americans killed in Southeast Asia, a figure proportional to the number of blacks in the US population at the time and slightly lower than the proportion of blacks in the Army at the close of the war" (Pedigo 2). This is backed up by Dunnigan and Nofi: "black Americans were not disproportionately represented in the ranks in Vietnam" (5).

Reporter Herr didn't underestimate King's assassination as trouble. "The death of Martin Luther King intruded on the war in a way that no other outside event had ever done. In the days that followed, there were a number of small, scattered riots, one or two stabbings, all of it denied officially. . . . A southern colonel on the general's staff told me that it was a shame, a damn shame, but I had to admit (didn't I?) that he'd been a long time asking for it (158). Later Herr met up with a black staff sergeant, a friend who'd ignored him when the news was everywhere. "'Now what I gonna do?' he said." Herr responded, "I'm a great one to ask." The sergeant: "'But dig it. Am I gonna take 'n' turn them guns aroun' on my own people? Shit!' That was it, there was hardly a black NCO anywhere who wasn't having to deal with that. We sat in the dark, and he told me that when he'd walked by me that afternoon it had made him sick. He couldn't help it" (158-9).

Report from the Skull's Diorama
by Yusef Komunyakaa

>Dr King's photograph
>comes at me from *White Nights*
>like Hoover's imagination at work,
>
>dissolving into a scenario
>at Firebase San Juan Hill:
>our chopper glides in closer,
>down to the platoon of black GIs
>back from night patrol

with five dead. Down
into a gold whirl of leaves
dust-deviling the fire base.
A field of black trees
stakes down the morning sun.

With the chopper blades
knife-fighting the air,
yellow leaflets quiver
back to the ground, clinging to us.
These men have lost their tongues,

but the red-bordered
leaflets tell us
VC didn't kill
Dr. Martin Luther King.
The silence etched into their skin

is also mine. Psychological
warfare colors the napalmed hill
gold-yellow. When our gunship
flies out backwards, rising
above the men left below

to blend in with the charred
landscape, an AK-47
speaks, with the leaflets
clinging to the men & stumps,
waving to me across the years. (156)

Captain Norman Alexander McDaniel (a POW) recalls "When Dr King was assassinated; they called me in for interrogation to see if I would make a statement critical of the United States. I said no, I don't know enough about it. They wanted all of us to make statements they could send abroad or make tapes they could play to the GIs. They wanted me to tell black soldiers not to fight because the United States is waging a war of genocide, using dark-skinned people against dark-skinned people. I would tell them no, this is not a black-white war. We're in Vietnam trying to help the South Vietnamese. It is a matter of helping people who are your friends" (Terry 137).

Maybe it was a black-white war, thought Don F. Brown, Staff Sergeant. "When I heard that Martin Luther King was assassinated, my first inclination was to run out and punch the first white guy I saw. I was very hurt. All I wanted to do was go home. I even wrote Lyndon Johnson a letter. I said that I didn't understand how I could be trying to protect foreigners in their country with the possibility of losing my life wherein in my own country people who are my hero, like Martin Luther King, can't even walk the streets in a safe manner . . . . Said a white guy a few days later, "I wish they'd take that nigger's picture off the TV. . . . And we commenced to give him a lesson in when to use that word and when you should not use that word. To play on the sympathy of the black soldier, the VC would shoot at a white guy, then let the black guy behind him go through, then shoot at the next white guy" (Terry 167).

○ *MASH.* Mobile Army Surgical Hospital. Some women who served as nurses were sometimes not considered "Vietnam Vets" because of a misguided notion that they never faced shelling, shooting, and combat. It wasn't until some Vietnam Veterans of America chapters admitted women that the prejudice was overcome.

○ *Medal of Honor.* The Highest award. Risk of life beyond call of duty, often mistakenly called "Congressional" Medal of Honor although Congress has nothing to do with it. Also, one does not *win* the MOH, one is *a recipient* of the Medal of Honor.

○ *MEDCAP.* **Med**ical **C**ivilian **A**ction **P**rogram, a program to help the South Vietnamese. "[MEDCAP] was designed to separate the Viet Cong from the civilian population on which it so heavily depended" (Anderson *Other War* 77).

"Once a week we take a corpsman out to a vill and give free [medical] treatment for whatever we find. There's a lot of skin infections, simple things like that. Villagers can't figure out why they don't heal up but they keep taking baths in the same stream they shit and piss in. We teach them how to use soap but the next time we go back we see the same new bars we gave them. If they got some serious illness or need an operation, we bring them into a hospital in Da Nang" (Anderson *Other War* 67).

Doc Holley, after six months in the bush ready, willing, and able to use his weapon, is just learning what his job at the rear will be: "I will be expected to make three or four trips per week to the local villages to treat their ill, in an effort to 'win the hearts and minds' of the natives. This is all part of a program called MEDCAP.... However, all the docs I've talked to stress the importance of being well armed as they are occasionally mortared or ambushed. What gratitude! Seriously though, this points out one of the biggest problems for any American over here—just who is the enemy, and how can you tell him from the typical peasant farmer who lives out in the paddies and wears black pajamas and thong sandals just like Charlie?" (21).

"Thousands of doctors, dentists, nurses, and medical technicians spent hundreds of thousands of hours administering modern medicine and teaching

basic standards of hygiene, in both large cities and tiny villages, under the Medical Civic Action Program (MEDCAP) of the US Command. Hundreds of clinics, hospitals and schools were built and thousands of Vietnamese trained to staff them. On their own initiative, thousands of American servicemen spent much of their off-duty time working in orphanages and schools" (Anderson *The Grunts* 203).

MEDCAP program doctors examining village children.

○ **Medevac.**

The chopper that performs Medical Evacuation to soldiers hurt in the field. Triage in the field determined where the wounded would be sent: to a field hospital or a rear area hospital. Naval hospital ships were also an alternative. Herr, who rode in choppers to find action to report, was not to worry.

"'If you get hit,' a medic told me, 'we can chopper you back to base-camp hospital in like twenty minutes.'

MEDEVAC wounded have been evacuated.

"'If you get hit real bad,' a corpsman said, 'they'll get your case to Japan in twelve hours.'

"'If you get killed,' a Spec 4 from Graves [Registration] promised, 'we'll have you home in a week'" (21).

○ **Medics.** Medics typically received eight weeks' training for *field* medicine, not *hospital* medicine. They typically called their introduction to war as "trial by death." The fear they experienced was first anger and then the need for survival. Survival was on everyone's mind. Spec 4 Ford confessed that "[we] had a medic that gives us a shot of morphine anytime you want one. I'm not talkin' about for the wounded. I'm talkin' about when you just want to get high. So you can face it" (Terry 38). Herr also saw medics giving out pills and drugs. "Going out at night the medics gave you pills, Dexedrine breath like dead snakes kept too long in a jar. I never saw the need for them myself" (4).

The Army had its own medics. Marine medics received medical training in the Navy and were then sent for four weeks of combat training including humping mountains and navigating through bush with only a map and a compass. They practiced triage on troops with artificial wounds made from plastic.

Heat exhaustion was common, but medics could do little for a heat stroke: red face, hot, dry skin, a fever. Medics would give fluids if they had any and start an IV if possible. Then they waited for Medevac. Another major problem was a fungus the grunts called jungle rot, especially on the feet which stayed wet a lot of the time. Dry socks and baby powder from home kept feet as dry as possible.

"Soldiers in past wars often drank themselves into numbness, and Vietnam was no exception. But Vietnam was also the first war in which the forces of modern pharmacology were directed to empower the battlefield soldier.

"The administration of tranquilizing drugs and phenothiazines on the combat front first occurred in Vietnam. The soldiers who became psychiatric casualties were generally placed in psychiatric-care facilities in close proximity to the combat zone where these drugs were prescribed by MDs and psychiatrists. The soldiers under their care readily took their 'medicine,' and this program was touted as a major factor in reducing the incidence of evacuations of psychiatric casualties" (Grossman 270).

Medic
by Randy Cribbs.

Crawling, bag in tow
Through enemies who still litter
This dangerous place he must go,
He moves with single-minded
Purpose from one still figure
To another,
From brother to brother,
Not dwelling on living or dying,
Through the screams and
crying.
Working in the
Hot days dusty veil
With forced patience,
Dispensing his magic
To relieve their hell.

Medic, sawbones, doc,
Call him what you like,
Always there to answer
In the thick of the fight,
Moving without hesitation,
Through the remnants and brass
Left in the battles aftermath,
While other soldiers pass,
Save those he directs to
Load the bird;
They respond
Without a word
To the soldier, who
Fights a different war,
Knowing
There will come yet more . . . (45)

MEDIC attending to a man's wounds.

○ *Mekong Hospital.* Civilian hospital located in Mekong delta. "Among the total number of 87 surgical patients, 21 had no connection with the war. The remaining 66 were war victims" (Honda 34).

○ **MIA.** Missing in Action. "And we tended to list the people as MIA as opposed to KIA until we were absolutely certain. We held out hope that they would be recovered, captured, anything but dead" (Terry 194).

The North Vietnamese had an MIA team (not the same as the US MIA) to find, identify, recover, and then bury the dead. To many North Vietnamese, the dead became shadows, or they became sounds. One MIA team was haunted by a song each claimed to hear; following the sound, the team came across a shallow grave, with nothing but bones and a guitar. After the burial, the song ended forever. (See **War Stories** below.) From the Vietnamese soldier, Bao Ninh, who was there: "True or not? Who's to know? The yarn became folklore. For every unknown soldier, for every collection of MIA remains, there was a story" (91).

"President Clinton has said that before he will lift the embargo, he must be satisfied that Vietnam has cooperated in the fullest possible accounting of the MIAs." Latest figures, as of 1994, show that there are 2236 Americans missing in action in Indochina. Of those some 1647 are still missing in Vietnam (*Roanoke Times* 29 January 1994, A4).

○ **Midnight requisition.** Obtaining items on your own, without any authority.

○ **Mike-Mikes.** Mounted on a C-47. Mike-Mikes fired 300 rounds per second and were often all fired at the same time for a short period of time. The C-47 was called Puff the Magic Dragon, but the Marines called it Spooky. Herr says "Every fifth round fired was a tracer, and when Spooky was working, everything stopped while that solid stream of violent red poured down out of the black sky . . . . If you watched at close range, you couldn't believe that anyone would have the courage to deal with that night after night, week after week, and you cultivated a respect for the Viet Cong and NVA who had crouched under it every night now for months" (133).

○ **Military Advisors.** Safer asked to go to Saigon and stay as long as there were stories (xvi). "Nothing prepared me for what I found in Saigon. Both the physical and psychological terrain was being prepared for a colossal American Intervention. Machismo was in the air. American military advisers—there were no full-scale units—were beginning to strut their stuff. They were giving up their role of bystanders and sideline coaches. The war was ceasing to be a Vietnamese show" (xvi-xvii).

○ **Million-dollar wound.** A wound serious enough for you to get sent home but not serious enough to cause permanent injury or disfigurement. "Some of the guys have stopped taking their malaria pills in the hopes of contracting that disease instead of a case of acute lead poisoning—compliments of Charlie. Some even shoot themselves in the foot to get a trip back to the World!" (Holley 128).

○ *Monday pills.* Weekly large, orange malaria pills caused diarrhea in many; grunts also took pink salt tablets which caused nausea (Reinberg 143, Holley 102).

○ *Monsoon.* "The climate shaped the activities of both sides. Vietnam is a tropical country that still has seasons. The most influential 'season' is the annual monsoon. In the north of South Vietnam, the rainy season is from September to January. In the south, especially in the Mekong Delta and the Cambodian and Laotian infiltration routes, the rains come between May and September. This period of heavy rains makes military operations difficult. It is time consuming and dangerous to make your way through the bush when in a monsoon rain. Visibility is low, the ground is muddy or slippery, and it's cold, at least compared to the normally tropical heat" (Dunnigan and Nofi 92). Monsoons took away physical comfort and changed attitudes as well writes Surgeon Holley to his future wife. "Well, today is truly a 'blue' Sunday as it's been gray and overcast and rainy all day long. The monsoons have arrived, and I've never seen such huge raindrops. I know that sounds crazy, but sometimes it looks like it's raining grapes, and it's not hail, just huge raindrops, and lots of time it comes down in buckets" (181).

Nurse Lynda Van Devanter noticed a change in the war depending on the weather. "The fall monsoons brought our greatest number of casualties. It was a good time for the V.C. because they knew the country and were at home with its seasons. To our soldiers, the elements were merely another enemy, which, in combination with the V.C., proved unbeatable" (179-180).

Spec 4 Strong (MOS machine gunner) and his guys got caught on a mission during the monsoon season. It wasn't anything like he'd ever seen before. "It rained 15 days and 15 nights continuously. We stayed wet 15 days. We started catching cramps and charley horses. And guys' feet got messed up. Well, they were trying to get supplies into us. But it was raining so hard, the chopper couldn't get in. After five days, we ran out of supplies. We were so hungry and tired we avoided all contact [with the enemy]. We knew where the North Vietnamese were, but we knew that if we got into it, they would probably have wiped a big portion of the company out. We were really dropped there to find the North Vietnamese, and here we were hiding from them. Running because we were hungry. We were so far up in the hills that the place was so thick you didn't have to pull guard at night. You'd have to take a machete to cut even 100 meters. It could take two hours, that's how thick the shit was. We starved for four days. That was the first time I was ever introduced to hunger" (Terry 55).

To a Vietnam veteran who went to war at 17, Claude Anshin Thomas, now a Buddhist monk, finds that rain "for want of a better word [is a flashback] (3). "For me, every time it rains I walk through war. For two rainy seasons I experienced very heavy fighting. During the monsoons in Vietnam, the tremendous volume of water leaves everything wet and muddy. Now when it rains, I am still walking through fields of young men screaming and dying. I still see tree lines disintegrating from napalm. I still hear seventeen-year-old boys crying for their mothers, fathers, and girlfriends. Only after reexperiencing all of that can I come to the awareness that right now, it's just raining" (3).

Monsoon Season
by Yusef Komunyakaa

A river shines in the jungle's
wet leaves. The rain's finally
let up but whenever wind shakes
the foliage it starts to fall.
The monsoon uncovers troubled
season we tried to forget.
Dead men slip through bad weather,
stamping their muddy boots to wake us,
their curses coming easier.
There's a bend in everything,
in elephant grass & flame trees,
raindrops pelting the sand-bagged
bunker like a muted gong.
White phosphorous washed from the air,
winds sway with violet myrtle,
beating it naked. Soaked to the bone,
jungle rot brings us down to earth.
We sit in our hooches
with too much time,
where grounded choppers
can't fly out the wounded.
Somewhere nearby a frog
begs a snake.
I try counting droplets,
stars that aren't in the sky.
My poncho feels like a body bag.
I lose count. Red leaves
whirl by, the monsoon
unburying the dead. (130)

○ **Montagnards or Yards.** Probably the original inhabitants of Vietnam. Forced into the mountains away from their fishing places, they hated the Chinese who took their farmland and fishing places. They farmed, smoked a lot of marijuana, and got on well with the US forces. They proved to be more dependable than the ARVNs (Devanter 215).

Strictly speaking, the Montagnards are not really Vietnamese at all, certainly not *South* Vietnamese, but a kind of upgraded, demi-enlightened Annamese aborigine" (Herr 93). Sometimes called Mountain Yards.

"In the highlands, where the Montagnards would trade you a pound of legendary grass for a carton of Salems, I got stoned with some infantry from the 4th. One of them had worked for months on his pipe, beautifully carved and painted with flowers and peace symbols. There was a reedy little man in the circle who grinned all the time but hardly spoke. He pulled a thick plastic bag out of his pack and handed it over to me. It was full of what looked like large pieces of dried fruit. I was stoned and hungry, I almost put my hand in there, but it had a bad weight to it. The other men were giving each other looks, some amused, some embarrassed and even angry. Someone had told me once there were a lot more ears than heads in Vietnam; just information. When I handed it back he was still grinning, but he looked sadder than a monkey" (Herr 34).

A favorite catch-and-cook for the Yards was the rat. Because rats hung around food and dirt, Special Forces in underground camps were overrun. After shooting the rats, sometimes with shotgun shells filled with rice, the Special Forces brought them to the Yards who didn't understand why the Americans wouldn't join them to eat (Dunnigan and Nofi 102).

One grunt who usually walked point dressed like a Montagnard. "I wouldn't wear conventional camouflage fatigues in the field. I wore a dark-green loin-cloth, a dark-green bandana to blend in with the foliage, and a little camouflage paint on my face. And Ho Chi Minh sandals. And my grenades and ammunition. That's the way I went to the field. I dressed like that specifically as the point man, because if the enemy saw anyone first, they saw myself. They would just figure I was just another jungle guy that was walking around in the woods. And I would catch 'em off guard" (Terry 244).

○ **Montagnard bracelet.** Usually worn by Special Forces who worked with the Yards. Others felt honored to be presented with one. After the war was over, the Montagnards lost their land in the mountains. The Yards were terrifically fierce fighters and comfortable with Special Forces; many

LRRPs and SEALs wore Montagnard bracelets which were brass, made with bullets.

○ **Mortar.** Tube that launched projectiles that made huge arcs, kept the enemy away and out of sight.

○ **MOS.** United States Army MOS. **M**ilitary **O**ccupational **S**pecialty. The soldier's individual MOS falls in one of a number of groups: for example 11B Infantry rifleman, 13B artilleryman and 91B medical specialist (Reinberg 145). Dunnigan and Nofi note that 18,465 men designated 11B died in Vietnam, "accounting for 31.76 percent of American deaths in Vietnam" (3).

○ **Move out.** Pick up and go. Not what a platoon wants to hear after a wickedly hot and long hump the day before, particularly when it thought it was going to stay put. They'd much prefer to RON (remain over night).

○ **MPC.** Military Pay Certificates in place of money; an attempt to cut out black-marketing. The Army would announce a change in color of the MPC so troops would turn in their old ones. Locals who had sold stuff to the Americans were not in a position to change any MPC they held. Sometimes called "Monopoly money."

○ **My Country, right or wrong.** Not meant to be how it is usually taken to be. This line is only part of what was originally said. The essence is that we, the United States, want to be right in our dealings with other countries. Within our own country, we can accept that we can be right and we can be wrong. Johnny said in one program about the protestors that he didn't resent them. It was their right to protest" (Vet Program 01/01/93).

An American Rescuing Vietnamese Children.

NOVEMBER (N)

"America has made no reparation to the Vietnamese, nothing.
We are the richest people in the world and they are among
the poorest. We savaged them, though they had never hurt us,
and we cannot find it in our hearts, our honor, to give them
help—because the government of Vietnam is Communist. And
perhaps because they won."
—Jean Baudrillard (1986); he was a French philosopher,
political commentator, and photographer

○ **'Nam or The 'Nam.** When your tour was over, you went back to "the World."
What does that say about where you are now? A place not in the World? A place
that doesn't exist? In a crazy war with no clear objectives grunts could see,
'Nam was hell. Even to the Vietnamese.

"'I've had nightmares since joining this team, but last night's was the
worst.'

"'No doubt,' the driver said, waving his hand in a wide arc. 'This is the Jungle
of Screaming Souls. It looks empty and innocent, but in fact it's crowded. There
are so many ghosts and devils all over the battleground! I've been driving for
this corpse-collecting team since early seventy-three but I still can't get used to
the passengers who come out of their graves to talk to me'" (Ninh 41).

"I watched the white rain, the mountains, the endless forests, battlefield
after battlefield, stretched out all the way to the horizon. This vast space
swarming with soldiers, armies of black ants, red ants, winged ants, fire ants,
bee ants, termites, all paddling about in the mud, running through scorched,
desolate fields" (Huong 246).

For reporters, there was "a standard question you could use to open a
conversation with troops, and [former Saigon CBS bureau chief] Fouhy tried
it. 'How long you been in-country?' he asked. The kid half lifted his head; that
question could *not* be serious. The weight was really on him, and the words
came slowly.

"'All fuckin' day,' he said" (Herr 179). There it is. That's the 'Nam.

○ *Napalm.* "Napalm is an incendiary chemical [stored in 55 pound drums] that burns at about 2,000 degrees Fahrenheit. It is made from gasoline and detergent, which form a jelly. Not only can it cause death by burning, but it also 'deoxygenates' the air, which can cause asphyxiation, and often generates enormous quantities of carbon monoxide gas, which is poisonous" (Dunnigan and Nofi 124). It is easily made at home with two ingredients: Styrofoam^R (any Styrofoam^R not covered in plastic: plates and cups) and gasoline mixed in a metal jar until it is sticky. It can be stored for a long time. Do not touch it. It produces third-degree burns. Ironically, because the napalm sticks to the skin and burns nerve endings just below, there is not as much pain as if a victim suffered second-degree burns. <*howany. com/how-to-make-napalm/*>.

"First used in World War II, napalm is an effective fire bomb. Its name comes from its two ingredients used by the military: naphthenic & palmiti acids. It's another defoliant, especially dangerous because it turns into a fire bomb. It was used in World War II by the US and by the U. N. in Korea. In Vietnam, it was used by both the US and the NVA.

"Napalm was also used by the VC and NVA. Their preferred method of dispensing it was by flamethrower, but they also occasionally used it in incendiary devices. There were never any protests against the use of napalm by the North Vietnamese Army" (Dunnigan and Nofi 134-135).

Bao Ninh, a North Vietnamese soldier and writer, reports on the effect of napalm. "That was the dry season when the sun burned harshly, the wind blew fiercely, and the enemy sent napalm spraying through the jungle and a sea of fire enveloped them, spreading like the fires of hell. Troops in the fragmented companies tried to regroup, only to be blown out of their shelters again as they went mad, became disoriented, and threw themselves into nets of bullets, dying in the flaming inferno" (5).

"In December 1969 the U.N. General Assembly resolved any use of chemical warfare—including herbicides—violated international law; the United States rejected this resolution as outside the scope of the General Assembly. In August 1971, however, the US and the Soviet Union jointly submitted a draft ban on biological weapons" (Kutler 114).

○ *NCO.* "An experienced draftee, [usually a sergeant] run through a special training course to make him an NCO; also sometimes a newly commissioned officer with no experience" (Dunnigan and Nofi 351). Non-commissioned officer; one that comes up through the ranks, not as a soldier appointed because of US education and military experience. An NCO was usually a squad leader or platoon sergeant. Fresh out of school, an NCO was called Shake'n'Bake, Ready Whip, Nestlé's Quick, or Instant NCO. Most of the men under him in a platoon knew a lot more than he did, but he didn't want to hear it.

○ **Net.** Radio frequency, from network.

○ **Newbie.** A newcomer. A newcomer to the war or a newcomer to a new task or job in the war. Newbies saw right away they'd better learn fast. A newbie has probably been trained for two weeks in South Carolina or Louisiana to put grunts into a Vietnam-like environment. And it included a basic eight-week course and specialty courses (Bobby Ward, Vets Program 1/28/93).

"New soldiers, the replacements, were not trusted by the more experienced soldiers. . . . Better to teach or ignore the FNGs and wait for them to prove they could survive and be reliable enough to work with" (Dunnigan and Nofi 78).

"One admirable quality I found in John Phillips was his leadership. Even as a new man, he walked point. He said his weapon was on automatic at all times. He could fire 18 times in three seconds, I think. It made me proud when he told us about becoming squad leader and remained point guard (is that what he was called?). I mean, the new men were treated so badly, yet John found it in himself not to treat them as everyone else had. That in itself makes him a hero in my mind" (Heather, Vets Program 1/28/93).

One of the major problems with newbies is the system: newbies operated under the individual replacement system. He went to a platoon with a hole to fill—a dead man, a wounded man not to return. So a newbie didn't arrive under the best of circumstances. His platoon needed his presence and hoped he had the skill it needed, too.

○ **Nicknames.** In a platoon of sixty or seventy, grunts rarely knew each others' names. First, it wasn't good to be close to a guy who might be dead next week. Secondly, the rotations in and out meant almost every grunt had a different DEROS—some were newbies with their whole term to serve; some were already counting down the days on their short-timer's stick. They didn't have a particular reason to make an effort to know newbies or grunts that'd been around a few months.

As with any nickname, it reflected something about **appearance**, Dog Face, Whiskers, Shorty, Pencil (tall and skinny like a . . .), Porky (who'd eat anything nobody else wanted); or about **some peculiarity**, Fruitcake (who carried around his grandmother's fruitcake, no doubt oblivious to the thought that would become her grandson's nickname—and would be safe from everyone, even Porky), Postman (who wrote a letter to his girlfriend every day), Peaches (he'd swap you almost anything for your can of peaches), Klutz (did everything wrong), Cowboy (for his gung-ho attitude), Magic ('cause he had that good set of ears and intuition, so he *always* knew if Charlie was hanging around), Einstein; and then **where a newbie came from**: Okie, Beach Boy, Dee-troit, I-away; or **a favorite team or favorite player**: Red Socks, Redskin, Yankee, Bull Dog, Stretch, Hank, Yogi; and **music**: Elvis, Stones, Lobo, Crystal, Soldier Boy; and **sometimes by ethnicity**: Chico, Bandit, Bro, Brother Willy (idea from Ebert 140-142). "According to veteran Roger Hoffman, nicknames were bestowed as an indication of acceptance as a new man moved up the infantryman's social ladder" (Ebert 140). (Note: this would be a real irony when vets went to the Vietnam Memorial—The Wall—much later; could a vet find Okie or Beach Boy or Dee-troit on the Wall? Maybe. A database allows a search for all PFCs from Oklahoma, or all men killed from Detroit).

o *Night.* "A night in the Nam always comes alive to some degree—things are either seen or heard. If something is both seen and heard, it usually turns out to be a tiger, rock ape or North Vietnamese" (Anderson *The Grunts* 128-129).

Night Enemy by Randy Cribbs	**Full Moon** by W. D. Ehrhart
Through the night nothing stirred; Pleasing to the ear, nothing heard. They come in the dark Leaving barely a mark, Slipping through shadows hidden, Guests unbidden.	We were on patrol last night; And as we moved along, We came upon one of the enemy. Strange, in the bright moon He did not seem an enemy at all. He had arms and legs, a head . . .
But not this night, Now giving way to light. So rest easy, you may; Soon comes the day. (27)	. . . and a rifle I shot him. (Rottmann 14)

o *NLF.* The National Liberation Front. Made up of the guerilla forces in South Vietnam until the Tet Offensive January 31, 1968. Then the NLF joined with the NVA, the North Vietnamese Army.

○ *Nobody said it was gonna be easy.* Life isn't always fair. "Life goes on" (Johnny, Vet Program). "Death is for everyone. I was 18 and young people don't die" (Bowman, Vet Program).

○ *No sweat.* It's no problem. A term tossed off even if what is being asked for is dangerous.

○ *Number one.* The best.

○ *Number ten.* The worst.

○ *Nung tribe.* Provided 15,000 troops, like Montagnards also a hill tribe and anti-Communist.

○ *Nurses.* About 7,350 women served as nurses during the Vietnam War, including the Air Force Nurse Corps (about 200), the Army Nurse Corps (6,250), and the Navy Nurse Corps (about 200). There were nine deaths reported for nurses (Dunnigan and Nofi 161-162).

○ *NVA.* "North Vietnamese Army or soldiers. One major problem in fighting them was a cultural

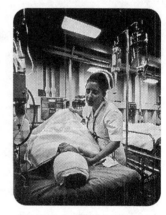

Nurse in hospital in Vietnam.

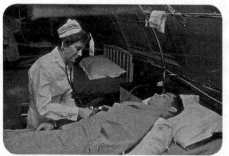

Da Nang US Navy Nurse.
LT. Commander Joan Brovilleffe attends to
pfc Charles Smith, Jan 6, 1968.

difference in time. In the west, our calendar has a beginning (Jan 1) and an end (Dec 31). For Vietnamese, time is a wheel that always flows, that never ends. A quick victory is a western concept. There is little sense of progress. History possesses little value and few goals. Hence, the Vietnamese are not impressed by a need to 'rush.' Their life span is already short; make do with what you have. With patience, perhaps in the next existence, your Karma will permit improvement" (The Religions of South

Vietnam in Faith and Facts, US Navy, Bureau of Naval Personnel, Chaplains Division [1967] at sacred-texts.com).

"The NVA were more like us in being oriented to organization, numbers, and to some degree firepower, although they didn't have as much as we did. But they were as motivated as we were. They didn't pay the same attention to detail, to preparing for battle, to digging in. They were there doing the basics, doing a job.

North Vietnamese troops on parade.

"[In contrast, the Viet Cong] were trained and familiar with the jungle. They relied on stealth, on ambush, on their personal skills and wile, as opposed to firepower. They knew it did not pay for them to stand and fight us, so they wouldn't. They'd come back and fight another day" (Terry 226).

OSCAR (O)

"I'm not going to be the first American president to lose a war."
—Richard Nixon (1969)

○ *O.J.* "A perfectly rolled marijuana cigarette soaked in an opium solution (Dickson 283).

○ *Operation.* "'Operation' is probably the biggest misnomer of all. There is nothing antiseptic, nothing surgically precise about a search and destroy sweep, nothing predictable like some anatomical structure or disorder. They usually start on the designated 'H-hour' as planned, but thereafter blunder on, in something closer to chaos than plan, to either a bloody climax or a quiet and uneventful conclusion. And there are days on which the worst enemies of an American field unit are exhaustion, stupidity, and the short-sightedness of its own leaders and troops" (Anderson *The Grunts* 27).

○ *o-dark-thirty.* "Very early in the morning: from the 24-hour system of military timekeeping in which the early morning hours start with zero—e.g., one a.m. is 0100 (stated as o-one-hundred hours)" (Dickson 283).

○ *Outgoing/outgoing mail.* "Friendly artillery fire" (Dickson 282) —that is, not from the enemy.

Men in helicopter.

A Vietnamese monk.

PAPA (P)

"I was proud of the youths who opposed the war in Vietnam
because they were my babies."
—Dr. Benjamin Spock (1988)

○ **Pacification.** "We had the war beat until they started this pacification program. Don't shoot, unless shot upon. The government kept handicapping us one way or 'nother. I don't think America lost. I think they gave up. They surrendered" (Terry 256). "The reporters call it [Civic Action Program or **CAP**] 'the other war.' The embassy calls it 'pacification.' And the politicians call it 'winning hearts and minds'" (Anderson *Other War* 68). According to the Army, "[P]acification was an unprecedented addition to the commander's mission. Although it was basically a civilian endeavor, the military played a vital and continuous part because the restoration of security in the countryside was a prerequisite to pacification" (Hay 181).

"The terms 'clearing,' 'securing,' and 'search and destroy' had served as doctrinal teaching points to show the relationship between military operations and the pacification effort. They had been adopted in 1964 for use by military and civilian agencies involved in pacification" (Hay 177).

○ **Papa-san.** A middle-aged or older Vietnamese man.

○ **Pathet Lao.** Laotian Communists under the control of the Vietnamese Communist Party.

○ **PAVN.** People's Army of Vietnam.

○ **Peace With Honor.** How do you win a war? With no peace or honor in sight, President Nixon turned to "Vietnamization," a gradual withdrawal of American forces to leave non-Communist South Vietnam forces to establish its own country with Saigon as the capital.

◦ **PFC.** Private Fucking Civilian. Private First Class.

◦ **Phoenix Program.** Set up by the C.I.A. in 1967 to combat insurgency. It was named Phoenix because it was "a rough translation of *phung hoang*, a mythical Vietnamese bird endowed with omnipotent attributes" (Karnow 601). Its two goals: 1) to identify and arrest VC suspects in areas controlled by South Vietnam; 2) to reach a target goal of 3,000 VC suspects per month. Those 3,000 VC suspects were to be arrested, were to give up information, and were then imprisoned. To meet that goal of 3,000 many innocent people were charged with being VC. From 1968-1972, about 28,000 people had been captured and imprisoned; another 20,000 were assassinated; 17,000 changed sides from "maybe VC" to NVA (Karnow 601). Those frequently targeted were VC organizers, propagandists, and tax collectors; 20,000 were "neutralized" and 6,187 killed (Karnow 602). According to Karnow, in 1971, all of the Phoenix Program information was released (601).

◦ **Piss tube.** Tube in ground for urinating.

◦ **Platoon.** Two or more squads or sections of approximately 45 men belonging to a company.

◦ **Pogue.** A rear echelon soldier; a term used in World War II and the Persian Gulf War. Known as an REMF (or Rear Echelon Mother Fucker) in Vietnam. A major goal of REMFs was to create a place as much like the World as possible so that "the GI could find all the baubles and goodies to help take his mind off Vietnam and its war, the unreal environment he wanted so badly to leave that he knew exactly how many more days and hours he had to endure before his 'Freedom Bird' would swoop down and take him away from it all" (Anderson *Other War* 6).

◦ **Point Man.** The first man on a combat patrol. The man behind him was the most vulnerable on the trail. He often missed what the point man saw. The point man would be the first to notice a booby trap.

    Sgt. Danny Phillips, an FNG, said he wanted to walk point. "The point was always doing something that was holding us up. After we would start to move I would have to walk by where all the action had been and I realized that if I were up front I could see and do and be part of what was going on instead of standing 100 yards back carrying a heavy weapon [M-79] and doing nothing. I guess what I am trying to say is if I was on point I would know what is going on and I could do something. That's one reason for me walking point and the next reason is everyday when I got to the bush the point was rotated, the Platoon Sgt picked someone different everyday and many did not want to do it and stated out loud their views. I figured why put someone up there who didn't want to do it or was scared? They were not going to be able to do the job safely so I volunteered .... I think I did a pretty good job, nobody behind me stepped on a mine and I didn't lead my company into any ambushes. I found a lot of mines and had them pointed out to everyone behind and I stopped several ambushes by paying attention to what was going on. I would like to say that I wasn't scared but that would be a big lie. I was scared many times but I kept doing what had to be done" (e-mail to Margaret Brown, 17 June 2009). (Note: Sgt. Danny Phillips walked point for 6 months until he was wounded. He received the Purple Heart and was awarded the Bronze Star for Valor during his one year tour in Vietnam).

"I went to Vietnam as a basic naïve young man of eighteen. Before I reached my nineteenth birthday, I was an animal. When I went home three months later, even my mother was scared of me.

"I was a cherry boy. Most cherry boys went on point in the LRRP team. I adapted so well to bein' a point man that that became my permanent position after this first mission" (Terry 236).

Herr's friend, Dana Stone (civilian photographer), would be "well ahead of the rest of the platoon on the trail, standard Dana and a break for the Marines, since he was easily the best equipped man in the party for spotting booby traps

Point man ahead of tank.

or ambushes. But that had nothing to do with his being on point. Dana was the man in motion, he just couldn't slow himself down" (Herr 196-197).

Johnny, a Vietnam vet, walked point with his rifle on automatic at all times. "It could fire 18 times in three seconds," he said (Vet Program, 2/4/93).

Point Man
by Randy Cribbs

If only I could see
What lurks behind that tree
Or around the next bend,
Enemy or friend.
What waits in the grass so thick;
Some harmless creature
Or that sharpened stick
Focus, if only I can;
My turn almost up,
Who's next—point man. (35)

○ **POW.** A Prisoner of War; The Third Geneva Convention detailed the Treatment of Prisoners of War (*first adopted in 1929*, last revision in 1949).

Welcoming home POWS.

"**Article 4** [of the Third Geneva Convention] defines **prisoners of war** to include:

4.1.1 Members of the armed forces of a Party to the conflict and members of militias of such armed forces.

4.1.2 Members of other *militias* and members of other *volunteer corps*, including those of organized resistance movements, provided that they fulfill all of the following conditions:
- that of being commanded by a person responsible for his subordinates;
- that of having a fixed distinctive sign recognizable at a distance (there are limited exceptions to this among countries who observe the 1977 *Protocol I*);
- that of carrying arms openly;
- that of conducting their operations in accordance with the laws and customs of war.

4.1.3 Members of regular armed forces who profess allegiance to a government or an authority not recognized by the *Detaining Power*.

4.1.4 Civilians who have non-combat support roles with the military and who carry a valid identity card issued by the military they support.

4.1.5 Merchant marine and the crews of civil aircraft of the Parties to the conflict, who do not benefit by more favourable treatment under any other provisions of international law.

4.1.6 Inhabitants of a *non-occupied territory*, who on the approach of the enemy spontaneously take up arms to resist the invading forces, without having had time to form themselves into regular armed units, provided they carry arms openly and respect the laws and customs of war.

4.3 Makes explicit that Article 33 takes precedence for the treatment of medical personnel of the enemy and chaplains of the enemy.

Article 5 specifies that prisoners of war (as defined in article 4) are protected from the time of their capture until their final repatriation. It also specifies that when there is any doubt whether a combatant belongs to the categories in article 4, they should be treated as such until their status has been determined by a competent tribunal" (Wikipedia).

"Sen. John McCain, who as a downed Navy pilot was tortured and held for five years in a North Vietnamese prison camp, recalled, 'many times I found myself asking to live just one more minute rather than one more hour or one more day, and I know I was able to hang on longer because of the spiritual help I received through prayer'" (Evan Thomas, *Newsweek*, 7 May 2007, 34). Charlie Plumb, six years as a POW, also found comfort in religion. "I consider my confinement in prison to be spiritually beneficial. I was given an opportunity that few men have –the time to pause, to reflect, and to establish priorities. I found that my previous value system was unrealistic. Stripped of all my material wealth, the only beacon I could home in on was my faith in an unchanging God" (232).

Col. Fred Cherry "was the forty-third American captured in the North. The first black . . . . The first place they tried to interrogate me appeared to be a secondary school. And they put me in this hut. I did what I was s'posed to do. Name, rank, serial number, date of birth. And I started talking about the Geneva Convention. And they said forget it. 'You are a criminal.'" . . . . "The next place I end up was Hoa Lo Prison, which we called the Hanoi Hilton. The first place Americans were brought for serious interrogation and torture" (Terry 272-274).

James B. Stockdale was a commander in the Navy when captured. He was a POW at Hanoi Hilton for over six years; he later was a recipient of the Medal of Honor.

According to Charlie Plumb, POW for over six years, he and other POWs were ordered on Christmas "to listen to a tape of a V Catholic priest giving a sermon in his native tongue. An interpreter translated it into English, a phrase at a time: 'We gather here of the occasion so to celebrate birth of Christ . . . which we do so many years . . . . This time we have special reason . . . multitudes of people are killed and injured . . . by bombs you American pilots drop . . . . You are instrument of devil . . . . Hope is for you and hope for world . . . . Jesus came to save world . . . . Now your opportunity, you American aggressors . . . . You commit sin, but if repent them now, will be clean white like snow . . . . You be able to forward in life . . . . Admit wrongdoing and thank Jesus . . . who born in lowly manger fight oppression from evil aggressors" (231).

Although the most famous Prisoner of War Camp was the Hanoi Hilton in North Vietnam, South Vietnamese and Americans also took prisoners.

South Vietnam POW Camp. Nov. 1968.

Captured Viet Cong, prisoners of war.

○ **Presidents Kennedy and Johnson.** Troops had strong opinions about each. Al, a Vietnam vet, thought that JFK would have gotten troops out faster. Maybe that's why he was killed, because war was a money-making proposition. And everybody knows that LBJ and his wife were interested in oil and there was a lot of drilling off the coast that could have been done (2/04/93). Some vets thought the whole war was about business. Johnny Phillips said they were lied to, that they weren't there to save South Vietnam; he said basic training "psyched us up so bad; we were scared into thinking the VC can move without making a sound—they shouldn't scare you so bad. He said the companies such as Goodyear, Michelin, Dow, IBM, Monsanto, and college research made money off the war" (Vet Program 1/21/93).

○ **Probe Sticks.** "Even more ominous, the point man, the platoon leader, and many of the other men carried probe sticks, long, slender poles, with which they tentatively poked the ground ahead of them. This indicated not only the threat of numerous booby traps and land mines but also the fact that we were operating in an area that belonged to the enemy most of the time" (Puller 114).

○ **Propaganda.** Attempts to dissuade any more fighting; come join *OUR* side. Leaflets and small booklets were dropped or handed out by both sides. Reporter Safer, back in Vietnam after the war, had to listen to a retired, drunken VC colonel praise his victory . . . : "I want my American friends to meet the brave fighters whose courage defeated the expeditionary forces of the imperialists. I welcome you to listen to the songs of our revolution, and you will understand how we were victorious over the Americans and their puppet regime" (72).

The colonel keeps going: "The vile acts and atrocities of the criminal American presidents, Eisenhower, Kennedy, Johnson and Nixon, could not defeat the progressive sentiments of our courageous men and women. Let us raise our glasses to their selfless sacrifice and their victory over the fascist war-making machine" (73).

Dr. Holley shared one of the leaflets with his wife. "I am enclosing a VC propaganda leaflet we found in hooch on one of our MEDCAPs in a local hamlet. Can you believe the spelling and grammar? You'd think they would have found someone to do a little better job with the English [all errors in the text are VC errors]:

AMERICAN GIs

"From the 1st to Nov 5th, 1.968. The united states commitec for demand of ending the US aggressive war in Vietnam hold "the week for united states armymen" which support to your opposing the war movement en demand for repatriation. Don't let

> american youths go on to south Vietnam and dic uselessly and senselessly. The Vietnam people and youths and students and pupil as well as the World people warmly wellcome and give whole hearted support and response to the creation of the united states committee.
> GI's
> ....Oppose the US aggressive war Vietnam.
> ....Demand the US government to stop immediately the US aggressive war in Vietnam and it must negotiate directly south Vietnam national front of liberation.
> ....Demand the US government brings home all US troops.
> ....Let the Vietnamese settle themselves their our affairs.
> ....Demand your repatriation refuse to go to the battefiel oppose your going to slaughler the Vietnamese people who are struggling for their independence, freedom and peace. That's the only way for you to defend the honer and pestige of america and save the happiness of your families and yousse lves (85).

The Americans had its own propaganda: In a leaflet printed by Veterans Alliance for Democracy in Vietnam, Ted Sampley addresses the "oppressed people of Vietnam." Following is the opening of the fifteen-page written appeal:

> Democracy for Vietnam
> is inevitable;
> Join its holy cause
> by Ted Sampley
> Veterans Alliance for Democracy in Vietnam

> "Dear oppressed people of Vietnam,
> "Stop for a moment and with your whole heart,
> your whole conscience, your whole body, study what the apostles of
> Ho Chi Minh's Communist Party have been telling you and learn
> what a terrible fate those professional revolutionaries have
> wrought upon you. Their Marxist-Leninist and Ho Chi Minh's
> 'utopian society' ideology is a deadly fraud of which the result
> is a poverty stricken Vietnam majority forced to live as slaves
> in one of the poorest countries in the world."

Bloods were not convinced. "They had us naïve, young, dumb-ass niggers believin' that this war was fought for democracy and independence. It was fought for money. All those big corporations made billions on the war, and then America left" (Terry 256).

○ **Protestors.** "The peace movement was not monolithic. Its adherents ranged across the political spectrum to include a surprising number of conservatives along with a lot more liberals and radicals. Although it did have considerable support, it utterly failed to mobilize a majority of the American people" (Dunnigan and Nofi 260).

Protest pins.

Three types of protestors: a) minority who believed in cause; b) leaders who would protest as long as they remained leaders and c) professional protestor who would protest anything (Idea from program 1/21/93). President Nixon showed his contempt and cynicism at the same time: "You know, you see these bums, you know, blowin' up the campuses. Listen, the boys that are on the college campuses today are the luckiest people in the world, going to the greatest universities, and here they are, burnin' up the books, I mean, stormin' around about this issue, I mean, you name it—get rid of the war, there'll be another one" (Isserman 167).

"In blustery voices [the career military, also known as lifers] made known, their version of truth on any and all subjects: 'America is the greatest country in the history of the world; the duty of every American citizen is to do all in his or her power to keep America the greatest; the best way to help keep America the greatest and to show one's love of country is to serve in the military; the line between dissent and treason is so vague that it can safely be ignored; communists and hippies are the most despicable life on earth and should be locked up forever if they can't be killed on sight; and, this Vietnam War is a great patriotic crusade that got off to a good start but recently turned into a chickenshit no-win thing because the pinko socialistic professors and politicians back in Washington won't get their hands off it . . ." (Anderson *Other War* 17-18).

"When I returned from Vietnam I was asked, 'Do you resent young people who have never been in Vietnam, or in any war, protesting it?' On the contrary, I am relieved. I think they should be commended. I had to wait until I was

35 years old, after spending 10 years in the Army and 18 months personally witnessing the stupidity of the war, before I could figure it out. That these young people were able to figure it out so quickly and so accurately is not only a credit to their intelligence but a great personal triumph over a lifetime of conditioning and indoctrination . . . . What they are against is our boys *being* in Vietnam. They are not unpatriotic. Again, the opposite is true. They are opposed to people, our own and others, dying for a lie, thereby corrupting the very word democracy" (Duncan 96).

○ ***PSYOPS.*** One effective psychological operation was to yell or scream at villagers or peasants over a loudspeaker while riding in a helicopter. In one situation, the sound of a baby crying came from the sky. "You wouldn't have wanted to hear that during daylight, let alone night when the volume and distortion came down through two or three layers of cover and froze us all in place for a moment. And there wasn't much release in the pitched hysteria of the message that followed, hyper-Vietnamese like an icepick in the ear, something like, 'Friendly Baby, GVN Baby, Don't Let This Happen to *Your* Baby, Resist the Viet Cong Today'" (Herr 53).

Often the villagers would hear the name or names of soldiers who had been captured or who had deserted. Herr relates a story by a Belgian mercenary. "'There were a lot of dead VC,' he said. 'Dozens of them were from the same village that has been giving you so much trouble lately. VC from top to bottom—Michael, in that village the fucking *ducks* are VC. So the American commander had twenty or thirty of the dead flown up in a sling load and dropped into the village. I should say it was a drop of at least two hundred feet, all those dead Viet Congs, right in the middle of the village.'

"He smiled (I couldn't see his eyes).

"'Ah, Psywar!' he said, kissing off the tips of his fingers" (173-174).

○ ***Puff the Magic Dragon.*** "One of the most unique weapons to emerge from the Vietnam War was the aerial gunship, a cargo plane loaded with automatic weapons" (Dunnigan and Nofi 126). Almost any fixed wing gunships, including AC 47 (also known as the C-47), which was the military version of the DC-3 (Wikipedia). These gunships were called Puffs, after the Peter, Paul and Mary song, because "when they're in action at night they look like a dragon spewing flame" (Dunnigan and Nofi 126). "The C-47 was a standard prop flareship, but many of them carried .20-and .762—mm. guns on their doors, Mike-Mikes that could fire out 300 rounds per second . . . They used to call it Puff the Magic

Dragon but the Marines knew better: They named it Spooky. Every fifth round fired was a tracer" (Herr 132-133).

∘ ***Punji stake.*** Homemade booby trap; a stake or sticks buried point-side up. The tip was allegedly smeared with excrement to cause massive infection, ["in fact a wound resulting from a wooden stake being driven through the foot that does not become infected would be quite surprising."] Punji stakes were also placed at the bottom of a ditch covered and camouflaged with sticks and leaves; other booby traps were explosives or hand grenades attached to trip wires activated by moving or lifting or stepping on them; booby traps accounted for about two percent of American casualties and virtually no deaths (Dunnigan and Nofi 70). These were also used against the French.

Avoiding Punji Stakes.

∘ ***Purple Heart.*** The **Purple Heart** is a *United States Military Decoration* awarded in the name of the *President* to those who have been wounded or killed while serving on or after April 5, 1917 with the *US Military* (Wikipedia).

"The system for giving out decorations, in recognition of battlefield performance, was corrupted. From Purple Hearts and Combat Infantry Badges, up to the highest awards, the standards fell as increased use of decorations was used to prop up falling morale and to enhance the careers of ambitious officers" (Dunnigan and Nofi 12-13).

"There was an unwritten policy . . . that the second Purple Heart was supposed to be a free ticket out of the bush, but the policy, of course, did not apply to officers" (Puller 151).

"I wish the people in Washington could have walked through a hospital and seen the guys all fucked up. Seventeen-eighteen-years old got casts from head to toes. This old, damn general might walk in and give them a damn Purple Heart. What the hell do you do with a damn Purple Heart? Dudes got legs shot off and shit, got half their face gone and shit. Anything you can mention that would make you throw up, that you can possibly dream of, happened" (Terry 54).

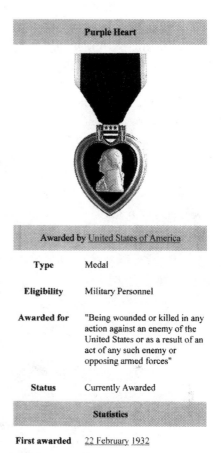

Purple Heart	
Awarded by	United States of America
Type	Medal
Eligibility	Military Personnel
Awarded for	"Being wounded or killed in any action against an enemy of the United States or as a result of an act of any such enemy or opposing armed forces"
Status	Currently Awarded
Statistics	
First awarded	22 February 1932

Purple Heart.

The Purple Heart
by Jim Gray

Frankly, I prefer the likeness of
George Washington
On a dollar bill rather than the one on this medal.

The Purple Heart, given by a grateful nation
To those crippled, unemployed "True Sons"
Who zigged when they should have zagged. (25)

"I [Byron Holley, a surgeon in Vietnam] got up and caught a cab out to the 3rd Field Hospital and was sewn up by a corpsman who insulted me by offering to put me in for a Purple Heart for my 'wounds sustained in combat zone!' I told him I knew hundreds of brave young men who had earned their Purple Hearts, some posthumously, and he ought to go out in the field and see for himself what goes over here in the real combat zone" (Holley 146).

o **PX.** Post Exchange, but rarely called that. Here is the place the REMFs tried to create an atmosphere as far away from war as possible. Servicemen could pick up needed personal items for next to nothing—if you include TV sets, cameras, and radios as personal items. A PX with nearly everything grunts would want to buy: peanut butter and jelly, soft drinks, candy, potato chips, soft drinks by the case, pearl necklaces, ruby earrings, perfume, the latest tunes, American magazines, transistor radios, Instamatic cameras, television sets, tape recorders, stereo record players, after-shave lotion, books and skin magazines, jewelry, and nearly every alcoholic beverage and snack food available in the States" (Anderson *Other War* 33). Television shows, weight rooms, and libraries were also available. Everyone there tried their best to put the war behind them (Anderson *Other War* 33).

Assisting wounded soldier.

QUEBEC (Q)

"What we need now in this country, for some weeks at least, and
hopefully for some months, is to . . . put Vietnam behind us and
to concentrate on the future."
—Secretary of State Henry Kissinger (April 29, 1975)

○ **Quartermaster or QM.** Officer in charge of supplies (and dead bodies).

○ **Quartermaster property.** Dead soldier. Taken to Graves Registration where
bodies were identified and embalmed (Reinberg 96).

○ **Quarters and Rations.** Room and board, Army style.

○ **Quick kill.** Veterans refer to this as the result of being "programmed"
(Grossman 257), "brainwashed" (Bobby Ward), "to some extent brainwashed"
(Grossman 257).

Setting up room and board army style.

Putting up a tent.

Picture of Marble Mountain.

ROMEO (R)

"I am the man I suffer'd, I was there."
—Walt Whitman

∘ **Race.** "I learned a lot about people in my platoon. I learned you have to take a person for what he feels, then try to mold the individual into the person you would like to be with. Now my platoon had a lot of Southerners as well as some Midwesterners. Southerners at the first sign of a black officer being in charge of them were somewhat reluctant. But then, when they found that you know what's going on and you're trying to keep them alive, then they tried to be the best damn soldiers you've got. Some of the black soldiers were the worse I had because they felt that they had to jive on me. They wanted to let me know, Hey, man. Take care of me, buddy. You know I'm your buddy. That's bull" (Terry 111). Bullets don't discriminate.

"After graduation, I was chosen to be a procurement NCO for Special Forces in California. The joke was made that I was now a procurer. After seeing how we were prostituted, the analogy doesn't seem a bad one. General Yarborough's instructions were simple: 'I want good, dedicated men who will graduate. If you want him, take him. Just remember, he may be on your team someday.' Our final instructions from the captain directly in charge of the program had some succinct points I stood in shocked disbelief to hear, 'Don't send me any niggers. Be careful, however, not to give the impression that we are prejudiced in Special Forces. You won't find it hard to find an excuse to reject them. Most will be too dumb to pass the written test. If they luck out on that and get by the physical testing, you'll find that they have some sort of a criminal record.' The third man I sent to Fort Bragg was a 'nigger.' And I didn't forget that someday he might be on my team" (Duncan 78).

"There was [a] guy in our unit who had made it known that he was a card-carrying Ku Klux Klan member. That pissed a lot of us off, 'cause we had gotten real tight. We didn't have racial incidents like what was happening in the rear area, 'cause we had to depend on each other. We were always in the bush.

"Well, we got out into a fire fight, and Mr. Ku Klux Klan got his little ass trapped. . . . And a brother went out there and got him and dragged him back. Later on, he said that action had changed his perception of what black people were about.

"But I got to find out that white people weren't as tough, weren't the number one race and all them other perceptions that they had tried to ingrain in my head. I found out they got scared like I did" (Terry 23).

"The racial incidents didn't happen in the field. Just when we went to the back. It wasn't so much that they were against us. It was just that we felt that we were being taken advantage of, 'cause it seemed like more blacks in the field than in the rear.

"In the rear we saw a bunch of rebel flags. They didn't mean nothing by the rebel flag. It was just saying we for the South. It didn't mean that they hated blacks. But after you in the field, you took the flags very personally" (Terry 38).

"They gave me the Bronze Star for pulling Rick out. And Rick wrote me this letter. It says, 'Sergeant Major, I thank you for my life.'

"Hell, he was one of my

"They gave me the Bronze Star for pulling Rick out." (Not actual photograph of the incident.)

men. Black or white, I would have done the same even if I got shot to hell in the process [he still has pieces of steel in him from rescuing Rick.] And I was forty-eight at the time, and that boy couldn't have been much over twenty-one" (Terry 151-152).

"'That [racial relations] was a tough situation for lots of people. I wouldn't have called myself [Parks, a Vietnam Vet] prejudiced, but a lot of those boys were when they got there. One thing is for sure, they weren't for long. It didn't matter who you were, we were in it together and you trusted them with your life'" (Ramsey 68).

○ *R & R.* Rest and Relaxation; once per year troops were given leave. Many took their leaves in Thailand, Japan, Malaya, Taiwan, the Philippines, Singapore, Australia, some even stayed in Vietnam at resorts like China Beach, but only a lucky few went to Hawaii. Troops referred to it as "I and I," intoxication and intercourse.

"I guess you are packing your bags to come see me. So, you probably won't get this letter until you return, but I've been thinking about you and had to write anyway. I am back at Dong Tam and have gotten my bags packed and my uniform ready. I can't really believe that in three days we will be together. I'm so excited I can hardly stand it. Baby, I'm still a little concerned about how I will seem to you. I know I've changed some. So much has happened to me and around me since I last saw you. One of my very good friends is in critical condition now, and another had his fingers shot off. I've had so many casualties brought in to my little aid station at Giao Duc. I know most of them well, and I can tell it's getting through to me. It's breaking my heart. A little bit of you dies each time you see one of your friends mangled, killed or mutilated. I can feel myself tied up in knots, so I hope I don't disappoint you" (Holley 143).

◦ **Ranger.** Elite commandos and infantry especially trained for reconnaissance and combat missions, also anyone who is a grad of the Army Ranger School (ARS).

◦ **Rations** (Note: letters meaningless except for "R.")
"A-rations—Regular fresh and frozen foods served in garrison mess halls and aboard ships.
"B-rations—Canned, dried, and preserved foods prepared in field kitchens.
"C-rations—individual one-day ration of six cans, three with meat/vegetables, three with crackers, plus candy and coffee. The complaint was that C-rations were heavy and greasy.
"D-rations—Enriched hard chocolate bar as an emergency ration, to be consumed only on order. Specifications said it was to 'taste little better than boiled potato' to prevent it from being eaten as a snack.
"K-rations—Three individual meals used in combat, containing canned meat/vegetables, crackers and spreads. The complaint was that they were not filling.
"R-rations—Based on the Chinese march ration, these consisted of rice and fresh bacon and were tested by the Marine 2d Raider Battalion. They were a failure as they required prolonged cooking, not just heating, the bacon went rancid, and they were not to American tastes.
"10-in-1 rations—Rations containing B—and K-ration components to feed ten men three meals for one day. They required little preparation. There was a less used 5-in-1 ration" (Rottman FUBAR 91).

◦ **Recon.** Reconnaissance, small scout patrol to search for the enemy.

Camouflaging the Chimera
By Yusef Komunyakaa

We tied branches to our helmets.
We painted our faces & rifles
with mud from a riverbank,

blades of grass hung from the pockets
of our tiger suits. We wove
ourselves into the terrain,
content to be a hummingbird's target.

We hugged bamboo & leaned
against a breeze off the river,
slow-dragging with ghosts

from Saigon to Bangkok,
with women left in doorways
reaching in from America.
We aimed at dark-hearted songbirds.

In our way station of shadows
rock apes tried to blow our cover,
throwing stones at the sunset. Chameleons

crawled our spines, changing from day
to night: green to gold,
gold to black. But we waited
till the moon touched metal,

till something almost broke
inside us. VC struggled
with the hillside, like black silk

wrestling iron through grass.
We weren't there. The river ran
through our bones. Small animals took refuge
against our bodies; we held our breath,

ready to spring the L-shaped
ambush, as a world revolved
under each man's eyelid. (137)

◦ **Red bird. Righteous anger.** It's easy to think you're entitled to be angry, to think that your anger is not misplaced.

◦ **Red LZ.** Soldiers would send up red flares in a potential Landing Zone warning pilots it is too dangerous to land there. (White flares meant okay, all clear.)

◦ **Refugees or DP (displaced person).** The total of Southeast Asian people fleeing their homeland for fear of reprisal is astounding. Many nations refused to accept any more boat people—the primary, cheap way to escape—and the United States limited the number who could come in legally. By 1975, twenty thousand boat people fled; by 1979, the number was up to one hundred thousand. In 2000, it is estimated that two million people left the country of Vietnam. Hmong tribal people who had been anti-communist settled in California and Minnesota—by the early 90s, a half-million were in this country (*Encyclopedia of the New American Nation*).

In 1984, the United States announced that "it will admit 8,000 Vietnamese children fathered by American servicemen over the next three years. These children, whom the law regards as US citizens, are persecuted in Vietnam because of their non-Asiatic features" (*Vietnam War Almanac 355*).

◦ **Religion.** Not necessarily traditional religion, but what got you through each day. Sometimes it was a one word chant, sometimes it was fetishes of all kinds from charmed soldiers to cookies. Johnny Phillips carried a peace sign and a little pocket Bible which never got wet (Vet Program 04/15/93).

"Flip religion, it was so far out, you couldn't blame anybody for believing anything.

"A few presidents have tried to conceal their dependence on prayer. On some nights during the Vietnam War, after picking bombing targets in the Situation Room, Lyndon Johnson would secretly pray with monks in a monastery" (Evan Thomas *Newsweek* 7 May 2007).

"Before withdrawing from the battlefield, we, the nineteen survivors, had organized the backbone of a new company and a farewell ceremony for our dead comrades. We knelt before an altar of bamboo covered with white gauze. I gave the order to light the pyre. It would take an inferno to conjure up the faces of more than a hundred dead. They would never leave us, those faces: ashen, drained of blood, twisted in pain, accusatory, demanding justice . . ." (Huong 237).

Johnny ditched his little G.I. Bible when he came home. In one of the Vet Programs he said that Vietnam made him lose his religion. "I can't go to church no more." In an April program, Clyde said he was caught in quicksand and God reached down and pulled him out. One time he came to a fork in the road and God told him to go right. So he did. He never found out what was going on to the left, but he learned to listen to God (04/01/93).

◦ **Reparation.** The United States had a policy of paying out money if we accidentally killed someone or destroyed their property. Forty dollars (or in Vietnamese currency, 4000 piasters) seems such a small amount for the family of someone who was accidentally killed. For a house, a family would receive $10 (Terry 80). For destruction of hooch, we could give 1,000 piasters which was the equivalent of about $9 (Terry 81). One vet, Banjo, killed a water buffalo, a working animal in Vietnam, and got fined $500; however, he couldn't remember how he paid the fine (Al, Vet Program 2/4/93). The Vietnamese were always out for money. People in villages were so poor they'd throw themselves in front of a Jeep just so the family could collect some money (Banjo, Vet Program 2/4/93). The VC hid in rubber plantations in order to attack. Not only were they well-hidden, they knew that American soldiers weren't supposed to fire into a plantation, because if a tree got damaged, the US had to pay reparations for it. Damage to a rubber tree cost about $500 (Bobby, Vet Program 2/4/93).

◦ **Repo Depo.** The gathering place for incoming replacements to pick up their assignments. Also where a grunt picks up his paperwork to go home.

◦ **Reporters.** Herr, a reporter, writes about his observations of the reporters near the end of his time there: "So there we all were, no real villains and only a few heroes, a lot of adventurers and a lot of drudges, a lot of beautiful lunatics and a lot of normals, come to report what was ultimately the normals' war; and somehow, out of all that, a great number of us managed to find and recognize each other. You could be hard about it and deny that there was a brotherhood working there, but then what else could you call it? It wasn't just some wartime clique of buddies, it was too large in number for that, including members of at least a dozen cliques, some of them overlapping until they became indistinguishable, others standing in contemptuous opposition to one another; and it was too small to incorporate the whole bloated, amorphous body of the Vietnam press corps. Its requirements were unstated because, other than sensibility and style, it had none. Elsewhere, it would have been just another scene, another crowd, but the war gave it urgency and made it a deep thing, so deep that we didn't even have to like one another to belong. There was a lot that went unsaid at the time, but just because it was seldom spoken didn't mean that we weren't very much aware of it or that, in that terrible, shelterless place, we weren't grateful for each other" (223-224).

○ **Re-supply.** As much as grunts could carry on their backs, they still needed re-supplies out in the field brought to them on helicopters. "The blunders, trials and missed chances of the day were set aside in the exhilaration over what the re-supply chopper had brought—carrots, cucumbers, tomatoes, C-rats, new socks and jungle uniforms, orange juice, grape juice, mail, water, and 300 mortar rounds, many more than the Company could carry. 'Hey, B.J., you see them boxes off to the side? Mortar rounds, hundreds of them. That means we stay for awhile, Man!'" (Anderson *The Grunts* 110-111).

Helicopter drops supplies to waiting soldiers.

"When no trees or brush over three feet above ground remained standing, the resupply chopper was called in . . . . Everything fell from the sky this time—orange juice, socks, new canteens, gallon cans of pickles, tins of foot powder, cigarettes, grape juice, bootlaces, Red Cross kits of stationery, candy bars, toothpaste and brushes, chewing gum, razors blades, and 'Oh Christ, that pilot better not drop it,' one hundred

Viet Cong supply cave discovered by Americans.

twenty gallons of clean water in twenty-four marine green cans" (Anderson *The Grunts* 89-90).

◦ **Reup.** Re-enlist for another year.

◦ **Rice robbery or relief rice.** The VC were used to showing up at harvest time for rice. Each year their demands were different. Sometimes, as a tax, they would take a quarter of a harvest, sometimes nearly all of it. Then "the peasants were made to carry the product of their own labor into the hills to the secret caches of the Viet Cong" (Walt 51). Once the Americans arrived, the South Vietnamese peasants no longer had to carry their rice to the VC hide-outs, although they still had to pay a tax to them. The VC, in retaliation, told the peasants not to harvest their crops, or else. Without the Marines, the peasants would never have been able to harvest their crop, store it, and plan its distribution. The VC, attempting to make good on its "or else" threats, were repelled by the Marines whenever a village was threatened. In this way, the VC were deprived of rice, and the peasants could have what they grew. Marine patrols also searched areas looking for rice that could be returned. They were successful in finding tons of rice hidden near the fields or in shelters (all information from Walt 51-53). A South Vietnamese man tells a quite different version of events. "American soldiers plundered peasants' rice and then rationed it out to refugee peasants as 'relief' rice. And the peasants are obliged to receive 'gratefully' the rice that they cultivated with their own labor . . . . Such an operation cannot but be called 'Rice Robbery' equipped with helicopters, automatic rifles, and machine guns" (Honda 11).

In his six month's duty in the field, Doc Holley learns how the peasants were treated. "From what I've heard from some of our grunts, these [search and destroy] missions can get real hairy because it is so hard to tell who is the enemy and who are the innocent peasant farmers . . . . It usually ends up with their hooches being burned by flame throwers and their rice hauled off to the ARVNs [the Army of the Republic of (South) Vietnam]. When the ARVNs come across large stockpiles of rice or other foodstuff, they automatically assume it is being held for delivery to the Viet Cong. I guess it never occurs to them that a rice farmer would have large amounts of grain on hand until he could get it hauled to the market" (48). US soldiers tried to avoid rice farms and their dikes as they were often booby-trapped.

◦ **Road Warriors.** Truck drivers. Most war supplies were brought to Vietnam in ships that landed in heavily fortified ports. Some equipment and soldiers could be transported to bases inland by helicopters or small aircraft, but the majority of supplies, equipment, and soldiers had to be trucked in convoys down thousands of miles of roads that had never been cleared of mines and were not patrolled. "Next to the infantry, the guys who saw the most combat were the long-haul truck drivers" (Dunnigan and Nofi 95). Truck drivers were armed with M-16s and some trucks were equipped with machine guns; however, at least one of the trucks in the convoy carried explosive or flammable material. For this reason, these trucks were placed at the end of the convoy, something that was not a secret to the VC.

Convoys were often ambushed when most heavily guarded (with helicopters above looking for ambushers) plus armored vehicles, and combat trucks scattered among the convoy. It was like swinging a red cape in front of a bull; the VC often ambushed the most heavily-armed convoys. "The truck companies lost about a quarter of their carrying capacity to these security measures, plus thousands of trucks damaged and destroyed by the attacks" (Dunnigan and Nofi 95). Bobby drove a truck. "You should have seen a thunder run. You got two fools in a tank, going as fast as they can, and hope a mine blows up when you're past it. Now top speed was only 30 mph. But somebody had to clear the roads and take out the bushes near the roads. Those APCs were all-terrain" (Vet Program 02/12/93).

○ *Rock'n'roll also Mad Minute.* Let's do it! Fire weapon on full automatic, just fire, put it in the bush.

○ *Rogues or pogues.* Rear-echelon personnel who tried to create an escape from the war for grunts coming out of the bush. They themselves worked in air-conditioned offices and wore starched uniforms.

○ *Rolling Thunder.* The biggest bombing mission of the war from March 2, 1965–October 31, 1968. During the war, US aircraft dropped approximately 13 million tons of bombs, six times the total dropped by US aircraft in WWII. "The explosive force was sufficient to displace 3.4 billion tons of earth—ten times that evacuated for both the Suez and Panama Canals—that caused an estimated 26 million craters and flattened 200 square kilometers of forest" (Dunnigan and Nofi 131). Rolling Thunder did not come without cost to the US At least 2,317 US airplanes were lost in air. Surprisingly, it was "old-fashioned cannon and automatic weapons fire that accounted for nearly 90 percent of the loss" (Dunnigan and Nofi 122-123).

Rolling Thunder probably came from the first four lines of the hymn, *How Great Thou Art* (words and music by Carl G. Boberg and R. J. Hughes):

> O Lord my God, When I in awesome wonder,
> consider all the worlds Thy Hands have made;
> I see the stars, I hear the rolling thunder,
> Thy power throughout the universe displayed.

(Note: for more on **Rolling Thunder**, see Appendix B.)

○ ***Rome Plow.*** A large bulldozer with a large blade used to clear brush for a safer operation.

○ ***Ronson***. Flame thrower. "Tunnel rats often succumbed to booby traps [or] died from oxygen starvation, having entered a tunnel too soon after it had been given a Willy Pete or Ronson (white phosphorus or flame-thrower) treatment" (Dunnigan and Nofi 105).

○ ***Rotate, Rotation.*** Could be called an individual replacement system. "Created during World War II (it didn't work then, either) and carried over to the Korean War (another failed attempt to make it work), *this system regarded a combat unit as a machine and the troops in it as parts of a machine. If a part became broken (i.e., killed or wounded) you just ordered up a new part (an individual replacement soldier) and the machine would keep chugging along*" (Dunnigan and Nofi 78). *[Emphasis added.]*

It shouldn't take a general to see what problems this would create: newbies (FNGs) appeared in a unit missing one man; no soldier already in that unit could trust that newbie until he proved himself in the field; only LRRPS and Rangers who worked together were consistently effective. As a newbie caught on, his tour was about over; the longer he could last, the better his chance of surviving or avoiding devastating injury. According to the researchers Dunnigan and Nofi, of a random 100 infantrymen who got killed, about 40% had been in country three months or less. "Only about 6% of the deaths were in the last three months of the one year tour" (77-78). No wonder the short-timers were considered good luck charms. (See Short-timers below.)

After the war, a retired colonel from the South Vietnamese Army spoke with Morley Safer. "Our soldiers had no fixed term for their duty. They knew they had to fight until the war was over. You send a man here for one year. Only one year! He spends six months learning; for three months he is a good fighter, but for the last three months he is trying to protect himself to make sure he stays alive. About the time he was ready to fight, he was ready to leave! I do not understand such a policy" (33).

See the End
by Randy Cribbs

Get through one day,
Then think about the next,
Always in our mind
Like a hex.

As the tour shortened,
We dwelled on it more,
Thinking of
That friendlier shore.

Then so short, can't
Get in the rack,
But more anxious; maybe
We would get back.

One digit midget, days
From the great silver bird;
Think it, but don't say it;
Bad luck.
Not a single word. (53)

Replacements brought with them the attitudes of the country, so units were under constant change. A young black might show up with an Afro and the new kind of comb necessary to maintain it. This broke two rules: the length and style of hair; the comb that protruded from the uniform pocket. Nothing could protrude from the top of a pocket. Other black American practices weren't forbidden, but were curious and thought improper: the ditty-bop, a style of walking to illustrate the new "I am somebody" pride; "the ditty-bop was accomplished by exaggerating the normal roll and swing of hips, shoulders, and arms, and locking one knee" (Anderson *Other War* 150). Then the Black Power salute to one another—the raised fist, followed by a ritual of hand movements, pats on the back of the hand, punctuated with questions such as "What's happening, baby? . . . . The complete soul greeting between two men might take as much as two minutes, and if one man or group met another group, as much as ten minutes might be taken up in a process of recognition that whites would accomplish with a one-second wave or nod of the head" (Anderson *Other War* 151). The whites were confused in other ways, too. At base camp, the blacks tended to hang together, but in the bush, they proved friendly, reliable, and co-operative. Anderson, from the rear echelon after hearing and seeing the behaviors, decided "The presence of the enemy in the field apparently caused blacks to postpone expression of their ethnic pride" (152).

○ *RTO.* **R**adio **T**elephone **O**perator; man who carries a PRC-class radio, weighing 25 pounds, on his back; its antenna was quite tall, so the RTO was an easy target; not many wanted to walk with him. Major use of radio was to call in air attacks on North Vietnamese troop positions. A newbie wasn't usually assigned to be an RTO because he might misread a map and call an air strike on his own forces.

○ *Rubber Plantations.* A good hiding spot for the VC. A good place from which to ambush an American unit.

Rubber plantations were excellent hiding spots for VC. If Americans fired into plantations and damaged a tree, we had to pay $500.00.

In A Plantation
by Basil T. Paquet

The bullet passed
Through his right temple,
His left side
Could not hold
Against the metal,
His last "I am" exploded
Red and grey on a rubber tree. (12)

○ ***Ruck.*** Rucksack issued to every soldier. It had straps to hold it on the shoulders and could carry a lot of weight, usually a minimum of 40 pounds.

Grunt carrying a rucksack.

○ ***Rules of Engagement.*** Set up by the Military, but authorized by the President. This policy left soldiers in precarious positions. The ROEs were formed to keep the war limited to Vietnam. Even though the Ho Chi Minh Trail snaked its way down the borders of Laos and Vietnam, United States soldiers were forbidden to fire into Laos or go into Laos. VC supply bases in Cambodia were also off limits. Banjo said if you got wounded in Cambodia, there was no compensation (Vet Program 2/4/93). Within Vietnam, the ROEs restricted soldiers to determine who was a VC and who was a civilian before taking action. This ROE was established to calm the tensions between villagers and the American soldiers who were combing the area for the VC.

Often accused of not fighting aggressively enough, the Military was severely hampered by the ROEs that seemed to favor the enemy. Soldiers could be shot from Laos but others in the unit were prevented from returning fire. In North Vietnam, the NVA could fire at bombers from protected areas. The ROEs, however, did prevent any other countries near and surrounding Vietnam from intervening. Because of this, the war remained a "limited war" (Kutler 481-483). "You have to go into war with the intention to win. You can't tie soldiers' hands. In Korea, MIGs could chase you up 'til the Yalu River' The lesson is there. Let generals run the war" (Jim, Vet Program 2/4/93).

Another soldier had major complaints about the rules. He watched a Marine walk over to a three-year-old kid running down the street. When the Marine touched him, they both blew up. "If those guys were low enough to use kids to bait Americans or anybody to this kind of violent end, well, I think they should be eliminated. And they would have been if we had fought the war in such a manner that we could have won the war . . . . The people in Washington setting policy didn't know what transpired over here. They were listening to certain people who didn't really know what we were dealing with. That's why we had all those stupid restrictions. Don't fight across this side of the DMZ, don't fire at women unless they fire at you, and don't fire across this area unless you smile first or unless somebody shoots at you. If they attack you and run across this area, you could not go back over there and take them out. If only we could have fought it in a way that we had been taught to fight" (Terry 110-111). Even tank drivers complained. "The fact that we couldn't legally hold land we had won created an extremely weird situation. We had to drive out of that town knowing damn well another group of VC would move in at any time, even against the wishes of the inhabitants. There simply weren't enough ARVN [Army of the Republic of Vietnam] to go around and sooner or later, we'd have to clean it out again" (Zumbro 54).

◦ **RVN.** Republic of (South) Vietnam; pronounced "Are-vin."

Cartoon depicting helicopters firing rockets.

SIERRA (S)

"And what about when your warrior's anger goes home?
What is it like with his wife and children? Is it useful then, too?
—Cicero*

○ **Saigon.** Also known as Sin City. Saigon was the center of everything. Like a spider, it felt the trembles of action here, there, and everywhere. It had a black market along with snake-skin shoes and obscene wooden carvings. "Sitting in Saigon was like sitting inside the folded petals of a poisonous flower, the poison history, fucked in its root no matter how far back you wanted to run your trace. Saigon was the only place left with a continuity that someone as far outside as I was could recognize. Hue and Danang were like remote closed societies, mute and intractable. Villages, even large ones, were fragile, a village could disappear in an afternoon . . . . Saigon remained, the repository and the arena, it breathed history, expelled it like toxin, Shit Piss and Corruption. Paved swamp, hot mushy winds that never cleaned anything away, heavy thermal seal over diesel fuel, mildew, garbage, excrement, and atmosphere. A five-block walk in that could take it out of you . . . . You'd stand nailed there in your tracks sometimes, no bearings, and none in sight, thinking, *Where the fuck am I?*" (Herr 43).

City in South Vietnam.

○ *Saigon Warriors.* Slang for a soldier stationed in Saigon, also known as a Saigon commando.

"I really have a thing about these 'Saigon warriors' who think they have been to war and have never left the relative safety of the city. They have never had to undergo the mental and physical strain that is part of a grunt's daily existence, where the highlight of any day is mail call. Half of these REMFs [Rear Echelon Mother Fuckers] have girlfriends with apartments or villas and live with them, but I have started looking into who sleeps in their beds and who doesn't, and all hell will break loose when I put a stop to their little pillow games. They are officially AWOL if they are sleeping off army property, and if we had an offensive, we would be in big trouble. None of them even clean their weapons, so I kind of feel like Hack [Colonel David Hackworth, author of *About Face*] did when he came to the HARDCORE, those not obeying authority. They need their asses kicked, and I'm in the mood to do it" (Holley 161).

"These warriors far from the war could go back to the States and say they were in Vietnam during the war. That statement would, of course, be technically true, but not completely true. No civilian listener would think to ask if the veteran had been in the field or the rear, since those who served in either area wore the same uniform and in most cases the same campaign ribbons. . . . Veterans of this type could, in effect, carry out a cover-up. . . . By declining to explain certain facts about their Vietnam experiences, they could conceal their earlier concealment of their loss of resolve to face danger head-on.

"Such veterans could thereafter claim to be tested combat veterans without ever having faced the test of combat they once sought, and they could then receive as much attention, respect, or even awe, as their unknowing listeners were willing to pay them" (Anderson *Other War* 42).

"A lament, popular among GIs and written by an anonymous grunt went:

> 'Scuse me General Westy, I hate to bother you,
> But I've got a couple of problems,
> And I don't know what to do.
> My air conditioner's broke,
> My sedan's outa gas,
> Besides all this, well, I can't get a seven-day pass.
>
> I'm a Saigon Warrior, I'm helping fight a war.
> Pushin' a pencil, my finger's getting sore

Well, now, since I've been 'In Country'—that's military
For "here"—I've learned to speak the language,
I'm winning hearts and minds.

I can say fluently . . ."Tudo," "Saigon
    Tea," . . ."I love you too much,"'
    "massage?" "Hey, where you go now?"
    "Money changed?"
    "dee-dee . . . . you buy for me . . . . "

I'm a Saigon Warrior, I'm helping fight a war.
Pushin' a pencil, my finger's getting sore." (Safer 259-260)

○ **Sapper.** VC or NVA commando using armed explosives. "The communists developed one type of elite soldiers . . . the sappers. Often half a dozen sappers would attack an American fortified base containing over a hundred troops. The sappers would get through all the mine-fields and barbed wire, blow up much of the American base, killing and wounding many of the American troops, and then get away, sometimes without taking any casualties. The main job of the sappers was to destroy things, not people. And they did so with remarkable success. Not just enemy bases, but also aircraft on the ground and ships anchored in South Vietnamese ports" (Dunnigan and Nofi 275-276).

○ **SAR.** Search and Rescue; also Sea, Air and Rescue, looking for downed pilots. "The US Air Force had their SAR . . . helicopters, but they often needed some knowledgeable people on the ground, and that's where one or more [Recon Teams, composed of US forces and Montagnards] came in" (Dunnigan and Nofi 171).

○ **Scavengers.** "The enemy had three main sources of supply: supplies carried overland through Laos and Cambodia and then into Vietnam; supplies carried in by sea from North Vietnam; and supplies captured from US and allied troops. Major efforts were made to stem the first two sources, but there was not enough being done about the third" (*A Distant Challenge* 84).

○ **SEAL.** Highly-trained Navy special warfare team members. A Navy version of LRRPS.

○ *Search and destroy.* Offensive operations designed to destroy enemy forces without maintaining holding actions. They had three purposes: locating the enemy and attacking them; clearing enemy forces from populated areas; and securing operations directed against the enemy in the hamlets, who were often farmers by day and Vietcong by night. "Each of the three missions supported the pacification program" (Hay 169-170).

According to a monograph published by the Department of the Army, "Search and destroy operations, by any name, were the tactics by which US units engaged the enemy. They were the right operations at the time, and they contributed to the essential function of shielding the pacification effort from the enemy's main forces. Without the shield, the South Vietnamese would not have had the opportunity to rebuild their forces, and the pacification effort in Vietnam would have been impossible" (Hay 178).

Search and Destroy Mission.   *Soldier saving children during*
                                        search and destroy mission.

"Early in the third phase the US command recognized that the term 'search and destroy' had unfortunately become associated with 'aimless searches in the jungle and the destruction of property.' Spec 4 Kirkland was in charge of a search and destroy mission: "you just clear the village and burn the hootches because the village is suspected of a Vietnam stronghold or VC sympathizers. We did not have the capacity as a platoon to take them and hold them. We just cleared them, because we wanted them secure . . . . Most of the time we just rounded the women and children up, and they would literally run out of the village. Then we started putting fire in the holes, throwing grenades inside the hootches, inside of the little bunkers, down the wells. Hoping that we could ferret out a couple of VC. Then we burn the village. A Zippo raid was standard operation procedure when we went into a village.

"My platoon did that to 50 to 75 villages. Like being in Vietnam, there are little villages all over the place.

"If we use the figure 50 villages, we found suspects in 12 of them. Maybe 30 suspects in all of them. We very rarely found a real VC" (Terry 93-94).

"In April 1968 General Westmoreland therefore directed that the use of the term be discontinued. Operations thereafter were defined and discussed in basic military terms which described the type of operation, for example, reconnaissance in force" (Hay 177). The attitude of South Vietnamese soldiers was search and avoid.

○ **SEATO.** Southeast Asia Treaty Organization, a regional system for defense. Because the United States signed it (with other nations such as France, Great Britain, New Zealand, and Australia), it gave permission for the US to be in Southeast Asia.

○ **Shitbird.** Someone always in trouble. "They called me a shitbird, because I would stay in trouble. Minor shit, really. But they put me on point anyway. I spent most of my time in Vietnam runnin'. I ran through Vietnam 'cause I was always on point, and points got to run. They can't walk like everybody else. Specially when you hit them open areas. Nobody walked through an open area. After a while you develop a way to handle it. You learned that the point usually survived. It was the people behind you who got killed" (Terry 7).

○ **Shit burning.** Sanitation of excrement through burning with kerosene; this job was often given to blacks. The platoon would take 55 gallon drums and split them in half. When they were full, the shit-burners would have to burn the shit in the drums in order to empty them.

"As we began to stir, we were struck by the most nauseating and putrid odor one could imagine. It smelled like something burning, but we couldn't identify it. . . . We asked [our briefing officer] what was stinking so bad. 'They're burning shit. They burn it every morning. There are no sewer systems over here, and the guys doing the burning are on shit detail as a punishment for some misdeed. This aroma *fills* the air around all the American military bases, and it has become known affectionately as the 'perfume of Vietnam'" (Holley 18-19).

○ **Shitters.** Those men, usually blacks, assigned the shit-burning detail. Most of the platoon avoided them, especially at meals, because they could never get the smell off them.

○ **Short-arm inspection**. Refers to checking for VD. Soldiers had a high VD rate in Vietnam . It was 396.3% higher than that of the Civil War, against which the ratio of all US Army is measured. In Korea, it was 178%; in World War II, it was 46% (Dunnigan and Nofi 166).

○ **Short or Short-timer.** Possibly borrowed from prison slang (Hynes 184). A short-timer was nearing the end of his tour of duty. He knew exactly how much more time he had left in country, almost down to the second. "I remember when I had two months, seven days, and eleven hours and thought I was short" (Bobby, Vet Program 01/21/93). Many of the troops had a ritual game . . . "How short are you?" The short-timer would reply with some appropriate remark. "'I'm so short,' he would say, 'I have to stand on a ladder to tie my bootlaces'" (Van Devanter 229). "I'm so short I'd have to parachute off a dime."

A Cartoon depiction of Short timer's Calendar.

Many short-timers who were two months from leaving would stick to their base camp and keep a low profile. "Short-timers still in the field were overly cautious by nature and sought to avoid any condition that might lessen by the smallest fraction their chances of completing their tours intact. Thus, [one man] soon learned that short-timers didn't want to be near a new guy; it was paranoia or bad luck" (Ebert 139). It was only later, much later, that researchers discovered that only six percent of the casualties occurred to men with less than three months to go (Dunnigan & Nofi 77-78).

Reporter Michael Herr observed that "odd things happen when tours are almost over. It's the Short-Timer Syndrome. In the heads of the men who are really in the war for a year, all tours end early. No one expects much from a man when he is down to one or two weeks. He becomes a luck freak, an evil-omen collector, a diviner of every bad sign. If he has the imagination, or the experience of war, he will recognize his own death a thousand times a day, but he will always have enough left to do the one big thing, to Get Out . . . .

"In this war they called it 'acute environmental reaction,' but Vietnam has spawned a jargon of such delicate locutions that it's often impossible to know even remotely the thing being described" (91).

"They [25 of my buddies from the 4/39] were very surprised and happy to see old Doc Holley there, and the feelings were mutual. Well, as of tomorrow I will officially become a 'two digit midget' with only ninety-nine days remaining until DEROS! Praise the Lord, I'm getting short!" (Holley 188-189).

"I sure am getting a short-timer's attitude. I don't feel like doing anything but eat, sleep, and drink. I wish I could just go to sleep and wake up one day before DEROS. But it's really best to keep busy, which I am doing with all the troubles at this dump" (Holley 191). The Short-Timer Syndrome became a preoccupation. Says an infantryman, Tom Schultz, "'You'd been there a long time, but you could have only one day left and make a mistake'" (Ebert 398).

"Almost every day the grunts ambled over to Epps' mortar pit, ate C's [combat rations] with him and helped him get things ready to go, as if by thus associating with and helping these short-timers, some of their shortness would rub off and help them get home sooner" (Anderson *The Grunts* 163).

Short Timer
by Randy Cribbs

So short you can't see me.
Days, not weeks, and I am free.

How glorious I begin to feel,
Hot food replacing the OD canned meal.
Not hiding from
The detail man,
Too short, but
Catch me if you can.

A different line of work, no doubt,
Even assembly line widgets,
Things OK to think about
If you are a one digit midget.

No more worry over
Ignition of fuse and primer,
Not for me,
I'm a short timer! (66)

A Short-timer.

○ **Shovel.** "With this tool, American firepower was rendered much less lethal. Communist soldiers not only dug the usual trenches and foxholes, but also underground bunkers and tunnel systems. Thus one of the more unique developments of the Vietnam War was the widespread use of underground installations" (Dunnigan and Nofi 103).

○ **Shrapnel.** Pieces of metal sent flying by an explosion.

○ **Slackman.** Second man in patrol, right behind point man.

○ **Slicks.** Hueys, helicopters, little to no armament used to lift troops, supplies. According to *Vietnam Studies: Tactical and Materiel,* the Vietnam War was full of innovations because of the guerilla war, the terrain, and the weather. Some innovations lasted only until the enemy countered it. "The widespread use of the helicopter was the most significant advance of the Vietnam War" (Hay 179).

Rain
by Jim Gray

I hate rain, low gray clouds and mist,
Tensed at the controls over my fate,
My senses strained beyond my visibility.
Looking for the obstacle
Whose gut-wrenching, split second avoidance
Is the gossamer thread between life and death
On which I hang.

I much prefer clear, blue spring skies
Where all the treacheries of the earth
Are plain, small and harmless
Maybe even beautiful.

I tell myself that what I see
Through this Huey windshield, tired eyes and rain
Is just an aberration
Of fear's flawed lens. (11)

○ **Slope.** Derogatory term for oriental person, also dink and gook.

◦ *Small Arms Fire or SAF.* Soldiers firing the following weapons: rifles, machine guns, or pistol bullets. Dunnigan and Nofi in *Dirty Little Secrets of the Vietnam War* include a list of causes of combat fatalities. Small Arms Fire accounted for some 55% of fatalities in the Vietnam War (245).

A report by the Adjutant's Office of the United States Army Vietnam to the Commander in Chief in the USA-Pacific details 353 incidents with American rifles, pistols, machine guns causing death or injury to Americans. The report excludes errant bombs, artillery or mortar fire, or injuries caused by American mines. The 353 incidents resulted in 68 killed (KIA) and 300 wounded (WIA) over six months. This report is on file at National Archives and Records Administration in College Park, MD. (Note: some of the oddest incidents are listed here.)

Sampling from six months' worth of small-arms fire, Jan 1-June 20, 1967:

1 KIA—machine gun caught in vines, pivoted on mount, and discharged
1 KIA, 3 WIA—hand grenade pulled out by heavy vegetation
1 WIA—man asleep, woke up, jarred weapon that discharged
1 WIA—man tripped, shot himself with his M16

1 WIA—an M79 trigger caught on pants leg; weapon discharged
1 WIA—man slipped in mud; weapon discharged
1 WIA—man held a grenade with white phosphorus too long; it exploded as it left his hand
1 KIA—hand grenade slipped from grasp in foxhole

1 WIA—man with .45 pistol attempted to shoot dog; shot self
1 WIA—a .45 discharged as officer was placing weapon in holster
1 WIA—a man slept with his loaded weapon which got tangled in bedding; discharged when removed
1 WIA—a .45 discharged during horseplay
1 WIA—a man shot while cleaning his M16

◦ *SNAFU.* Situation Normal All Fucked Up.

◦ *Snake.* Slang for taking a nap; also the nickname for the AH-1G Cobra or Hueycobra.

But there were real snakes, too, constrictors, cobras, kraits (extremely venomous), vipers, and twenty foot pythons. "The most common snakes were usually encountered by the point man . . . where the reptile is startled by the slow and cautious approach of some guy with a gun. If the snake is one of several species of constrictors . . . the encounter is usually non-fatal . . . But there are also several species of cobra . . . . Soldiers . . . believed that cobras traveled in pairs, mated for life, and sought revenge if you killed its mate. For that reason, killing a snake in a bunker or hut did not bring relief but anxiety over where the vengeful mate was" (Dunnigan and Nofi 101).

Reptiles of Southeast Asia
by Larry Rottmann

There are two kinds of snakes in Vietnam
Mr. One Step
And Mr. Two Step
Named for how far you go after being bitten. (Rottmann 27)

○ **Sneaking and peeping; snooping and pooping.** Reconnaissance usually by Special Forces to gather intelligence for a possible Operation.

○ **Sniper.** Sterile kind of killing in which the killer is not at all in fear of danger. "In Vietnam it took an average of 50,000 rounds of ammunition to kill one enemy soldier. But the US Army and USMC snipers in Vietnam expended only 1.39 rounds per kill" (Grossman 254).

Killing for the ordinary soldier was also becoming passionless because of "the development of new weapons systems [enabling] the soldier, even on the battlefield, to fire more lethal weapons more accurately to longer ranges: His enemy is, increasingly, an anonymous figure encircled by a gunsight, glowing on a thermal imager or shrouded in armor plate" (Richard Holmes, *Acts of War* in Grossman 169).

The enemy, avoiding the massive firepower of the US, had success as snipers. Sometimes that was the only contact between grunts and their enemy. It became more of a nuisance than anything else, although there were times that snipers did cause damage since they used a variety of weapons. A unit could call in for fire-power, but it was usually too late. The sniper or snipers were long gone (Ebert 248-250).

○ **Soft target.** A person; hard target is a building.

○ **SOL** Shit out of luck.

○ **SOP.** Standard Operating Procedure.

○ **Sorry ass.** You get called this when you really mess up. You better learn so you won't be a sorry ass.

○ **Sortie.** An air mission.

○ **SOS.** Same Old Shit.

○ **Soul brother.** A black man.

○ **Southerners.** "American regionalism also contributed to racial tension during the Vietnam War. In the American South military service has long been considered not only a duty but an honor . . . . These regional attitudes affected personnel composition of the military; during the Vietnam War there was a higher proportion of southerners in uniform than the regional distribution of the American population would lead one to expect.

"The result of the southern character of the military was to heighten the suspicion and tension between young blacks in the lower ranks and white authority figures. Young blacks from large northern cities were brought into close contact with a kind of white man they had only heard about secondhand from parents and grandparents who had migrated from the rural South" (Anderson *Other War* 154).

○ **Souvenirs.** "When we first started going into the fields, I would not wear a finger, ear, or mutilate another person's body. Until I had the misfortune to come upon those American soldiers who were castrated. Then it got to be a game between the Communists and ourselves to see how many fingers and ears that we could capture from each other. After a kill, we would cut his finger or ear off as a trophy, stuff our unit patch in his mouth, and let him die" (Terry 244).

○ **Special Forces.** President Kennedy, upon watching increased Vietcong guerilla activity, ordered anti-guerilla training for US troops. The Special Forces were known as Green Berets. Other special forces were the Navy SEALS, and CIA operatives. In the Vietnam War, the "most successful operations against the Viet Cong and the North Vietnamese were by small groups of specialists in irregular warfare. These were the Army Special Forces, the navy SEALS, CIA operatives, and several other groups" (Dunnigan and Nofi 168).

In another program, Dallas talked about his experiences: "I was in a community college in Kentucky, and I enlisted. I wanted to be a helicopter pilot. I went to Officer Candidate School, came out a second lieutenant. Then I went to Fort Bragg to get trained to be in Special Forces. In December of '68, I went over alone in a 707; I didn't know anybody. I went from Hawaii to Japan to Saigon in 22 hours. My first memory is walking behind a C130 transport and smelling kerosene. Awful, I can still smell it. I went to the receiving station and I was assigned to Fifth Special Forces Group.

"I wasn't Rambo. We were doing counter-insurgency or insurgency in hostile country. There were teachers of other forces who taught us how to protect ourselves; how to kill face-to-face; there were teachers who ran camps all over Vietnam in the jungle, training us in warfare. There were six missions: area reconnaissance, bomb damage assessment, wiretap, prisoner snatch, road mining, and ambush.

"How do you gather intelligence? In a small plane you recon the area; you look for landing zones; you come back; set up code words to use when everybody gets out there; figure out artillery co-ordinates; give a report to others—about twenty men—to see if you've got it all correct. The helicopters would take us forward, we'd have to wait for the weather, then get dropped on an LZ, and call for extraction when supplies ran out. We communicated back three times a day. Each of us carried two gallons of water, three rounds of ammo, 5-day food, and 4-5 grenades. Sometimes there'd be flybys, and we could call in airstrikes if we needed to.

"I was on some pretty neat missions. We measured the level of traffic on the Ho Chi Minh Trail. Now it wasn't a trail. It was more like a highway. Hard-packed road with communication wires and spurs off-road. The trucks moved at night. We tried to mine the roads, and the Air Force dropped earth-moving bombs with a slower explosive charge to crater the road, not destroy it.

"We were also in Cambodia and Laos, even though we weren't supposed to be. I saw bunkers, but I didn't see any tunnels—this was *their* territory. Didn't see any civilians. Sometimes we'd be ordered to RON—or remain over night. (Frank interrupted: we called it snooping and pooping.) I was always the one to go get our supplies. They never got dropped in the right spot. But everybody'd say, "Here comes Rat." And I'd be lugging coolers full of beer and soft drinks in a hill" (Vet Program).

○ **Spider hole.** Camouflaged enemy foxhole.

○ **Spooky.** Ghost-like. Herr said the grunts would go back for a body count after a battle only to find no VC casualties. Soon they learned that the NVA or VC had dragged their dead into nearby tunnels. Messing with grunts' heads (95). One night, a patrol is getting ready for a combat assault. The first problem the men encountered was swarms of black ants that sting. Off go all their clothes so ants don't get in them and sting. But they knew they were making too much noise. "Here comes Charlie . . . . They had to hear us. But they came walking right on up the trail. I still can't understand this. We sprung the doggone ambush in our undershorts, supposedly killed four of 'em. And we don't have no bodies. Haven't got a damn thing to show for it. You can go out there and see where there was some blood. I don't know where these guys go when you kill 'em. It's just that they just vanish. Somewhere. I don't know. Maybe the Twilight Zone" (Terry 177).

Grunts shared spooky with the NVA. Although many had been smoking *rosa canina* (made from a plant and its flowers), they told stories about smelling their own blood as a prediction of death and monsters chasing them. "Many said they saw groups of headless black American soldiers carrying lanterns aloft, walking through in Indian file. Others paled in terror as horrible, primitive wild calls echoed inside their skulls in the rainy, dewy mornings, thinking they were the howls of pain from the last group of orangutans said to have lived in the Central Highlands in former times . . . . Soon there sprang up tiny altars in each squad hut and tent, altars to the comrades-in-arms" (Ninh 13-14).

◦ *Spooky.* The name for the C-47 gunship called in for air support, also called *Puff the Magic Dragon.*

◦ *Stand-down.* Back to base camp. A three-day rest from the bush for Military units when all operations other than security are curtailed.

◦ *Starlight Scope.* The starlight scope is another innovation made for the Vietnam War. Lieutenant General Hay writes the "device weighs only six pounds and, when mounted on an M16 rifle [another innovation for the war] or the M60 machine gun, soldiers can fire effectively at night out to 300 meters" (52). It was readily available. "Each mini-platoon had an M-16 outfitted with a Starlight Scope, a device like a telescope which amplifies available light to allow you to see at night" (Holley 53).

"The infantry kills the enemy up close and personal, but in recent decades the nature of this close-in battle has changed significantly. Until recently in the US Army the night sight was a rare and exotic piece of equipment. Now we fight primarily at night, and there is a thermal-imagery device or a night-vision device for almost every combat soldier. Thermal imagery 'sees' the heat emitted by a body as if it were light.

"Night-vision devices provide a superb form of psychological distance by converting the target into an inhuman green blob" (Grossman 169). A young enlistee just out of basic training: "War becomes more impersonal. Will war become like playing a video game?" (Dee, Vets Program 01/28/93).

Starlight Scope Myopia

by Yusef Komunyakaa

Gray-blue shadows lift
shadows onto an oxcart.

Making night work for us,

the starlight scope brings
men into killing range.

The river under Vi Bridge
takes the heart away

like the Water God
riding his dragon.
Smoke-colored

Viet Cong
move under our eyelids,

lords over loneliness
winding like coral vine through
sandalwood & lotus,

inside our lowered heads
years after this scene

ends. The brain closes
down. What looks like

one step into the trees,
they're lifting crates of ammo
& sacks of rice, swaying

under their shared weight.
Caught in the infrared,
what are they saying?

Are they talking about women
or calling the Americans

beaucoup dien cai dau?
One of them is laughing.
You want to place a finger

to his lips & say "shhhh."
You try reading ghost talk

on their lips. They say
"up-up we go," lifting as one.
This one, old, bowlegged,
you feel you could reach out
& take him into your arms. You

peer down the sights of your M-16,
seeing the full moon
loaded on an oxcart. (139-140)

○ **Stars and Stripes.** US Military newspaper. It is free to Army personnel even outside the US.

○ **Stay behind.** Ambush technique, if a moving force thinks it's being followed a small detachment stays behind.

○ **Stay off the trail.** Another "take care of yourself." Do what you have to do. "I made it a policy not to follow trails and paths. That way you avoid ambushes and punji sticks" (Terry 23). An identical statement by an Army sergeant: "Make yer *own* way through the jungle out there. It's a lot safer and you'll avoid the mines and booby traps" (Anthony 61).

○ **Suckin' wind.** Talking without saying anything.

○   **Survivor.** "He was a moving-target-survivor subscriber, a true child of the war, because except for the rare times when you were pinned or stranded the system was geared to keep you mobile, if that was what you thought you wanted. As a technique for staying alive it seemed to make as much sense as anything, given naturally that you were there to begin with and wanted to see it close; it started out sound and straight but it formed a cone as it progressed, because the more you moved the more you saw, the more you saw the more besides death and mutilation you risked, and the more you risked of that the more you would have to let

Stay off the trail.

go of one day as a 'survivor.' Some of us moved around the war like crazy people until we couldn't see which way the run was even taking us anymore, only the war all over its surface with occasional, unexpected penetration" (Herr 8).

○ **Survivor's Guilt.** Wounded Marine Lewis Puller, Jr. describes the feeling: "I felt guilty for years that I had abandoned them [the South Vietnamese] before our work was finished. I was to feel even worse that I was glad to be leaving them" (187). "To make matters worse, I suddenly felt guilty to be feasting on prime rib and drinking chilled wine while real marines were trying only to make it through another day in the arena" (273).

Jail
by Jim Gray

If life can be thought of as a prison
In which we serve a term prescribed
By the ultimate Supreme Court,
Then surely my solitary confinement
Is cruel and unusual punishment.

What I did for love of country
Was not cold and premeditated,
It was a crime of passion
And I was a juvenile offender. (27)

North Vietnamese soldiers suffered from survivor's guilt as well. Says popular North Vietnam writer and veteran, Bao Ninh, "What remained was sorrow, the immense sorrow, and the sorrow of having survived. The sorrow of war" (192).

For Lew Puller
by Hoa Binh and Mike McDonell

I remember the first time I ever heard of you, Lew,
it was in the late fall of '67 and word came down
from the lieutenants' net that Chesty Puller's son
was at the Basic School in Quantico and I thought
"The poor sonofabitch" because you were your father's son
and would never be able to fill his boots
and everyone would expect you to.
But I was wrong—you more than filled them—
but in a totally different way
and so

I write to you while you transit between life and legend.
Like you, we knew where you would go: to VietNam and I Corps,
to the 1st Marine Division and the First Marines.
It was written in the stars, the Southern Cross,
under which we fought each night and which surrounded
the blood-red "One" branded with "Guadalcanal."
If Chesty was the Marine Corps' god, then he was the son of the
1st Marine Division: his son would come to us.
"God save him," I thought and pissed off into the monsoon rain,
stumbling towards Tet, near death and enlightenment.
Four months after I made my bird to El Toro,
you made yours to Danang, as green as I once was;
brown bitterness had not begun its work on you yet
as it had begun on me.
Shuffling papers in Barstow, I heard you were blown away
by a 105 rigged as a mine—
"One of ours got one of ours thanks to them," I thought
and without looking back, I climbed through
the hole in my soul and never thought of you again
until I emerged from the other side
and found you there before me.
We shared the same wounds to the soul, Lew,
and you showed me how to heal them
one day at a time and in God's time
not mine.
You made us proud and humble,
two contradictory feelings held together
by your example of courage and service
to your brothers and sisters and to God.
Two years ago you dedicated my copy of your book,
thanking me for my service to my country,
welcoming me home and signing it "Semper Fi."
You ended by telling me to "Keep coming back"
and we have come back—
to the World,
to this Wall and the memory of the others
and of you.
Rest in peace and in our hearts,
Fortunate Son.

(Note: The last line, *Fortunate Son*, is the title of Puller's Pulitzer-prize winning auto/biography. This poem was written after Lew Puller's death on May 11, 1994; it appeared in the Fall 1994 newsletter of the *Memorial Day Writers' Project* (MDWP). According to its newsletter, MDWP will once again be at the Wall to provide a public performance space for aspiring poets, song writers, and musicians.)

Hueys—The mules of Vietnam.

Marines take to water.

Statue of a god at entrance to cave.

TANGO (T)

> "If you look too deeply into the abyss,
> The abyss will look into you."
> —Nietzsche

○ **Take care.** "With their different training duties and outlook, leaders and troops held as completely different interpretations of unnecessary harassment as they held of the *take care* concept.

○ **Television War.**

> Thanks to television, for the first time the young are seeing
> history made before it is censored by their elders.
> —Margaret Mead

"The postwar generation was the first to grow up with television, a medium of communication whose profound effects are still not fully understood. In the fifteen years before American troops were sent to Southeast Asia, television gave illustration and emphasis to several values and habits of mind that were not helpful to people who would have to adjust to a rapidly changing and increasingly complex world. Television glorified violence and at the same time kept it at a safe distance. The viewer was encouraged to accept the idea that swift and violent action usually yielded positive results. He could also see that he didn't really have to get involved in the problems of others if he didn't want to, he could let somebody else do it . . . .

"Television helped many Americans, young and old, to adopt an escapist mentality. With the aid of television one could leave far behind him the numbing repetition of his own existence. Things unpleasant could be made to seem far away, for other people; things fantastic could feel close and credible. The 'boob

Walter Cronkite, CBS News
(back middle with microphone) interviews troops.
TV camera filming Cronkite.

tube' encouraged both superficial and black and white thinking. Viewers quickly learned they didn't have to exert any effort at analyzing people and events—the tube did it all for them" (Anderson *The Grunts* 193-194).

"The television generation was getting its view of the World smashed today. From the boob tube they had learned that for every problem there is a simple, instant solution. With the right pill you can banish acid indigestion or the aches and pains of fatigue. With the right deodorant, one need never fear social ostracism or unpopularity. And if you're pressed for time, throw in a TV dinner. Here the grunts were, though, faced with a new one that wouldn't go away. They had been gulping water and Kool-Aid and salt tablets, frantic to relieve an agony that defied relief. Slowly the hard reality came through: there was no alternative, no time-out, no falling out from this 'field problem.' All this would have to be endured—second by second, minute by super-heated minute, with no excuses from mother good enough to get one out of it. The grunts were being beaten to a psychological pulp. The dream of returning to the great dreamland America was looking more hopeless every minute" (Anderson *The Grunts* 62).

Malik views TV from the other side of the world. "I'm in the Amtrak with Morley Safer, right? The whole thing is getting ready to go down. At Cam Ne. The whole bit that all America will see on the *CBS Evening News*, right? Marines burning down some huts. Brought to you by Morley Safer. Your man on the scene. August 5, 1965" (Terry 1). Later, Malik comments on what he calls the whole thing: "[Morley] Safer didn't tell them to burn the huts down with they lighters. He just photographed it. He could have got a picture of me burning a hut, too. It was just the way they did it. When you say level a village you don't use torches. It's not like in the 1800s. You use a Zippo. That's why people bought Zippos. Everybody had a Zippo. It was for burnin' shit down" (Terry 3).

General Westmoreland caught hell from the military that wanted him to control reporters. Herr says the higher highers kept saying they were winning the war; it was "you people" who are making us look like losers (228-229).

"In Vietnam, television, most of journalism, merely confirmed to Americans that the entire affair had a certain stench to it. Westmoreland and many others fully believed the stench came from the lies, inexperience, and manipulations of journalists" (Safer 134). Covering a war was a dilemma for Herr and no doubt for others, too. "[If] you photographed a dead Marine with a poncho over his face and got something (money, prestige, something) for it, you were some kind of parasite. But what were you if you pulled the poncho back first to make a better shot, and did that in front of his friends? Some other kind of parasite, I suppose. Then what were you if you stood there watching it, making a note to remember it later in case you might want to use it?" (228).

Another dilemma faced by Morley Safer (CBS) and Susan Brownmiller (ABC) were "photo ops." Morley Safer, watching Marines arrive on the beach, said that was his introduction to the phrase, "photo opportunity." The Marines were greeted by "cameramen and photographers fetched up from Saigon to record the event . . . . For Marine Corps recruiters it would be an especially stirring device to remind eighteen-year-olds that they, too, could stand in the same salty Pacific that John Wayne had liberated so many times before" (161-162). Brownmiller in the United States watched a tape of the "US Marines wade ashore seven months after the Gulf of Tonkin Resolution. The amphibious landing was a bit of a stunt, a rerun of "Sands of Iwo Jima" [1949, starring John Wayne as a tough Marine] for the older generation, a recruiting-poster image for the kids who were going to fight in the war. Brigadier General Karch flew in by helicopter for the photo-op on the beach—a nice little ceremony, short and to the point. Speech by the local mayor, bunch of schoolgirls carrying flowers. Children waved from the side of the road as the truck convoys followed the heavily secured route to the airbase . . ." (77). Print reporter Michael Herr saw the effect of television on the grunts. "I keep thinking about all the kids who got wiped out by seventeen years of war movies before coming to Vietnam to get wiped out for good. You don't know what a media freak is until you've seen the way a few of those grunts would run around during a fight when they knew that there was a television crew nearby. . . . They were insane, but the war hadn't done that to them" (209).

Quickly Vietnam "was no longer a war in which a few people were being killed. Large, large numbers of people were being killed. And everybody knew about it. It was in the papers, on television" (Terry 194). It was a new fight. "The new policy, as any follower of evening TV newscasts can perceive, is one of all-out war against the countryside. Its aim is to make the rural areas in which the Vietcong operate unlivable. It is assumed that the populace, for one reason or another, supports the Viet Cong and that the United States with its saturation bombing, is going to make the price of that support too high. The result will be increasingly large numbers of refugees from the bombed areas" (Scheer 75).

They Watched Television Together
by Kellan Kyllo

> Late at night
> the house was still and quiet
> His best friend,
> killed
> in Vietnam,
> sat on the basement sofa with him
> and shared
> only a glance and a few words. (Eichler 70)

○ *Tell it like it is.* Just say it. No matter if anyone believes you or not.

○ *Tell it like you mean it.* Say the truth. Or tell someone to tell you the truth. No bullshit because you might not see that someone again.

○ *Tell me this ain't happening.* I don't believe it, but I figure I will get beyond it.

○ *Tet.* The lunar holiday once a year in January; Buddha's birthday; major uprising of VC and VC sympathizers coordinated attacks against military installations and provincial capitals occurred January 31, 1968 at 3:00 AM.

"The North Vietnamese launched this massive attack [the Tet offensive, January 1968] because they had been beaten on the battlefields out in the countryside, but thought one major attack would reverse their declining fortune. They thought that they had support in the towns and cities, and a major Communist attack would trigger a general uprising among the people. The communists guessed wrong. Militarily, the attack was a disaster, with some 50,000 communists dead and many more wounded. This was over ten times American and South Vietnamese losses. The population did not rise in support of the VC" (Dunnigan and Nofi 258).

"The Tet offensive had an electric effect on popular opinion in the United States. The banner headlines and the television reports of fighting in the cities brought the shock of reality to what was still for many Americans a distant and incomprehensible war. The pictures of corpses in the garden of the American embassy cut through the haze of argument and counterargument, giving flat contradiction to the official optimism about the slow but steady progress of the war" (Fitzgerald 493). "At the height of the Tet Offensive alone, there were between 600 and 700 correspondents accredited to the Military Assistance Command, Vietnam [MACV]. Who all of them were and where all of them went was as much a mystery to me and to most of the correspondents I knew as it was to the gentle-tempered bull-faced Marine gunnery sergeant assigned to the department…which issued those little plastic-coated MACV accreditation cards" (Herr 220). It seemed to Herr that a member from every group, town, and state showed up. Gun magazines, religious groups, hometown papers managed to send its man in for a quick look (220-221).

○ ***There it is.*** "*There it is*, the grunts said, like this: sitting by a road with some infantry when a deuce-and-a-half rattled past with four dead in the back. The tailgate was half lowered as a platform to hold their legs and the boots that seemed to weigh a hundred pounds apiece now. Everyone was completely quiet as the truck hit a bad bump and the legs jerked up high and landed hard on the gate. 'How about that shit,' someone said, and 'just like the motherfucker,' and 'There it is.' Pure essence of Vietnam" (Herr 254).

○ ***There's only one bullet that's got your number.*** Watch out for that one bullet. But for Americans fighting in Vietnam, the odds were very good. "There was a 1.8-percent chance of being killed in action, a 5.6-percent chance of being seriously wounded but surviving the experience" (Dunnigan and Nofi 242). Still, it only took one bullet. Only one bullet had your name on it. A North Vietnamese soldier says, "Why bother running for cover? I thought: Bullets may miss people, but no one dodges a bullet" (Huong 36).

Reggie O'Neal says, "1st bullet hole on my 3rd or 4th flight. I knew then they meant business."

○ ***Thousand Yard Stare.*** Herr reported about the first thing he noticed about grunts that'd been in 'Nam too long, seen too much. "He had one of those faces, I saw that face at least a thousand times at a hundred bases and camps, all the youth sucked out of the eyes, the color drawn from the skin, cold white lips, you knew he wouldn't wait for any of it to come back. Life had made him old, he'd live it out old" (16).

Thousand Yard Stare
(The Siege of Khe Sanh)
by Joseph Greene

Iron falls like rain,
day after day of earth slamming
bone ripping indifference as I watch
one boy after another being smashed
into hash by jagged chunks of death;
it's been falling for weeks—
       waiting my turn.

Mirror images: red shadows,
filthy, intimate with rats,
hollow eyes, thousand yard-stare,
gaunt, beyond terror, no black, white or brown,
just sick down to the marrow—
       heroes are in myths.

Rockets slam as I run
zigzag playing tag with death,
trying to escape the unending barrage
of hatred that leaves meat
scraps strewn over the landscape—
       without even a "by your leave."

Six marines huddled close for safety
in their own coffin dug in red earth.
I scramble to get in but come up short;
one hundred-and-fifty-two-millimeters
of revenge with a debt to pay, slams home—
       all died but me;
          all died but me. (Eichler 51-52)

Morley Safer notices that the Vietnamese also have that thousand yard stare: "I look away from Van Le's face; it is bent to one side, his eyes focused past me. Again, the thousand-yard stare of boys who aged overnight" (247).

○ *Tiger Cage.* A small cell made of bamboo out in public. A POW couldn't stand or stretch.

○ *Tiger Scouts.* "They [two young Vietnamese kids suffering from malaria] were hired by our line companies to serve as Tiger Scouts, i.e., to go out in the field on operations and help point out booby traps, etc." (Holley 84).

A tiger scout.

○ *Titi.* Slang for a little. From the French "petit," meaning little.

○ *TOC.* Tactical Operations Center.

○ *Tracer.* Round of ammo treated to glow or give out smoke so that its flight can be seen.

Red smoke from tracer assisted in locating the enemy.

○ *Triple canopy jungle.* That was the 'Nam. Triple canopy means that plants grow at three levels; they intertwine. There's moss, and the growth is so dense that no sun gets through. A perfect place to rest or hide.

○ *Tunnel rat.* A soldier who goes into tunnels to find the enemy or discover enemy resources. "[Rat] was the one who went down in any bunker or tunnel encountered to search for weapons, supplies, or North Vietnamese. No extra pay was offered for the extra danger, so other were glad to see Rat come along and volunteer" (Anderson *The Grunts* 95). Rat is proud because he found something he liked: "I got to like it after I found out I could be good at it. I've only had to kill two guys I found so far—brought thirteen out alive when I was doing it. I think it was cuz I took the fear out of them, I'd just flash my flashlight on my face when I knew there was one there, and I'd smile—real big, like I'd just knocked off a piece, you know—and they'd come right out. I even brought out two at once one time" (Anderson *The Grunts* 95).

A dangerous job in Vietnam because a tunnel rat could look like the enemy: small and dark with dirt popping out the camouflaged entrance. Some Hispanic soldiers were tunnel rats. Some Australians also were tunnel rats; dangerous because you went into darkness alone, knowing nothing and expecting the worst. Sometimes, however, a tunnel rat would come out and say the tunnel was cold (empty).

Tunnel rat coming out.

Tunnel rats had to overcome fear and feelings of claustrophobia in tunnels that were so low you had to bend over to walk, that were so narrow you had to walk sideways. Some of the tunnels were so small and narrow that crawling on your belly was the only way to get through. Tunnels were dark, so the sense of smell was critical. Tunnel rats didn't smoke (smoke could be smelled 1/2 mile away), chew gum, eat candy, or eat before going into a tunnel. Most tunnel rats tossed in CS or tear gas before entering, and a knife was the weapon they carried because the sound of a weapon discharging was painful. Tunnel rats developed a sixth sense—they knew when Charlie was there. They often felt or smelled the enemy was nearby in one of the cut-outs, just waiting.

Marine Puller's platoon discovers a tunnel hidden on a hill. Puller was surprised at how many of his men volunteered to investigate "since there was no way of knowing what was inside, but the element of the unknown seemed to spark the enthusiasm of some of the men. After a volunteer was selected, we tossed a couple of grenades into the shaft. The volunteer's quick foray produced nothing but some sacks of rice and medical supplies from an American pharmaceutical company. Apparently the shaft was used only for storage, which was a relief to me but a disappointment to the tunnel rat, who was looking for the in-country R&R that a kill would bring him" (107).

Tunnel rat teams explored tunnels using CS (or tear gas) first to flush any enemy out. Once in, the tunnel rat's progress was followed by a "Tunnel Explorer Locator System" that also mapped the tunnel. After a tunnel had been searched, it was then destroyed to prevent further use (Hay 34).

One tunnel rat decided on his own not to confront an enemy in a tunnel. "Then I cautiously raised the upper half of my body into the tunnel until I was lying flat on my stomach. When I felt comfortable . . . I switched on the flashlight, illuminating the tunnel.

"There, not more than 15 feet away, sat a Viet Cong eating a handful of rice from a pouch on his lap. We looked at each other for what seemed to be an eternity, but in fact was probably only a few seconds.

"Maybe it was the surprise of actually finding someone else there, or maybe it was just the absolute innocence of the situation, but neither one of us reacted.

"After a moment, he put his pouch of rice on the floor of the tunnel beside him, turned his back to me and slowly started crawling away. I, in turn, switched off my flashlight, before slipping back into the lower tunnel and making my way back to the entrance. About 20 minutes later, we received word that another squad had killed a VC emerging from a tunnel 500 meters away.

"I never doubted who that VC was. To this day, I firmly believe that grunt and I could have ended the war sooner over a beer in Saigon than Henry Kissinger ever could by attending the peace talks" (Grossman 1-2).

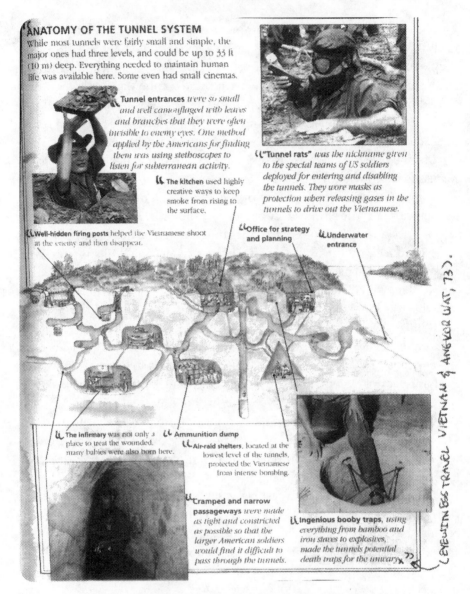

ANATOMY OF THE TUNNEL SYSTEM

While most tunnels were fairly small and simple, the major ones had three levels, and could be up to 33 ft (10 m) deep. Everything needed to maintain human life was available here. Some even had small cinemas.

Tunnel entrances *were so small and well camouflaged with leaves and branches that they were often invisible to enemy eyes. One method applied by the Americans for finding them was using stethoscopes to listen for subterranean activity.*

The kitchen used highly creative ways to keep smoke from rising to the surface.

"Tunnel rats" *was the nickname given to the special teams of US soldiers deployed for entering and disabling the tunnels. They wore masks as protection when releasing gases in the tunnels to drive out the Vietnamese.*

Well-hidden firing posts helped the Vietnamese shoot at the enemy and then disappear.

Office for strategy and planning

Underwater entrance

The infirmary was not only a place to treat the wounded, many babies were also born here.

Ammunition dump

Air-raid shelters, located at the lowest level of the tunnels, protected the Vietnamese from intense bombing.

Cramped and narrow passageways *were made as tight and constricted as possible so that the larger American soldiers would find it difficult to pass through the tunnels.*

Ingenious booby traps, *using everything from bamboo and iron staves to explosives, made the tunnels potential death traps for the unwary.*

(EYEWITNESS TRAVEL VIETNAM & ANGKOR WAT, 73).

The complexity of tunnels, over 4800 hundred were found.

○ **Tunnels.** End of 1970, 4,800 tunnels had been discovered (Hay 34). Not tunnels in the ordinary sense of the word: "there were three basic precepts: 'Walk without footprints, cook without smoke, and speak without a sound.'

"Not every tunnel, with its requisite air vent and camouflaged escape hatch, had the advantage of good hard soil and wood-beam reinforcement. Untold numbers of tunnels collapsed, burying the inhabitants alive under the cave-ins caused by aboveground tank movements, or by bombs and shells that scored a direct hit or landed close enough to produce fatal tremors" (Brownmiller 173-174).

Tunnels were honey-combed to make a tiny village. The Vietcong believed in fighting first, comfort second. Tunnels had workshops for producing homemade weapons, military storerooms, conference rooms, printing and even temporary graveyards. Tunnels also had air-raid shelters near the surface to allow the sound of approaching aircraft to penetrate. They also had complete living facilities: places for sleeping and eating, latrines, a hospital, a kitchen, and a well. Their kitchens were smokeless because smoke was sent through

Cross section of V.C. Tunnels 12 miles from Saigon in CU CHI was one entrance-120 miles.

many ducts. Tunnel entrances usually had false entrances, ones that led nowhere; there were hidden entrances usually a small square with dirty water and vegetation to cover it up; there were booby-trapped entrances.

Tunnel entrance to surgery room—entrance in lower middle at the sign.

Many North Vietnamese tunnel complexes had booby trapped entrances.

Some tunnels were a thousand years old; others were over twenty miles in length. They were hand-dug by villagers early in the war. The US attempted to map tunnels but proved unsuccessful. Some land was bull-dozed in attempts to collapse tunnels; entrances were blown up as well (Dunnigan and Nofi 103-105).

Tunnels
by Yusef Komunyakaa

Crawling down headfirst into the hole,
he kicks the air & disappears.
I feel like I'm down there
with him, moving ahead, pushed
by a river of darkness, feeling
blessed for each inch of the unknown.
Our tunnel rat is the smallest man
in the platoon, in an echo chamber
that makes his ears bleed
when he pulls the trigger.
He moves as if trying to outdo
blind fish easing toward imagined blue,
pulled by something greater than life's
ambitions. He can't think about
spiders & scorpions mending the air,
or care about bats upside down
like gods in the mole's blackness.
The damp smell goes deeper
Than the stench of honey buckets.
A web of booby traps waits, ready
to spring into broken stars.
Forced onward by some need,
some urge, he knows the pulse
of mysteries & diversions
like thoughts trapped in the ground.
He questions each root.
Every cornered shadow has a life
to bargain with. Like an angel
pushed up against what hurts,
his globe-shaped helmet

follows the gold ring his flashlight
casts into the void. Through silver
lice, shit, maggots, & vapor of pestilence,
he goes, the good soldier,
on hands & knees, tunneling past
death sacked into a blind corner,
loving the weight of the shotgun
that will someday dig his grave. (138)

Blind entrance into the tunnel.

○ **Two-digit-midget.** A short-timer down to 99 days or fewer (two digits) until DEROS (date of return from overseas). Then the Freedom Bird would take you home. "It's amazing how much hate man can build up against his enemy. I'll sure be glad to get back home where I can experience love instead of hate. I'm so tired of hate and killing and death" (Holley 141).

○ **2.5 tons.** Standard deuce and a half truck.

○ **201 file.** A US Army personnel file for each member of service. It contains information on promotions, mobilization orders, service School Academic Evaluation Reports (DA 1059s), MOS (Military Occupation Specialty—a number assigned to designate your specialty), awards, transcripts, SGLV 8286 (Single Group Life Insurance), SGLI (Single Group Life Insurance traumatic brain injury), NCOERs (measurement of an NCO—non-commissioned officer), OER (Officer Effectiveness Report). [Note: the 201 file is also known as OMPF, Official Military Personnel File. Copies can cost $15-$50; fax a request to 314.801.9195 or write NPRC, 9700 Page Avenue, St. Louis, Missouri 63132; or submit a request through eVetRecs. The 201 is important because it proves your military service; you are advised to keep copies of it and everything in it in case the military misplaces your 201. (Note: Information found at <*http://201file. com/dd214.php>.*)]

2.5 ton truck.

UNIFORM (U)

"It's time that we recognized that ours was in
truth a noble cause."
—Ronald Reagan (October 1980)

○ *Unclassified matter.* Official information that is not sensitive enough to be a security threat; but unclassified doesn't make the information open to everyone (Dictionary of US Military terms for joint usage from Joint Chiefs of Staff Feb. 1964).

Wounded soldier helped aboard Huey.

Troops exiting a Huey.

○ **Uncle Sam.** The United States. Popular wartime poster: Uncle Sam Wants you. Also uncle, uncle sucker, and uncle sugar.

The Chu Lai USO Club opened in September 1966. It was originally housed in Quonset huts, and was moved to new tropical frame building on the beach in October, 1967. This was due to the fact that the new runway on the airfield was extended—terminating just short of the original club location. This is one of the fifteen facilities USO operated in Vietnam. These were made possible by the generous contributions given by the American public to USO through their United Funds, Community Chests, Combined Federal Campaigns and other voluntary donations.

○ **Unit.** A subdivision of a group within a task force.

○ **United States Army Special Forces.** Military personnel trained to aid, supply, and enlist locals in guerilla warfare. They were also trained in specialized skills in order to combat the enemy in unconventional ways. LRRPS were Army; later called Rangers. The Navy had SEALS. The Marines also had LRRPS.

○ **USO.** The United Services Organization. "Established by request of the President [Franklin Roosevelt], the USO [is] a private, non-profit organization providing morale and recreational services to [armed] forces . . . and sponsored by the National Catholic Community Service, National Jewish Welfare Board, National Travelers Aid Association, Salvation Army, Young men's Christian Association, and Young Women's Christian Association" (Rottman *FUBAR* 112-113). It

Bob Hope, in beige suit coming to entertain the troops Dec 19, 1966.

operated many centers around Vietnam with goodies such as books, milkshakes, and company. The USO is usually linked to its Christmas Show that featured Bob Hope for years, plus a starlet or two. The show, welcomed by the troops, was also a source of danger; the enemy knew exactly where a large group of soldiers would be (Herr 7).

At one center, the USO sponsored a Seder for Jewish servicemen. "The largest of the celebrations was held at the United Service Organization's clubhouse here [unidentified]. It was attended by more than 500 men, ranging in rank from private to colonel. Many, wearing their green combat fatigue uniforms, arrived on special passes from their division defending the capital. Other observations were held in Nha Trang and Danang. "The armed forces shipped 18 tons of 'Kosher for Passover' delicacies, including sacramental wine, gefilte fish, matzoh and boiled chicken, to Vietnam for the celebrations. New kitchen utensils were provided for their preparation" (*The New York Times* qtd. in *Vietnam War Diary* 80). Birthdays, Easter, and Christmas were also celebrated; anything they could do to bring a sense of normalcy to the soldiers' lives.

USO Christmas party.

*USO Christmas party.
Susan Wimmers is on the right.*

In an interview with a former USO member, Susan Wimmers, she explained that she wanted to be in Vietnam in some capacity because she was patriotic. "I was too old to join the Red Cross," she said with a laugh. "You had to be between the ages of 22-25 and I was 26. I went to many of the centers in Vietnam. One of them was in a combat zone, although I don't think it was supposed to be. In our club facilities, we offered 13 shops, a restaurant or two, a rec room, a library, and a small chapel. We also had the first base phones to the US—instead of that MARS thing you had to wait to use. Now we didn't have plumbing; we had a "Squat-a-toilet." We had luncheons for the women in Vietnam. We heard about an ambulance standing around that was a brothel, but I'm not sure about that."

Outside a USO.

○ **Utilities.** Marine slang for combat fatigues. During the war, the fatigues were changed to camouflage—greens and yellows. Because of the wet weather or 100% humidity on dry days, plus elephant grass, plus dirt and dust, the fatigues didn't last long. They ripped and shredded. Some Marines actually lost the seat of their fatigues.

VICTOR (V)

"This war has already stretched the generation gap so wide that
it threatens to pull the country apart."
—Sen. Frank Church (May 1970)

○ *VC.* Short for Viet Cong, Victor Charlie, the enemy; many soldiers could not distinguish between which Vietnamese individual might be VC. "The term is a contraction of Viet-nam Cong-san and was the equivalent of 'commie.' It was originally used by Ngo Dinh Diem, who was President of South Vietnam from 1955 until 1963. The term 'Viet Cong' refers specifically to the guerilla fighters of the National Liberation Front [North Vietnamese Army]" <http://*mazalien. com/viet-cong.html*>. The VC conducted its attacks against the South Vietnamese from home bases in Laos and Cambodia and were resupplied by locals coming down the Ho Chi Minh Trail.

"I suppose one of the things that bothered me from the very beginning in Vietnam was the condemnation of the ARVN as a fighting force: 'the Vietnamese are cowardly . . . the Vietnamese can't be disciplined . . . the Vietnamese just can't understand tactics and strategy, etc., etc.' But the Viet Cong are Vietnamese. United States military files in Saigon document time and again a Viet Cong company surrounding two or even three ARVN companies and annihilating them. It became obvious that motivation is the prime factor in this problem. The Viet Cong soldier believes in his cause. He believes he is fighting for national independence. He has faith in his leaders, whose obvious dedication is probably greater than his own" (Duncan 91).

"I had a great deal of respect for the Viet Cong. They were trained and familiar with the jungle. They relied on stealth, on ambush, on their personal skills and wile, as opposed to firepower. They knew it did not pay for them to

*A Viet Cong Soldier
in a tunnel.*

263

stand and fight us, so they wouldn't. They'd come back and fight another day. We knew that we could not afford to get careless with them because you pay the price. But they were not superhumans. And they did not scare us" (Terry 226).

"The ability of the Viet Cong continuously to rebuild their units and to make good their losses is one of the mysteries of this guerilla war. . . . Not only do the Viet Cong units have the recuperative powers of the phoenix, but they have an amazing ability to maintain morale" (General Maxwell Taylor from a briefing November 1964; see Fitzgerald 173).

○ *VC Death Squads.* These squads committed many atrocities on the civilian population. "[They] systematically murdered village leaders, clergy, medical personnel, social workers, teachers, small merchants, and, of course, landowners" (Dunnigan and Nofi 286).

○ *VC MIA.* This term describes policing the area after a battle. The VC would remove all of their dead and retrieve whatever they found: spent ammunition, an American M16 left behind, shell casings, ammo—anything they thought they could use. Some American soldiers were shocked when they returned only to find no traces of any dead VC. Many of them were pushed into tunnels whose entrances were hidden. After a battle, several Marines were assigned the body detail to remove wounded and dead US soldiers from the battlefield (Herr 82).

This dead soldier and his possessions would be taken away by the VC-MIA. This cadre was responsible for cleaning up, gathering weapons left behind and taking bodies for burial.

○ *Vietminh.* Vietnam nationalists organized by Ho Chi Minh to get the French out of Vietnam so that it would no longer be a French colony.

○ *Vietnam.* Vietnam has become synonymous with War. Were you in Vietnam—as a question means "Were you in the war?" Twelve years earlier, the Korean War did not become Korea. Korea was Korea. But Vietnam simply doesn't exist. To so many veterans, Vietnam was unreal, didn't mean anything, spooky, ghostly; exists in dreams, nightmares, flashbacks, all of the war.

○ **Vietnamese culture.** The greatest culture shock for one of the soldiers landing in Vietnam was that the country was 130 years behind: he noticed people defecating in public and other things that we in the US would consider vulgar.

"The Vietnamese have no sense of time the way we understand it, that their mental and body clocks are tuned more to history than to the ticking urgencies of ordinary life. That is why small, seemingly weak men and women were able to lug tons of supplies hundreds of miles through impassable and dangerous foot trails for years on end. [That is why] many of them will cycle thirty to forty miles [in the middle of the day] simply to say hello to a cousin or to deliver some firewood to a sick granny" (Safer 4).

○ **Vietnamization.** The American plan to turn over more of the defense of South Vietnam to the South Vietnamese trained by Americans. Ironically, the North Vietnamese called this same plan "de-Americanization" (Safer 102).

"Little by little, as all these facts made their impact on me, I had to accept the fact that, Communist or not, the vast majority of the people were pro-Viet Cong and anti-Saigon. I had to accept also that the position 'we are in Vietnam because we are in sympathy with the aspirations and desires of the Vietnamese people,' was a lie" (Duncan *Ramparts* 91).

○ **Ville.** (also vill) A village. Made up of many hamlets and hooches.

A Vietnamese hooch with people working in the fields.

○ **Volunteers.** A Japanese reporter interviewed several men in a US field hospital. "Two of the four were draftees, one a volunteer, and the other said, 'Formally, I am a draftee. But, as I was thinking of volunteering, in fact, I may be counted as a volunteer.' What was common to all of them was that they had a very strong sense of duty, and were of the opinion that it was right and proper for citizens to accept the war policies being taken by statesmen elected by themselves. They had very little of the so-called 'Holy War' consciousness, and said that they wanted to go home as soon as their obligatory term of one year would be over" (Honda 32). [Note: The idea that is "right and proper" goes back to the Romans: *Dulce et decorum est pro patria mori* (it is sweet and fitting to die for one's country).]

Jim Bowman volunteered in 1965 at the age of 19. "Somebody has to do it, might as well be trained people. I didn't go on blind faith. I had an oath to serve/obey orders. I considered it my personal responsibility" (2/4/93). Bobby Ward volunteered at age 18. "For me, it was an escape, not just from poverty or college, but to make some money." Unlike Bobby Ward who had no friends, Jim Bowman said he had four good friends there; two died. "Maybe the worst was the jungle rot, worse than in WW2. I got malaria, which was like being crushed in a car. When I got home, I had some mental problems but nobody to help me. Maybe the ABC (Alcohol Beverage Commission) store" (Vet Program 2/4/93).

Just as Bowman said, volunteering was a personal responsibility. The young Vietnamese felt the same way. "I ran my fingers through the hair of a corpse, that of my youngest soldier, Hoang. He had been the purest soul in the company. Barely eighteen years old, Hoang was the son of an intellectual couple; the father a doctor, the mother a schoolteacher of the third rank. There were two sisters. He had taken first place in the math competition that selected students for study abroad. But he had volunteered for the army instead. 'No, the college classrooms aren't as important as the battlefield. There have been and there always will be classrooms for those who want them. Only the war gives me a chance to participate in our country's historic mission. I've heard the sacred call'" (Huong 219-220).

"Being the only son in my family, I did not have to accept the orders to Vietnam. I accepted the orders because I wanted to see what the war was all about. And I thought that if we were there it must be right. We have to stop communism before it gets to America. I was just like all the other dummies" (Terry 63). Some, however, were forced to volunteer, like Robert E. Holcomb who evaded the draft for over a year and when finally caught by the FBI, he was told to say the oath. He'd be a problem for the Army next time. When he refused, he was told either he served in the Army or he would spend the rest of his life in prison. "I raised my hands and said the oath. I was sworn into the Army in manacles" (Terry 200).

WHISKEY (W)

"Vietnam is what we had instead of happy childhoods."
—Michael Herr

○ *Wait-a-minute.* A vicious vine. Ed Emanuel, a member of the "Soul Patrol," the first all-black LRRPSs, says "The vines hung down from the canopy of the jungle, sprouting sharp barbs at one-foot intervals. I learned on the first day in the boonies that you have to cover up all exposed skin because the 'wait-a-minute' vines would always triumph when it came to the slice-and-dice battle. It was unbelievable how badly the vines or even tall blades of grass [probably Elephant grass] could cut up your arms and hands, anything that was exposed. The barbs from the vines would hook onto your clothes or equipment and pull you backward down to the ground when the slack played out. The 'wait-a-minute' vines were one of nature's many annoying jokes designed only to piss you off" (45).

○ *Wake-up Call.* The end of a grunt's tour. The wake-up call was to get you onto your Freedom Bird and get back to the World. The tour was twelve months in the Army, an extra twenty days for being a Marine. The wake-up call would vary within a platoon or unit since each soldier might be a replacement for another Medevaced out or KIA. That replacement might have ten months left in his tour; several others in the unit he joined might be short-timers. It made for a lack of cohesiveness. Every new guy was suspect until he proved himself.

○ *War.* "The essence of both the practical and the ethical problem of warfare is '**Whom shall we kill and why?**' [emphasis added] . . . . The craft of the military leader is to cause death and destruction in the manner most likely to prevent the enemy from effectively continuing the fight" (Seabury & Codevilla 226-227). In the Vietnam War, the "whom" was the first problem. The enemy was not obvious. Any Vietnamese person could have been the enemy. When the practice of body count was established, the soldiers said if it's dead, it must have been VC. The "why" was the more troubling.

In the theory of a so-called "just" war, there are five sanctions for war: 1) are there goods or resources at stake; 2) that they have been seriously threatened; 3) violence is the only way to protect them; 4) is there a reasonable chance of success; 5) evils that are committed in war do not outweigh the value of the goods (Seabury & Codevilla 215). Those soldiers who participated in fighting against Germany and her allies considered they were fighting a "good war." People and countries were at stake, with minority groups singled out for death, peace talks and treaties were broken, and the United States once it joined Germany's enemies tipped the balance against Germany. Number five, the use of nuclear weapons, can be argued both ways. But what is important, many American soldiers fighting in Vietnam (and more of them were volunteers than draftees—see Appendix C) knew their fathers fought in a "good" war; they thought they would be, too.

○ **War Powers Resolution.** A President could send troops abroad on his own for 90 days without approval from Congress. The law was passed on August 4, 1964 after the Gulf of Tonkin incident in which the commander of the US Maddox reported being fired upon. The War Powers Act gave the President of the United States unlimited power to use military force at his command only. After ninety days, the President can ask for an extension unless Congress declares war. As of 2010, the War Powers Resolution is still in force.

○ **War versus Conflict.** Some called the Korean Police Action/Conflict World War 2½. Vietnam Conflict or Vietnam War depended with whom you were speaking. The United States chose not to declare war in Vietnam. It wanted its involvement seen as short-term, winning hearts and minds, and keeping the North from invading the South. The United States was not to capture territory, was not to drive an enemy away into its own territory, and was not to invade another country, even relatively small ones such as Laos and Cambodia. So when the war wasn't short-term, when the VC (guerillas from the South) didn't seem to be changing their hearts and minds to say nothing of the North, and when we invaded Cambodia (disguised as an "incursion"), why didn't the United States *declare* war?

○ **War Stories.** Michael Herr always found a story wherever he went. "In war more than in other life you don't really know what you're doing most of the time, you're just behaving, and afterward you can make up any kind of bullshit you want to about it, say you felt good or bad, loved it or hated it, did this or that, the right thing or the wrong thing; still, what happened happened" (20-21). Writer Henry Miller just wanted a good story, true or false.

"When a story is good I listen. And if it develops afterwards that it was a lie why so much the better—I like a good lie just as much as the truth. A story is a story, whether it's based on fact or fiction" (Miller 134).

The grunts Herr talked with sometimes told him stories that he'd heard before; sometimes the stories would tumble out, barely articulate as if they couldn't get it out fast enough. He found the "mix [of grunts] so amazing; incipient saints and realized homicidals, unconscious lyric poets and mean dumb motherfuckers with their brains all down in their necks; and even though by the time I left I knew where all the stories came from and where they were going, I was never bored, never even unsurprised. Obviously, what they really wanted to tell you was how tired they were and how sick of it, how moved they'd been and how afraid" (30).

"But once in a while you'd hear something fresh, and a couple of times you'd hear something high, like the corpsman at Khe Sanh [during the 90-day siege] who said, 'If it ain't the fucking incoming it's the fucking outgoing. Only difference is who gets the fucking grease, and that ain't no fucking difference at all" (Herr 30).

A LRRP on his third tour thought Herr was "a freak because [I] wouldn't carry a weapon.

"'Didn't you ever meet a reporter before?' I asked him.

"'Tits on a bull,' he said. 'Nothing personal.'

"But what a story he told me, as one-pointed and resonant as any war story I ever heard, it took me a year to understand it:

"'Patrol went up the mountain. One man came back. He died before he could tell us what happened.'

"I waited for the rest, but it seemed not to be that kind of story; when I asked him what had happened he just looked like he felt sorry for me, fucked if he'd waste time telling stories to anyone dumb as I was" (Herr 6).

A "No Bullshit" War Story
by Jim Gray

We went to Vietnam,
And some of us came back.

That's all there is . . .
Except for the details. (21)

Herr said the grunts told their stories differently. "[They] were afraid they might not get to finish, or saying it almost out of a dream, innocent, offhand and mighty direct, 'Oh, you know, it was just a firefight, we killed some of them and they killed some of us'" (Herr 30). He heard so many stories that after a year he thought even the dead were trying to tell him their stories. It didn't matter "whether I'd known them or not, no matter what I'd felt about them or the way they'd died, their story was always there and it was always the same: it went, 'Put yourself in my place'" (31). "War story—I worked at US Army, had a job, nothing more nothing less" (Bobby Ward, Vet Program 1994).

"Killing comes with a price, and societies must learn that their soldiers will have to spend the rest of their lives living with what they have done . . . society must now begin to understand the enormity of the price and process of killing in combat" (Grossman 192).

That was part of Herr's problem about the war story that he didn't think had ended. He hopped on helicopters and went wherever they were going. He talked to grunts. He humped his own gear. He spent overnights in the bush (67). "Talk about impersonating an identity, about locking into a role, about irony: I went to cover the war and the war covered me; an old story, unless of course you've never heard it. I went there behind the crude but serious belief that you had to be able to look at anything, serious because I acted on it and went, crude because I didn't know, it took the war to teach it, that you were as responsible for everything you saw as you were for everything you did. The problem was that you didn't always know what you were seeing until later, maybe years later, that a lot of it never made it in at all, it just stayed stored there in your eyes. Time and information, rock and roll, life itself, the information isn't frozen, you are" (Herr 20).

○ **Wasted.** Killed. Greased. Zapped. Fried. Blasted.

○ **Waxed.** Killed. Wiped out. Erased.

○ **Weed.** Marijuana. Pot. Reefer. Roach.

○ **We gotta get outta this place.** Everybody said it. Everybody felt it. (From a song by Eric Burden and the Animals). "This was the national anthem for guys in 'Nam. The *geographical cure* is what we call it back here in the World. It made sense to want to get the hell outta Nam. Even so, we had to put in our 365 days.

If we made it through every one of those days—one day at a time—it meant we were going home alive" (Anthony 35).

○ **Well, good luck.** That was "the Vietnam verbal tic" (Herr 55). It was said in many ways—automatically, said too many times. "Sometimes, though, it was said with such feeling and tenderness that it could crack your mask, that much love where there was so much war" (Herr 56).

○ **Wet job.** An assassination, usually by Special Forces.

○ **WHAM.** Winning Hearts And Minds.

○ **What are you gonna do, send me to 'Nam?** If reprimanded or threatened with punishment, a grunt could say it and did. What was worse than where I am right now? "There is some consolation in just being where we are, in that certain place, wherever that may be. Just by admitting who we are and what our situation is, our life starts to get better. That's the simple secret of acceptance—to stop fighting it, whatever it is. Only then do we start to find peace (Anthony 81). Maybe this is another way of expressing acceptance of the situation. With that acceptance should come that Drill Sergeant who trained you—sitting on your shoulder reminding you that nobody said war was going to be easy.

○ **What you don't know can kill you.** Every unit was constantly getting a replacement. Listen to those in your unit who have experience that basic training couldn't do for you. Watch your back. Be aware of everything around you.

○ **White mice.** The Vietnam police, who wore white uniforms.

○ **WIA.** Wounded in Action.

○ **Widow maker.** Also known as the M-16, the standard rifle.

○ **Willie Peter.** Also known as Willie Pete, **WP** or **White Phosphorus;** its use was banned by the Geneva Convention, but it was used by both sides. One purpose was that of a marking round. "Sometimes the chopper you were riding in would top a hill and all the ground in front of you as far as the next hill would be charred and pitted and still smoking, and something between your chest and your stomach would turn over. Frail gray smoke where they'd burned off the rice fields around a free-strike zone, brilliant white smoke from phosphorus, deep black smoke from 'palm, they said that if you stood at the base of a column of napalm smoke it would suck the air right out of your lungs" (Herr 10).

Its other use was that of injury or death when it was packed into grenades or shells. It caused third-degree burns. Handling the victims of WP was just one more nightmare in Vietnam. "Just about dusk tonight, a white phosphorus ('willy peter') artillery round landed on top of a thatched hut in a small village . . . . It set the roof on fire, and the locals believed one of our rounds was accidentally fired short. They brought three women, who were really a mess, into my aid station. They had severe WP burns, and their skin was barely hanging on. I couldn't identify any veins to start an IV, so I had to do veinous cutdowns on each of their ankles and then have them dusted off to Saigon. I doubt very seriously that any of them will survive as it's pretty damn difficult to live with a total-body skin graft, which is what each one of them will need if they are to have a Chinaman's chance of survival—poor choice of words!

"White phosphorus is a very potent, caustic, and deadly agent, which will burn straight through any human tissue it comes into contact with. It will also burn through most manmade materials as well . . . . Both sides use WP as marking rounds because it produces an intense white smoke cloud that is easily seen from a considerable distance, therefore making it an ideal reference for adjusting artillery fire on a given target" (Holley 133).

○ **Wire.** The barbed wire that lined the perimeter of a bunker.

○ **Women in war.** "About 260,000 women served in the armed forces during the Vietnam War, about 3 percent of the total personnel in uniform. It is not possible to determine the number of American women who served 'in country' during the Vietnam War. It was certainly in the thousands" (Dunnigan and Nofi 161).

○ **The World.** For most of the men and woman in the 'Nam, there were only two places: the 'Nam and the World. ("World" meant the "USA" and "home" at the same time.) "About 2.5 million served in Vietnam . . . [and] were "dispersed within a population of over 200 million. Thus, the veterans had only about a one percent chance of meeting each other. Back in the World the veterans were surrounded by persons unable to understand their thoughts, their actions, or even their words" (Anderson *The Grunts* 176).

Back to the World
by Randy Cribbs

Back to the world.
Always in our mind.
Waiting for that day,
Putting in our time.

Each day things
Grow more insane
For the pawns in
This political game.

Back in the world
They blame
The warriors for the war,
Those brave youth who
Heeded the call,
nothing more.

We remind them,
Back in the world, of
Things not right,
Of us and them,
For and against,
Flee or fight.

But still,
Over here,
Not getting back
To the world
Is our worst fear . . . (92)

Leaving a rifle behind or out of sight was impossible at the end of a tour. The vets knew only one thing to do with it. "'I just can't hack it back in the

World,' he said [to Herr]. He told me that after he'd come back home the last time he would sit in his room all day, and sometimes he'd stick a hunting rifle out the window, leading people and cars as they passed his house until the only feeling he was aware of was all up in the tip of that one finger. 'It used to put my folks real uptight,' he said. But he put people uptight here too, even here" (Herr 5). Charlie, one of our vets, was out in the woods the first day of deer hunting, and all of a sudden he realized that he was looking for a gook to kill. "I took that rifle straight home and put it away" (3/04/93).

Coming home meant facing many problems. When Lynda's tour was over, she was dropped off at the Oakland Airport in uniform and had to hitchhike to San Francisco. When someone finally picked her up, he spit on her. "We're going past the airport, sucker, but we don't take Army pigs" (Van Devanter 247).

The Army provided booklets to parents (continuing today) that included what to expect once their loved ones came home. For those coming home from the 'Nam, parents were told: Don't be surprised if: your son grabs a bar of soap runs outside in the rain and strips. It's a bush shower. They may crave ice cream. Milk. Canned peaches. Long showers. Careful about that weapon under the bed. Hours on the phone (Van Devanter 229-230).

"Vietnam veterans seem no less well-adjusted than were those of the nation's earlier wars, though perhaps public awareness and tolerance of problems among them has been more acute. There have been a few genuinely objective surveys of Vietnam veterans. These suggest a considerably different picture from the common one. Some 91 percent of Vietnam veterans are proud to have served, and 74 percent believed their service was necessary. The overwhelming majority (91 percent) of Vietnam veterans received discharges that were honorable, the same percentage that had prevailed in the decade before the war. Nor have most of them found adjustment to civilian life unusually difficult. About 88 percent of them made the transition without difficulty, and the average income of Vietnam veterans is about 18 percent higher, and their unemployment rate rather lower, than that for their non-veteran contemporaries. Drug abuse patterns among Vietnam veterans and non-veterans of the same era are not particularly different; remember that it was the era of 'turn on, tune in, and drop out.' Fewer than 0.5 percent of them have been in jail, in contrast to a national incarceration rate of about 1.5 percent" (Dunnigan and Nofi 22-23).

"To [the Vietnam veteran], logic looks absurd, absurdity looks logical. They can't make realistic decisions about the future because they are no longer sure what reality is. The war was madness in motion; it was a surrealistic landscape brought to life and yet it was a real historical event, real enough to wrench once solid values out of all recognizable and useful shape. Now for the confused veterans the mad play of life on the planet Earth goes on, bouncing back and forth between reality and illusion, and they feel strapped to a seat before that stage. Action is okay, passivity is okay, brutality is okay, love is okay—they're all okay, they're all worthless, 'who gives a shit?'" (Anderson *The Grunts* 231).

"I'm tired of hating. I want to return to a place where people don't hate so much, but I can't help hating **CHARLIE.** He is so ruthless and has killed so many of my friends. Baby, I know I will never forget Vietnam, but I do hope I will be able to put it way back in a distant corner of my mind. All this hatred and killing have really brought out the worst in me." And two pages later, Holley continues, "I don't worry about getting killed like I did before coming over here. I guess I just have too much faith to worry about such things. But I do worry about the effect all this killing and dying and sorrow has had on me. I may come home without any visible scars, but I can assure you there are many scars way down deep inside me that may never heal. You can't be exposed to all that I have seen, felt, smelled and heard and not have it affect you" (Holley 151, 153).

"And I see many people back here stateside killing as many people as they were killing in Vietnam. Vietnam really gave me a respect for human life. I value people. People make me happy now. And I don't feel inferior anymore. When I was six or seven, I used to wonder why I was born black; I should have been born white. See, I found out from reading about my past before slavery—my ancestors built the pyramids that still stand today. They omitted the small things the Caesars of Rome studied in a university in Africa before they became Caesars. I learned that as a black man the only problem I had was that I wasn't exposed to things. I feel equal to everyone, and I walk humbly among men. I'm studying to be a computer programmer, but that doesn't make me better than a garbage man" (Terry 61).

○ *World of Hurt.* One Vietnam vet from Florida told me (Margaret Brown), ten years later: "So I'm in a World of Hurt figuring there's a fucking grenade out there with my name on it. I'm scared. I got 104 days left, not even short. I'm so fucking scared I'm walking point so I have some control. I can get off 18 shots in 3 seconds before I reload. If somebody's gonna fuck up, let it be me. A guy who got himself a Million Dollar wound gave me

A lucky charm.

his Ace of Spades. I've got it in my pocket. It's a little dog-eared by now, but it kept him safe, well, safe enough. Lost three fingers on his left hand, what the hell, he's right-handed. Maybe his card will keep me safe. I need some boonie magic bad" (interview with Randy Cribbs Jan 2008). This attitude affected numbers of grunts. Herr describes talking with a man worried about his friend. "So when he told me that he saw ghosts whenever they went on night patrol I didn't laugh," But I got really worried when he said he saw his own ghost, but it was okay since his ghost was behind him. "'It's when he goes and moves up in front that you're livin' in a world of hurt'" (252).

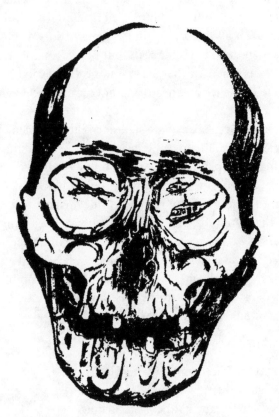

Cartoon depicting Ho Chi Minh.

X-RAY (X)

"The Vietnam War was a limited war, with limited objectives,
prosecuted by limited means, with limited public support.
Therefore, it was destined to be (and was) a long war,
a war so long that public support waned and political decisions
by Congress terminated our involvement, resulting in a victory
by the North Vietnamese Communists."
—General William Westmoreland

○ *Xenon Light.* Mounted on tanks. It has a 75-million candlepower, white and infrared. "In an emergency, its power can be doubled for short periods of time" (Zumbro 247).

○ *Xenophobia.* Fear of strangers.

○ *X-ray.* It wasn't only the Americans who needed to laugh. Herr reports a joke from the VC. "Once after an ambush that killed a lot of Americans, they [the VC] covered the field with copies of a photograph that showed one more young, dead American, with the punch line mimeographed on the back, 'Your X-rays have just come back from the lab and we think we know what your problem is'" (35).

Effects of Defoliants.

*Picture of Danny Phillips
during the conflict.*

*Picture of Danny Phillips in
dress uniform.*

YANKEE (Y)

> "Today, American can regain the sense of
> pride that existed before Vietnam.
> But it cannot be achieved by refighting a war that is
> finished. . . . These events, tragic as they are, portend neither the
> end of the world nor of America's leadership in the world."
> President Gerald Ford (May 7, 1965)

◦ ***Ya get what ya need.*** Taken from a Rolling Stones' song. "When something really bad goes down, I always ask myself, 'Why me?' The answer usually comes—but at its own speed and in its own time" (Anthony 57).

◦ ***Yards.*** Affectionate term for Montagnards. These mountain people were helpful to the United States' forces, especially LRRPs. Yards often gave them a special bracelet as a sign of friendship.

◦ ***Yes, sir.*** You learn it right away. You keep saying it. War correspondent Herr reported that soldiers and Marines didn't know what to call reporters. "They didn't always know what to think about you or what to say to you, they'd sometimes call you 'Sir' until you had to beg them to stop, they'd sense the insanity of your position as terrified volunteer-reporter and it would seize them with the giggles and even respect" (206).

◦ ***Your dick falls off and you step on it.*** That's when you really feel stupid.

◦ ***You're not alone.*** War is a lonesome time. You can feel isolated, but everybody around you feels the same: scared.

◦ ***You're your own best friend.*** Another "take care of yourself." Be proud of yourself, and others will treat you with respect.

Soldier in muddy hole—perhaps tunnel exit.

ZULU (Z)

"I see the light at the end of the tunnel."
—Walt Rostow, National Security Advisor (December 1967)

◦ *Zap list.* Crude, cruel term used by some for lists of war dead.

◦ *Zapped.* Killed. Wasted.

◦ *Zip.* A Vietnamese woman; a slut (Dickson 296).

◦ *Zippo.* Zippo lighters were made in the US and some were etched with military insignia there. Every grunt had one; if it was lost, stolen, or sent as a gift, it could be replaced at a PX for $1.80. Many Zippos were hand-decorated with names or a slogan or a picture or a peace sign. "And in every unit were a few individuals dubbed the 'Zippo squad,' who liked to burn villages to the ground whether the combat situation dictated such" (Anderson *The Grunts* 204). Zippo became one more thing to mark and show thoughts: etchings of peace signs, marijuana leaves, slogans, rock lyrics, combat slang, antiwar mottos, and social protest. All on what became an instrument of destruction. "Zippo" would never be the same.

◦ *Zippo raids or jobs.* Burning villages. Zippo lighters were used, and if Ronsons instead, it was still a Zippo.

Zippo Raid. The usual end of search and destroy mission.

Zippo Raid
by Randy Cribbs

Palms dried
And thatched, woven
On thin bamboo pillars;
No match for
That chromed menace.
Flick of a thumb
And huts disappear
In a brief
Spiral of smoke;
Never sure,
Enemy or friend,
But a village put to its end.

Hut to hut,
Giants dizzy with that strange
Mixture of power and sadness
Trod over small gardens,
Then gone,
Leaving behind the heats wavering
Décor and bewilderment,
Standing quietly, unmoving, alone. (95)

◦ *Zulu report.* A casualty report.

◦ *Zulu time.* Military time. A 24-hour clock, e.g. 1400 hours = 2 PM.

Zippo Lighters, one with the Ace of Spades on it.

APPENDIX A
(American's Longest War (before Afghanistan)

PHASE ONE (1950-1954): THE DOMINO THEORY

By the end of 1950, US has shelled out $133 million in aid to French-controlled region of Indochina, although French are suspicious of our motives. By 1952, US is paying for ⅓ the cost of the war against Ho Chi Minh, rebel leader of Vietnam (who has repeatedly asked for US help for independence against the French, comparing his war to our War of Independence). By 1953, US spent $400 million: new president Eisenhower thinks we have no choice but to defend the region ("Domino Theory" –if one country goes communist, another will, and then another . . .). The French are defeated in battle of Dien Bien Phu; Vietnam partitioned into North and South Vietnam along 17th parallel; free elections scheduled for 1956; cease-fires established in Laos and Cambodia.

(Total aid from the United States to the French from 1950-1954: $2.6 billion.)

PHASE TWO (1954-1961): BUILDING DEMOCRACY IN SOUTH VIETNAM

Late 1950s: 1,500 advisors

French aid to region stops: South Vietnam's economy in ruins because of fourteen years of war. New premier of South Vietnam is the unpopular Diem: US stops several coups to unseat him. American advisors are in South Vietnam trying to build a democracy that will vote against Ho Chi Minh. The strength of Ho Chi Minh leads US to block scheduled elections in 1956 that would have reunified the country under one leader. The United States believes a united Vietnam will become a communist country. Diem makes a crucial mistake in abolishing local elections in South Vietnam that would have named village and provincial officials. Instead he wanted to appoint his own officials that would be loyal to him. The NLF (National Liberation Front) in North Vietnam vows to overthrow Diem, a dictator.

PHASE THREE (1961-1963): TESTING OUR DETERMINATION: LIMITED INVOLVEMENT

Late 1961: 8,000 advisors
Late 1962: 9,000 advisors

By 1961, South Vietnam is 5th on a list of countries receiving economic aid from the United States. Military advisors include engineers, troops, and medical personnel. In the fall of 1961, President Kennedy is unwilling to commit troops to stop what he saw as a civil disturbance. When the Viet Cong step up attacks in South Vietnam, and Diem wants more aid to build an army in South Vietnam: advisor to Kennedy, Walt Rostow, visits, warns situation is serious.

By late 1962, there are 9,000 advisors flying combat missions and dropping South Vietnamese troops into battle. First hints of problems to come: can't tell the Vietcong (South Vietnamese communist guerillas) from civilians; everyone in South Vietnam is a target to Vietcong.

PHASE FOUR (1963-1965): OPEN-ENDED COMMITMENT

Mid 1964: 23,300 advisors
December 1965: 184,000 troops

Diem and his brother are murdered; three weeks later, JFK is assassinated. Vietnam becomes huge problem for new president Johnson because JFK reacted to crises instead of planning long-term strategies. Johnson moves away from Kennedy's limited response by July 1965. Kennedy's advisors stay with Johnson. Major event: Gulf of Tonkin incident, April 7, 1964. US ship bombed off the coast of North Vietnam in Haiphong Harbor. Johnson uses incident to win Congressional support for Gulf of Tonkin Resolution which allowed him to use "all necessary measures to repel any armed attacks against the forces of the United States and to prevent further aggression," in essence, a blank check to run the war. (The Senate voted in ten hours, 48-2; the House took 40 minutes, unanimous vote.) This marked major change: no longer defending South Vietnam but now responding to North Vietnamese provocations. Gen. William Westmoreland requested Marines. Gen. Maxwell Taylor warns US not prepared to fight guerilla war, that South Vietnamese would be all too happy to have the US fight their war for them. Johnson personally approves each air strike and target. He deploys 50,000 and promises another 50,000. New government in South Vietnam headed by Nguyen Ky and Nguyen Van Thieu.

PHASE FIVE (1965-1967): ESCALATION INTO GROUND WAR

December 1966: 385,000 troops

December 1967: 485,000 troops

US still has no strategy to win the war. Several assumptions are in the way. US assumed US equipment superiority mattered and US assumed its optimism mattered. By 1967, US dropped more bombs than in all of World War II. Cost of the war was $2 billion per month.

Contradiction: US wanted limited war (so near-by Communist countries larger than the United States were not threatened, but it also wanted a quick war (so critics at home wouldn't try to stop it).

Problems: (1) no strategic guidelines for use of American power, so military fought conventional war—without reference to jungles, limitations of South Vietnamese Army, the problems of resupply to troops half-way round the world, and restraints imposed by politicians; (2) bombing more palatable at home, but North Vietnamese responded by keeping bombed roads open and by using over 30,000 miles of tunnels built during other wars; (3) impact of weather on planning operations, weapons, armored vehicles, planes, helicopters, down to fatigues, boots, and equipment suitable for monsoons, fog-shielded targets, targets hidden in a triple canopy jungle.

(4) "Body count" eventually became only way to measure success because the US was not taking and holding territory. After the war, experts think the body count was inflated as much as 30%; (5) Hanoi (government of North Vietnam) showed no signs of weakening; (6) US split into "hawks" (Vietnam was a global struggle against Communism) and "doves" (who questioned the morality of war).

Oct 21, 1967: over 30,000 demonstrate at the Pentagon. Secretary of Defense Robert McNamara resigns.

PHASE SIX (1968): TET OFFENSIVE

December 1968: 536,000 troops

Jan 30, 1968: During the Tet offensive Vietcong assaults all major urban areas of South Vietnam, including assault on US embassy in South Vietnam; many Vietcong deaths but Vietcong come across as winners because they brought war to every place in South Vietnam at the same time. Tet includes battle for Hue and siege at Khe Sanh (Jan 20-Apr 14, 1968).

Shock in US over much-publicized statement: "We had to destroy the town in order to save it." (You can hear it in the documentary "Hearts and Minds".)

Sen. Eugene McCarthy challenges Johnson in Democratic primary. Sen. Robert Kennedy announces his candidacy for president; administration blames hostile news media, not realizing its own contribution to public's misunderstanding. US unduly optimistic, deliberately deceptive in assessments of war.

Formal peace talks begin in Paris, May 13, 1968: first order of business was to decide what shape will the peace table take. (For real!) ARVN (Army of the Republic of South Vietnam) troops expanded but many desert, officers in short supply, soldiers not unhappy that Americans doing bulk of fighting.

March 1968: My Lai massacre during which 200+ South Vietnamese villagers are killed. Robert Kennedy assassinated; Johnson chooses not to run for re-election; Nixon wins presidential election.

PHASE SEVEN (1969-1973): FIGHTING TO WIN AN HONORABLE PEACE

December 1969: 475,000 troops

December 1971: 175,000 troops

New president Nixon says, "The true objective of this war is peace. It is a war for peace." 'Peace with honor" was the slogan. Any pull-out of American troops could not look like defeat; any pull-out had to leave South Vietnam independent with a reasonable chance to survive on its own.

North Vietnam escalates war: Nixon begins policy called "Vietnamization," the gradual take-over of the war by the South Vietnamese army. By 1970, it had become one of the largest, best-equipped armies in the world.

"Incursion" into (invasion of) Cambodia, April 30, 1970: major demonstrations on college campuses such as Jackson State (MS) and Kent State (OH); 100,000 protestors come to Washington in May.

Senate revokes Tonkin Gulf Resolution (see *Phase Four*); Nixon continues to withdraw troops; by the end of 1971, only 175,000 troops are left—75,000 were combat troops. Summer of 1971, 71% of the American public believe the US has made a mistake by sending troops to Vietnam; 58% said the war was "immoral."

Secretary of State Kissinger starts secret peace talks with North Vietnam.

March 1972: North Vietnam invades South Vietnam. Nixon orders bombing of Haiphong Harbor and Hanoi and a naval blockade of North Vietnam. US agrees to let North Vietnamese remain in South Vietnam and to accept a tripartite election: Saigon government, Vietcong and neutralists. In October, South Vietnamese (Saigon government) leader Thieu rejects this plan. Nixon delivers more than $1 billion dollars in military hardware to Thieu, making the South Vietnamese Army the 4th largest air force in the world.

Christmas, 1972: over twelve days, Nixon drops more bombs on North Vietnam than had been dropped from 1969-1971. Peace negotiations start with a negotiated settlement imposed on South Vietnam.

PHASE EIGHT (1973 TO PRESENT): POST-WAR

November 1973: War Powers Act. President required to notify Congress within 48 hours of deployment of American troops; must withdraw them within 60 days unless Congress okays the use of force.

Fall 1974: balance of power shifts to North Vietnam. December, North Vietnam invades South; US fails to respond. Congress authorizes $33 million to evacuate Americans and for humanitarian purposes. By 1975, South Vietnam has collapsed. Saigon renamed Ho Chi Minh City.

Americans fighting to take hill.

APPENDIX B

THE VIETNAM MEMORIAL, WASHINGTON, D.C.

"THE WALL"
Dedicated November 13, 1982

The idea for a Vietnam Memorial was conceived by Jan Scruggs in 1977 while doing graduate research at American University on the psychological problems facing many fellow Vietnam veterans. Scruggs had served in the 199th Light Infantry Brigade from 1969—1970; he was wounded and earned a medal for gallantry. He wrote a proposal for a Vietnam Memorial and gave it to the Senate. When Scruggs had heard nothing for two years, he decided to build it with private funds. After six weeks, he had collected $144.50. After national publicity, veterans eventually raised $8.4 million. Scruggs envisioned the memorial near the Mall, not near Arlington National Cemetery. Because the Vietnam War produced no major battle to

Massachusetts vigil society gather at the wall.

commemorate, nor did it have a hero who emerged from the war, Scruggs saw the memorial as a list of names of those who died in an undeclared war.

He sought a place between the Washington Monument and Lincoln Memorial and said no government money would be needed. The Senate overwhelming approved the location, an empty grassy spot exactly where

Scruggs wanted it. President Jimmy Carter signed the bill in July, 1980. The next step was the design. Without government involvement, Scruggs put out a call for submissions, assembled a group to judge them, and watched as over 1400 designs came from every part of the country, from veterans, artists, housewives, and civilians. The submissions were given to the group of judges anonymously. Designs were to contain the names of the dead and to be neutral about the results of the Vietnam War or anything else political. Scruggs saw the memorial as one way to assuage the millions who needed a positive sign that their sacrifices would never be forgotten.

No one needed to see the memorial built more than Lt. Lewis Puller, Jr., a Marine so severely wounded that he was moments from death that October 11, 1968 when medevaced to the naval hospital in Da Nang (187). A booby-trapped howitzer (a round from a short cannon) took away fingers and a thumb, but the first man to get to him said, "Pray, Lieutenant, for God's sake, pray" (186). Puller didn't know then that he'd also lost his right leg at the torso and was left with a six-inch stump at his thigh where his left leg had been; he'd also lost huge portions of his flesh and muscles. He was not expected to survive. But once he was medevaced to the States *via* a hospital in Japan to face many major and reconstructive surgeries and to begin years of physical therapies, he was comforted by his wife, Toddy, and captivated by their new baby, Lewis III (Lewpy) —Toddy had been seven months pregnant when Puller was nearly killed.

Now home, Puller watched college kids hold vigils against the war, Nixon's call for the silent majority to make their voices heard, demonstrations in Washington, an incursion into Cambodia in 1970, and organized protests on college and universities (291). "What bothered me the most, however, was the shift in the mood of the country. Increasingly the war seemed to be regarded by more and more Americans as just not worth fighting, and if that were so, I had lost my legs and several good friends for nothing" (291-292).

Years later after making remarkable progress but preferring a wheel chair to any prostheses the VA could design, Puller graduated from law school and in 1978 was strong enough to run for a congressional seat from Virginia (he lost). When he heard about Jan Scruggs and that a design for a memorial to Vietnam veterans had been selected, he briefly considered volunteering in the project but he was "too incapacitated" (401) by alcohol to make a decision. "Nevertheless, in moments of lucidity I realized that something important was taking place for all of us who had served, and as if it were a lifeline thrown a drowning man, I was buoyed by the effort that others were making on my behalf" (401).

Since 1981 Puller had "followed with keen interest the vicissitudes of the Vietnam Veterans Memorial. On a positive side, funding for the memorial topped eight million dollars, the majority of which came in individual contributions of ten dollars or less. It appeared to me that the wherewithal was in place to build the memorial, and I was most proud that the government that had shattered the lives of so many of us had not been called upon to contribute one red cent. We had gone to war to do our country's bidding, to offer up our lives and limbs without thought of personal reward. But we had come home to indifference and rejection on the part of the government that demanded of us so much, and I thought it particularly fitting that it now be excluded from taking any credit for such a powerful symbol of the healing process. I was also pleased to learn that in conjunction with the expected completion date of the memorial, November 1982, a national salute to Vietnam veterans would be held. Even if such an event was coming ten or fifteen years too late, it would at least help validate the service we had given" (423-424). Puller couldn't have anticipated the reaction to the chosen design.

The selected design was announced in 1981. It was submitted by Maya Lin, a twenty-year old born in the United States to Chinese immigrants. She was an undergraduate at Yale. Upon first seeing the design, some called it "a black gash" or a "black gash of shame" or a "tombstone." Why did it look like a V—for Vietnam? Did it mean we won or lost? Why was it black when so many memorials near it were white? Why did it have no statues? No famous quotations? No height. No columns. "Many of those who disputed the winning design did so on the grounds that the completed memorial would fail to evoke healing because it was not, in effect, a *traditional* monument" (Beattie 44). If the chosen design would evoke "a reconciliation of the grievous divisions wrought by the war"—part of the charge given to those who planned to submit a design for the memorial (Beattie 44), many couldn't see how. "To many interpreters the names . . . [have] the potential to redirect the meaning of the memorial away from unity toward sorrow and loss" (Beattie 45) . . . . The public reactions are "The waste," "Such a waste," "Oh God, the waste," (John Lang qtd. in Beattie 45). But Maya Lin, however, in moving away from the traditional to "privileges of names" (Beattie 46) allowed for private reactions. Touch a name on the smooth, shiny black granite, slide your fingers down a row of names, rub in paper that precious name, leave a personal tribute—a letter, a rose, a flag, a teddy bear, a photograph, a boot.

Names on a plain, black wall. Despite opposition, the project went forward, and Maya Lin's design—the design that memorialized no war, that offered no important battle, and that had no conquering hero took shape.

1) 140 polished black granite panels in the shape of a chevron; black granite to reflect your image to make you a part of the wall of names:

Λ

West Side   East Side
May 1968-1975   1959-May 1968

2) West points to the Lincoln Memorial; east points to the Washington Monument.
3) Each panel holds engraved names (middle initial, not middle name) of those KIA or MIA.
4) Each name (one-half of an inch high) is separated from another by O.
5) Names listed in alphabetical order consecutively over time.
6) When a visitor comes to a name not following the previous alphabetically, this indicates a new day in the war.

Example: last name SANDERS O followed by last name HENRY O are not in alphabetical order; so SANDERS O marks the end of one day of death in the war; HENRY O then, begins a new day of death in the war.

7) The total length is 500 feet long.
8) The memorial begins eight inches high at each end; it rises to ten feet at the center.
9) The names of the first and last killed have a prominent place: "The names etched in the stone begin at the vertex . . . with the name of the first casualty, Dale R. Buis, in 1959, and run east 'in the order taken from us.' The list resumes at the low, west end of the Wall, and runs to 1975, where the last casualty, Richard Vande Geer [*died May 15, 1975 in the last combat of the Vietnam War which took place on the Mayaguez, an American ship commandeered by the Khymer Rouge after the fall of Saigon*] is listed, making the ten-foot high 'fold' in the Wall the place where the killing begins and ends" (Meyer 10).

(Note: the first actual casualty was US Air Force Technician Richard B. Fitzgibbon who died June 8, 1956; the Buis name was moved and in 1999, Fitzgibbon's name was engraved on the Wall as the first casualty.)

10) The architects, the officers of the Vietnam Veterans Memorial Fund, and the designer's name, Maya Lin, appear at the top of the Wall.

At the dedication of the memorial on Nov 13, 1982 there were 58,183 names on "The Wall," as it came to be called. One-third of the names on the Wall were draftees; there were eight female names; over one thousand names were marked with a † to indicate "MIA" status; after time, some were declared "KIA" so ◊ was put around the cross.

"A number of figures associated with the memorial's construction, including Ross Perot, who helped fund the design competition, objected to the final proposal. Perot's objections were partially met in Reagan's acceptance speech, in which he reinterpreted the memorial as a reflection of nearby traditional monuments. More specifically, those who were dissatisfied with the memorial were assuaged, to a degree, through a compromise in which a life-size bronze statue of three Vietnam War combat soldiers was installed near the memorial. Ironically, this addition re-invoked and refocused criticisms of memorial designs. Maya Lin, the designer of the Wall, called the statue 'trite,' and its sculpture, Frederick Hart, rejoined by calling the memorial 'contemptuous of life'" (Beattie 44-45). As part of the compromise, a flagstaff was installed with "the addition of a brief inscription to the memorial itself" (Beattie 45-46).

Dedicated on Veterans Day, 1993, another dimension added to the Lin/Hart "debate" was a statue "depicting a wounded combat GI attended by three female nurses, foregrounds the injured (male) body in a context of (female) healing. The realistic style and size of the bronze work parallels Hart's conception of an *appropriate* monument" (Beattie note #143, p. 169). The sculpture by Glenna Goodacre was the result of the efforts of an Army nurse, Diane Carlson Evans. RN, Vietnam 68-69. One of the nurses appears to be in prayer or waiting for a Medevac helicopter.

Three and a half million visitors come to the Vietnam Veterans Memorial "The Wall" each year. In their own way, they say "Welcome home."

Statue of three grunts installed near the wall.

One nurse comforts wounded soldier. The other (in back) looks skyward, perhaps in prayer, perhaps waiting for the Medevac to deliver more wounded.

ADDENDUM

"If you got there, you could hardly avoid the chubby old man stretching to reach for a name just off his fingertips, a woman with her eyes closed crouching with one finger on a name, two men hugging in front of a panel, a young soldier in full dress uniform saluting a panel, a ten-year-old boy sitting on a man's shoulders to get a rubbing of a name way high up. So much pain not just on the faces but evident from the teddy bears, the roses, the flags, the letters, the medals, and the photographs left each day, maybe left for someone you might have known. Was that chubby old man Mad Dog's Dad? The grieving woman Lucky's wife who bore his child long after he was dead? Your private demons pop up, you don't even know why you came, what made you believe anyone who told you that you had to do this, that it healed them, that the healing began after this pain ripped you loose from your moorings, names, and names, and names and I don't remember none of them" (part of a letter written to me by a vet who wishes to remain anonymous, 1974).

That remains the terrible irony of the Wall. In platoons, the soldiers went by nicknames based on a physical feature, where he was born, what MOS (job) he did, how he was regarded. Plus each soldier had a different number of days left, so that one soldier who pushed you into a bunker just in time might be "Red"—and that's all you know because he was three days from his Freedom Bird. "All our vets said they didn't remember any names" (Ann Olek, Vet Program 04/15/93).

Friends of the Vietnam Veterans Memorial pin.

"You can't view the Wall without becoming a piece of it. You are there in the past. There is no denying that fact. Our vets have been to hell and they survived. They took themselves back to the memories at the Wall; how will we ever be able to thank them for what they did for us" (Dora Perada, Vet Program at the Wall, 1993).

"As haunting as the memorial is, when you get there, you can hardly avoid the hawkers selling deluxe brass P.O.W. bracelets (only $7.95) and T-shirts ($16.95) and buttons ($1) and bumper stickers ($3) and military patches ($3) and books (any price) and mugs ($5) and tie clips ($4.95) and lighters (from $15.95) and post cards ($1) and posters (from $5 to $50) and belt buckles ($9.95) and dog tag key rings ($4.95)and an aircraft made out of beer cans ($20) and videotapes of combat ($29.95) and license plate frames ($9.95). All sold by guys adorned with buttons ('POW/MIA WANTED DEAD OR ALIVE'; *'POWS NEVER HAVE A NICE DAY'*; 'I GUESS YOU HAD TO BE THERE'; *'REMEMBER VIETNAM VETS'*), infantry patches, ribbons, medals on their T-Shirts ('WAR IS A 24-HOUR JOB') or camouflage shirts, faces older than their years. Flags everywhere, for sale, of course. Had those dudes really been to the 'Nam or were they just jerking everybody around?" (Part of a letter written to me by a vet who wishes to remain anonymous, 1974). All of these hawkers are keeping alive the memories of those who may remain MIAs or POWs. "Rolling Thunder" also helps keep those memories alive.

Rolling Thunder 2005. Maybe 200,000 Harleys.

Rolling Thunder is an annual Memorial Day parade in Washington, DC to remind the United States that it can leave no one behind. The parade for POWs and MIAs draws bikers from nearly every state. The route begins at the Pentagon and ends at the Vietnam Memorial. As many as 400,000 bikers clog up the capital to remind the nation of POWs and MIAs that still exist.

"Some had ridden across the US in a pilgrimage to 'The Wall,' the name given to the stark yet moving monument that records the names of the 58,000 US servicemen who died in Vietnam" (Anne Davies, <www.theage.com> 5/30/97). The ponytails might have greyed, and they're not as lithe as they were 40 years ago, but for the Harley-riding Vietnam veterans who descended on Washington for Memorial Day, it's a chance to remember and reflect on the war that changed their generation.

"An estimated 400,000 motorcyclists swarmed the capital at the weekend for the 20th Rolling Thunder event. Many were veterans sporting leather vests advertising their platoon, their tour of duty, fallen comrades—and their devotion to their Harley-Davidson. They are sometimes called 'Nam Knights,' even with their middle-aged potbellies" (Davies). In a VVA Chapter in SW Virginia, a company usually loans them a flatbed truck to haul their motorcycles. Sometimes you think you're in a convoy of pick-up trucks full of motorcycles, motorcycles riding side-by-side, no helmets, and American flags in stickers, license plate holders, bandanas, painted on trucks, and American flags of all sizes hanging from houses and businesses along the route.

Veterans History Project

"I urge all Americans to participate in the Veterans History project. Capturing stories of those who served in uniform in their own words will provide the inspiration future generations need when it is their turn to defend the nation Abraham Lincoln once called, 'the last best hope on earth'" (Anthony Principi, Secretary of Veterans Affairs).

"It is in the nation's best interest to collect . . . oral histories of American war veterans so that . . . Americans will always remember those who served in war and may learn first-hand of the heroics, tediousness, horrors, and triumphs of war" (Public Law 106-380).

Contact one of our Official Partners in your state. If there is an organization or institution that is an Official Partner of the Veterans History Project in your state, you can contact them and volunteer to assist them in the creation of their oral history project and collection. A list of our Official Partners is available on our website at <www.loc. gov/folklife/vets/partners/partners.html>.

Contact Information

Veterans History Project   Telephone: (202) 707-4916
American Folklife Center   Fax: (202) 252-2046
Library of Congress web: www.loc.gov/folklife/vets
101 Independence Ave, SE   message line: 1-888-371-5848
Washington, DC 20540-4615   E-mail: vohp@loc.gov

The POW-MIA dinner table, black for sadness, empty plates for loss, and a vase for tears part of an exhibit held on Memorial Day 2011 in St Augustine, FL.

APPENDIX C

"Of the 2,709,918 Americans who served in Vietnam, less then
850,000 are estimated to be alive today, with the youngest
American Vietnam veteran's age approximated to be 54 years old."

WHO IS A VIETNAM VET?

MYTHS SURROUND THE "who" who went to war. Average age of nineteen, mainly draftees, an abundance of minorities, uneducated, prone to suicide once home, homeless when they got home, divorced once or twice, constantly unemployed, suffering from PTSD or the effects of Agent Orange or alcohol or other drugs. Images of homeless vets in tatters crouched on a street corner begging for money, a bedraggled, whiskered man bent over and sobbing at the Wall—these myths are reinforced by books, magazine articles, pictures, and movies.

Who went? Volunteers made up two-thirds of the 9,087,000 military personnel who served during the Vietnam era. Of that number 2,709,918 served in uniform in Vietnam. Average age? Twenty-two. 97% were honorably discharged; 91% are glad they served their country; 74% would serve again. But that leads to another problem: What is the Vietnam era? Defining that has been a problem. "The Veterans' Improvements Act of 1996, Public Law (P.L.) 104-275, Section 505 enacted October 9, 1996" (Hanafin) changed the date of the Vietnam era into two dates depending on where the veteran served: (1) *Vietnam era vets* must have served in the Republic of Vietnam at any time between February 28, 1961 to May 7, 1975; (2) *Vietnam era vets* must have served at any time between August 5, 1964 to May 7, 1975. The legal status and the access to veterans' benefits impact a veteran who served at any time from 1961 to 1964. That veteran will now be a *Vietnam era vet* if he served within the Republic of Vietnam. This change allows for a longer period of time to be a Vietnam era vet (1961 to 1975) for those men who served in-country; this change allows for a shorter period of time to be a Vietnam era vet (1964 to 1975) for those men who served elsewhere (Hanafin).

Were they prone to suicide, homeless, divorced, unemployed or suffering from PTSD, alcohol or other drugs after they returned home? The following information refuting many of these myths comes from a document that has been circulating on line for months; the article, "Vietnam Facts *vs.* Fiction" presented by Bobbie G. Pedigo, former Commanding Officer of the 68th AHC and researched by Capt. Marshal Hanson, U.S.N.R. (Ret.). The Viet Cong did try to convince the bloods (black men) that they were fighting Whitey's war. According to his research, Vietnam veterans have done well. In their age group, Vietnam veterans have a lower unemployment rate than non-vets; their personal income exceeds non-Vietnam vets by 18%. A Veterans Administration Study concluded that drug usage in this age group is the same, vet or not. They are less likely to be in prison; only one-half of one percent of Vietnam vets have been jailed. According to Hanson's research, 85% have made a successful transition from military to civilian life (Pedigo 1-2).

The myth about suicide? Some vets did commit suicide, but not fifty to a hundred thousand. No. More like nine thousand. During the first five years after discharge, the Vietnam vet is 1.7 times more likely to commit suicide than the same age group of non-vets. After the five years, however, the rate is less than that of non-vets (Pedigo 3).

Another myth that will not go away concerns the number of black men who were killed in the war. Black fatalities (12%) represent the percentage of blacks in the United States at that time. 86% of the men who died were Caucasian. Approximately 70% of those killed in Vietnam were volunteers (Pedigo 3).

Hanson in his "Vietnam War Fact *vs.* Fiction" made two main points. One, the United States did not lose the war; two, "that a surprising high number of people who claim to have served there, in fact, DID NOT" (Pedigo 1). Some people are still convinced the United States lost a war it should have won. The United States did not lose the war. As one of my vets, Bobby Ward, said, *"Do you see the flag of Vietnam flying at the White House?"* Researcher Hanson needs no convincing: "How could we lose a war we had already stopped fighting? We fought to an agreed stalemate. The peace settlement was signed in Paris on 27 January 1973. It called for release of all US prisoners, withdrawal of US forces, limitation of both sides' forces inside South Vietnam and a commitment to peaceful reunification. The 140,000 evacuees in April 1975 during the fall of Saigon consisted almost entirely of civilians and Vietnamese military, NOT American military running for their lives" (Pedigo 5).

"THE WALL WITHIN"

Even CBS fell into the myth about vets and suicide. In an hour-long documentary, "The Wall Within," Dan Rather claimed without giving a source that "[p]ossibly as many as one hundred thousand vets had been driven to suicide over the war" (Burkett and Whitley 88).

This 1988 documentary, "The Wall Within" about Vietnam vets played to Americans who had "grown to believe about the Vietnam War and its veterans: They routinely committed war crimes. They came home from an immoral war traumatized, vilified, then pitied. Jobless, homeless, addicted, suicidal, they remain afflicted by inner conflicts, stranded on the fringes of society" (Burkett and Whitley 87).

The CBS documentary, "The Wall Within" was introduced by Walter Cronkite and available for $150. Dan Rather called the six vets with him "outcasts, broken spirits" (88) willing to tell their stories. These six men did not lie about being in service in uniform during the Vietnam War, but at least five of them grossly enhanced the experiences they described to Rather and the TV audience: assassinating Vietnamese under orders from the hush-hush "Phoenix Program"; forced into skinning 50 Vietnamese of all ages alive; traumatized by seeing a friend on the flight deck walk into a moving propeller. Burkett knew that war crimes had no statute of limitations, so why were two of the men telling of incidents they could be arrested for? Rather never gave his sources of information. Half of them said they were on "secret" missions or were highly-trained Special Forces. Secret missions and Special Ops (Operations) allowed men an excuse not to talk about what they did. It's a secret, you know? If I tell, someone will die. Whatever the reason, Burkett took it upon himself to determine if the so-called documentary were truth or fiction. He surprised himself by finding information about the six with phone calls and requests for military records under the FOI (Freedom of Information Act), something CBS fact-checkers failed to do. After reviewing the military records, Burkett concluded that only one of the six vets could be called a "true combat grunt. He was the recipient of the Purple Heart and the Combat Action Ribbon, which for Marines demonstrates at least 30 days under active fire" (Burkett and Whitley 91).

The vet who supposedly skinned people alive under orders as part of a covert ops served for three-and-a-half years but spent 300 days either AWOL or in the stockade; upon his return, he had been diagnosed as schizophrenic, not something that is war-related. But he does receive money from the government for PTSD (94-95). The SEAL who claimed he was 16 when he became a SEAL was an "internal communication repairman who went AWOL six times; the only special training he received was not training to become a SEAL, but training in motion picture operations" (92-94).

The vet who saw his friend walk into a propeller was on the Ticonderoga and part of a secret mission (96). But he was not listed as being on the flight deck when the vet said it happened—and access to a flight deck is strictly controlled. An incident that he described did occur, but at midnight, a time a repairman (the vet) was unlikely to be on the deck. Burkett reports that this man is receiving money from the government for PTSD disability for a story he heard happened (97). One of the men served his tour as a guard with a USMC helicopter unit instead of being a grunt "walking point." He received "no valorous combat decorations or Combat Action Ribbon" (91-92). The last of the six held a friend who died in his arms. The only man with the name the vet told Rather died in Vietnam a hundred miles from where the vet was stationed; the man's death in 1968 occurred months before Rather's vet arrived in country (92). All of the six, however, reported flashbacks, hostile behavior, drug or alcohol addictions, and PTSD.

So CBS shows us one type of Vietnam vet: exaggerating what happened or what they heard happened, relating horrifying incidents people expect to hear, showing their own pain and suffering, their ruined lives while sometimes making themselves appear important because they were on special or secret missions. Playing a victim of the war racked with PTSD, and in some cases profiting from it.

THE EFFECT OF MISCONCEPTIONS

Vietnam vet and long-time researcher in the National Archives, B.G. Burkett and Glenna Whitley, an award-winning investigative reporter, wrote *Stolen Valor* in 1998. Burkett saw first-hand what others thought about Vietnam vets when other professionals were surprised that he was both a professional (a stockbroker) and a Vietnam vet. "'You're kidding me,' [a long-time client of his] said, looking at me as if I had just confessed I had syphilis. Another said, 'Hell, I've dealt with you for years, and I never figured you were a Vietnam veteran.' I was confused. How was it supposed to show?" (42).

Then he knew how it was supposed to show—because of the public's misconceptions about Vietnam vets. "They were losers, bums, drug addicts, drunks, derelicts—societal offal who had come back from the war plagued by nightmares and flashbacks that left them with the potential to go berserk at any moment" (42). But from his own experience, he knew differently, and in trying to raise money for a Texas Vietnam Veterans Memorial, he saw what a challenge he faced. He had to ask for money to memorialize veterans stuck in an offensive stereotype, so if he were to be successful, he had to change the public's notion that the okay vet (as in not going berserk) or the surprise vet (as in—Gee, I never would have guessed) was not an "exception" (43)—that he was not an exception.

A series of setbacks in Burkett's fund-raising attempts gave him time to wonder if Vietnam vets *because of their experience in the war, [were] more likely than their peers who didn't go to Vietnam to suffer problems or commit crimes?"* (46) He knew many men had come home from the war able to function. Of course, some had problems, but those problems were not anything out of the ordinary. Divorce and alcoholism were not limited to Vietnam vets. But Burkett heard from others whenever a "Vietnam vet" was involved in a crime or accused of a crime. Bobby Ward, one of our vets, said if he were eighty and robbed a bank, the headlines would scream *Vietnam Vet Suspect in Robbery.*

VIETNAM ERA VETS VS. VIETNAM VETS VS. WANNABES

Another "who" is determined by definitions: an infantryman who fought in the bush, or crawled down into a tunnel with a knife and a rope, or carried out "search and destroy" missions, or a LRRP who spied, targeted, and killed? Or, engineers who built roads or kept them clear, who built or rebuilt bridges, who worked without weapons and were easy targets for snipers. They had one of the highest mortality rates of any other MOS. Vietnam vets? How about C.O.s? some of them going to war without a gun for religious or moral reasons. Vietnam vets? What about the eight people it took to keep one grunt in the field? Vietnam vets? The cooks on the base? The servers at Officers' nightclubs? The resupply guys? The chopper pilot who flew dead bodies to a Graves Registration Point? And nurses stationed in combat areas? USO employees who came to combat zones to make a homey place at a base camp? Then there were the Vietnam era vets who served in Germany in hospitals? Or chaplains of any religion who went where called. Somewhere around five million Americans served in the Vietnam War.

Nurse Lynda Van Devanter when she got home went to a Vietnam Veterans of American chapter meeting but was not welcomed. She was not considered a Vietnam vet because she was only a nurse. Now the hospital was under attack at times; there were serious and fatal injuries among the personnel. Vietnam vets? As Van Devanter explains, "There were only a few women in that room. They seemed lost. Some clustered together; others, like me, stood alone, not yet knowing anyone well enough to feel comfortable. When we moved outside to line up, I took a place near the front. However, one of the leaders approached me. 'This demonstration is only for vets,' he said apologetically.

"'I am a vet,' I said. 'I was in Pleiku and Qui Nhon.' . . .

"'Do you have a sign or something I can hold?' I asked.

"'Well,' he said uncomfortably, 'I . . . uh . . . don't think you're supposed to march.'

"'But, you told me it was for vets.'

"'It is,' he said. 'But you're not a vet.'

"'I don't understand.'

"'You don't look like a vet,' he said. 'If we have women marching, Nixon and the network news reporters might think we're swelling the ranks with nonvets'" (271-2).

And then there are the wannabes and virtual vets.

"In 1984 Connecticut representative Robert Sorensen assured everyone that—although he was opposed to a proposal to open each session of the legislature with the Pledge of Allegiance—he was patriotic. Sorensen's proof? 'My patriotism should not be questioned by anyone because when it was necessary, and when my country called me into service, I fought in Vietnam,' the thirty-two-year-old Sorensen said on the floor of the state house." Forced by his opponent, he admitted to fellow legislators that he had lied (Burkett and Whitley 173).

He then had the *chutzpah* to claim he really *was* a Vietnam vet because he watched television. "'For the first time ever, the American public had before them a war in their living rooms,' he said. 'Every single person in this United States fought in that war in Vietnam. We were all a part of that war in Vietnam because of what was coming to us, what we were feeling, what we were seeing. We all felt the pain. We all felt the anguish that those people felt. So in a sense a part of us was there with every single person that fought there. So in a sense I was there'" (Burkett and Whitley 173).

Unfortunately, his explanation was not unique.

Five million out of a population of 200,000 million served. Can you pick those millions out? That's the worst problem. Of course you can't pick them out. Not by their t-shirts, their caps, their medals, their patches, or wounds. There are wannabes out there. Most books say that 80% of those you meet that claim to be a Vietnam vet is a wannabe. They claim to be P.O.W.s. They share the incident that won them a silver star. They go to the Wall and find the location of friends, leave tokens, or letters, or flags, or a can of peaches. Vietnam Veterans of America doesn't check up on who wants to be a member. Wannabes can see dozens of movies, read dozens of "I Fought in the War" books, read history books, and glossaries so they can talk the talk. They pass.

Why does anyone claim to be part of an unpopular war? To be seen as someone who answered the call of his country? To be seen as someone who endured the spitting of peaceniks? To be called "baby killer"? Why? Why when doing so, they take money and resources earned by others: VA medical care, money for incapacitating injuries, money for retraining, lower rates for mortgages?

A wannabe is viewed as a hero or a villain. It depends on the reaction he wants. He can claim to have survived a stretch of time at the Hanoi Hilton, telling others' stories as his own or making up his own. He must be a John Wayne, but John Wayne didn't lie.

To sum it all up, listen to Charles Anderson, in *Vietnam: The Other War*, explain the behavior of Vietnam era soldiers:

"For those who, after their return to the States, felt the need to present themselves as something they were not, there was a real advantage to serving in units like 3d MPs. There was built into each man's assignment to the rear the means of covering up not only that assignment but also all the embarrassing reordering of values and the frantic searching for excuses it had provoked. At the end of their tours these warriors far from the war could go back to the States and say they were in Vietnam during the war. That statement would, of course, be technically true, but not completely true. No civilian listener would think to ask if the veteran had been in the field or the rear, since those who served in either area wore the same uniforms and in most cases the same campaign ribbons. The veteran would be assumed to have faced and survived an extraordinarily demanding experience. Veterans of this type could, in effect, carry out a cover-up of a cover-up. By declining to explain certain facts about their Vietnam experiences, they could conceal their earlier concealment of their loss of resolve to face danger head-on.

"Such veterans could thereafter claim to be tested combat veterans without ever having faced the test of combat they once sought, and they could then receive as much attention, respect, or even awe, as their unknowing listeners were willing to pay them. They were then forever protected from anyone questioning their courage or their manhood or whatever it was they valued so highly as to put themselves through that whole elaborate charade" (41-2).

VETS TODAY

Many vets today both American and Vietnamese visit the Wall. Morley Safer, in an interview with Bui Tin, Colonel in the People's Army of Vietnam, is surprised to learn that the Colonel has been to the Wall. "I [Morley Safer,] ask him if he has heard or read about the Vietnam Memorial in Washington, DC.

"'Yes, yes, I have been to it . . . also the memorial in New York.'

"I am jolted by this piece of information. I wonder what those veterans who still visit the wall in their old Vietnam fatigues would have done, or thought, had they known that the squat man in the beret near them was possibly responsible for the presence of some of those fifty-eight thousand names on the wall.

"'It is very important, the wall,' [the Colonel continues]. 'All the memorials. You must remember all those young men . . . . You must also remember the kind of bravery those young men had. They may not have had much understanding of the aims of that war. But the sacrifice, so much sacrifice, must not be forgotten. The spirit of young people must not be forgotten'" (Safer 39-40).

In a similar manner many American Vietnam Vets return to Vietnam. They remembered the beauty of the country. "A group of American veterans, from an outfit called 'Vets with a Mission,' are in Ho Chi Minh City [formerly Saigon]. They have been touring the country, more as an attempt to heal themselves than out of any curiosity about Vietnam" (Safer 68-69). In 1988 Vets with a Mission supported the opening of a health clinic in Vietnam. See the picture below.

VETS with a mission support a health clinic in Vietnam 1988.

Later in an interview with Bill Baldwin, a former Marine, Safer learns why Baldwin returned to Vietnam. "'I think all veterans are drawn back here . . . . Everybody has a sense of unfinished business. I've longed for Vietnam ever since I came home. I've longed for it. I've dreamed about it. I think when I go home, the chapter will be over'" (Safer 76).

Van Le, a North Vietnamese, wrote the following poem about American GIs returning to Vietnam:

> There's an American soldier
> Who returns to northern Cu Chi
> He bends his back to the tunnels
> What does he see? What does he think?
>
> There's a Vietnamese hero
> Now a grandfather.
> He asks the American to share wine
> Outside the tunnel.
>
> Each man is silent
> As he looks into the other's eyes.
> Something is rising like a deep pain.
>
> The war was terrible
> All that time past.
> The dead lost their bodies
> The living lost their homes
>
> How many American soldiers
> Died in this land?
> How many Vietnamese
> Lied buried under trees and grass?
>
> The pain still lingers.
> Why should we remember it?
> We are old, our era past.
> Our mistakes belong to bygone days.
>
> Now the wineglass joins friends in peace
> The old men lift their glasses.
> Tears run down their cheeks. (Safer 250-251)

*Some of the weapons used in war from an exhibit held on
Memorial Day 2011 in St Augustine, FL.*

*The Travelling Vietnam Memorial Wall, from an exhibit held on
Memorial Day 2011 in St Augustine, FL.*

APPENDIX D

THE FOLLOWING PROVIDES a context for the Vietnam War. Below are the major wars in which the United States participated. The dates range from 1775, the beginning of the Revolutionary War to the end of the Vietnam War (May 15, 1975, when the last serviceman left the country). Some figures are not known, such as Confederate casualties during the Civil War. Military personnel killed in the Vietnam War changes when newly-discovered evidence is found. The format of this information is the writer's; Ms. Fischer in no way is at fault for any inaccuracies. The website at the end will list casualties by branch of service as well as the number serving by branch.

HANNAH FISCHER, INFORMATION RESEARCH SPECIALIST, KNOWLEDGE SERVICES GROUP

Updated July 13, 2005
Principal Wars in Which the United States Participated
from 1775-1975

WAR & DATE	# SERVING	DEATHS	NON-FATAL
Revolutionary War (1775-1783}	———	4,435	6,188
War of 1812 (1812-1815)	286,730	2,260	4,505
Mexican War (1846-1868)	78,718	13,283	4,152
Civil War, Union (1861-1865)	2,213,363	364,511	281,881
Spanish-American War (1898)	306,760	2,446	1,662
World War I (1917-1918)	4,734,991	116,516	204,002
World War II (1941-1946)	16,112,566	405,399	671,846
Korean War (1950-1953)	5,720,000	36,574	103,284
Vietnam Conflict (1964-1973)	8,744,000	58,209	153,303

Source: <*http://web1.whs.osd.mil/mmid/casualty/WCPRINCIPAL.pdf*>

Vietnam Conflict Only: Casualty Type	Total	Army	Air Force	Marines	Navy
Killed in Action (KIA)	40,934	27,047	1,080	11,501	1,304
Died of Wounds	5,289	3,604	51	1,482	152
Missing In Action (MIA)—Declared Dead	1,085	261	589	98	137
Captured—Declared Dead	116	45	25	10	36
Total Hostile Deaths	47,424	30,957	1,745	13,091	1,631
Missing—Presumed Dead	123	118	0	3	2
Other Deaths	10,662	7,143	841	1,746	932
Total Non-Hostile Deaths	10,785	7,261	841	1,749	934
Total In-Theater Deaths	58,209	38,218	2,586	14,840	2,565
KIA No Remains	622	181	221	123	97
MIA Declared Dead—No Remains	737	216	366	75	80
Captured—Declared Dead—No Remains	53	32	7	4	10
Non-Hostile Missing—Presumed Dead No Remains	97	92	3	2	0
Non-Hostile Other Deaths—No Remains	336	70	30	37	199
Total—No Remains	1,845	591	624	242	388
Wounded—Not Mortal	153,303	96,802	931	51,392	4,178
Number Serving Worldwide (B)	8,744,000	4,368,000	1,740,000	794,000	1,842,000
Number Serving SE Asia (B)	3,403,000	2,276,000	385,000	513,000	229,000
Number Serving S Vietnam (B)	2,594,000	1,736,000	293,000	391,000	174,000

Source: <http://web1.whs.osd.mil/mmid/CASUALTY/vietnam.pdf>. Prepared by Washington Headquarters Services, Directorate for Information Operations and Reports.

a. **Inclusive dates are November 1, 1955, to May 15, 1975.** Casualty dates after the end date represent service members who were wounded during the period and subsequently died as a result of those wounds and those service members who were involved in an incident during the period and were later declared dead.
b. **Estimated figures.** The National Archives and Records Administration (NARA) has published statistics derived from Southeast Asia. The National Archives and Records Administration (NARA) has published statistics derived from its Southeast Asia Combat Area Casualties Current File. This includes tables on Vietnam casualty data by branch of service, race, religion, state, and other categories at <http://www.archives.gov/research_room/ research_topics/vietnam_war_casualty_lists/statistics.html>.

The Women in Military Service to America Memorial (WIMSA) presents casualty data on women in principal wars as researched by its historian's office at <**http://www.womensmemorial.org/historyandcollections/history/ lrnmreqacasualty.html**>.

A nurse checking the medical chart of an injured marine.

Shadow box created by Margaret Brown, entitled "The Fog of War."

APPENDIX E

MIA Facts Site
SSC Report
Private Efforts Section, Part 2
1 July 1991
(From the Senate Select Committee on POW/MIAs)
<www.miafact.org/money.htm>

"DOG TAG" REPORTS

"Over the past decade one type of report has been received most often by the Defense Intelligence Agency's Special Office for POW/MIAs. These accounts are referred to as 'dog tag' reports. Since mid-1982, over 6,300 of these reports have been received and more arrive daily.

"In most dog tag reports a person or persons—many of them residents of Vietnam—claim to possess the remains of one or more Americans. As proof they offer data copied from military identification tags (dog tags), tracings or photographs of dog tags, authentic dog tags or other identification documents. More than 5,100 US military men have been named in these reports. Of these, 91 percent served in the United States armed forces, but were not casualties of the Vietnam war. Another six percent were killed, but their bodies were recovered, identified and returned to the US for burial. Thus, it is impossible that their remains are held by the people claiming to have them. Only three percent of the dog tag reports name a man who is missing, suggesting that his remains or personal effects have been recovered from battlefields or crash sites. However, the evidence indicates it is unlikely that these items were recovered by private citizens.

"In many cases several different people claim to have the remains and/or personal effects of each of the named men. Frequently, sources profess to have recovered the same items on a different date or at a different location. This indicates that the people did not obtain their data by recovering items from battlefields or crash sites. For instance, two of the men whose remains and dog tags several persons claim to have found, are in fact former POWs who returned alive—their dog tags had been kept by their captors.

"Further, throughout the war the communists enforced a policy to find and bury Americans killed in action and to send to central authorities a report of the burial site along with the personal effects and identification taken from the body. They continually stressed that this was important to the 'political struggle.' Thus, the governments of Vietnam and Laos should have knowledge of the missing men whose names have appeared in dog tag reports.

"Often there are tragic aspects to the dog tag reports. Many of the sources have been led to believe that possession of American remains will assist in their resettlement in the US. This has prompted some people to pay for the dog tag data. In fact, the US provides no rewards or assistance for POW/MIA information.

"Considering the policy and practices of the Indochinese governments to collect material on US war dead, coupled with the patterns in the dog tag reporting, the evidence indicates that the majority of reports reflect information and personal effects recovered by Vietnamese forces, not private citizens. Years of investigation and analysis have shown that the dog tag reports have been instigated by elements of Vietnam's government in an effort to influence and exploit the POW/MIA issue. Nevertheless, each report is carefully analyzed to determine its validity."

The full report is available at <http://1cweb2.loc.gov/frd/pow/senate_home/pdf/report_S.pdf>

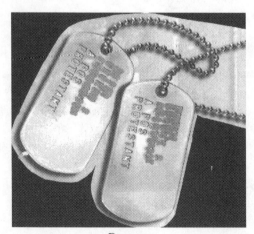

Dogtags.

WORKS CONSULTED

. . . "Bill Clinton and the Draft." *Roanoke Times,* 21 September 1992, A10.

. . . *Charlie Ration Cookbook.* Avery Island, LA: McIlhenny Co., 1966.

. . . "C. Religious Discipline and Concepts Affecting Behavior. *<http://www.
sacred-texts.com/asia/rsv/rsv/16.html>.*

. . . "How to Make Napalm." *<http://howany.com/how-to-make-napalm>.*

. . . "Jungle Rations and Delivery Systems especially by Radio Guided Parafoils.
<http://www.junglesnafus.com/chapter17.html>.

. . . "List of United States Army MOS." *<http://absoluteastronomy.com/topics/
List_of_United_States_Army_MOS>.*

. . . "Missing Americans in Indochina." *Roanoke Times,* 29 January 1994, A4
from AP dispatch.

. . . *US Army Survival Manual.* NY: Barnes and Noble, 1992.

. . . "USO® Until Everyone Comes Home®." *<http://www.uso.org/other-services.
aspx 2011>.*

. . . "Vietnam: America's Conflict." 4 DVD set. NP: Mill Creek Entertainment,
1969.

. . . "Vietnam: Endless War." *Monthly Review* 20 (April 1969): 1-11.

. . . *Vietnam War Diary.* NY: Military Press, 1990.

. . . "Viper's Vietnam Veterans Pages, Military Wannabe's [sic], Fake's [sic], and
Fraud's [sic]." *<http://vietnam-veterans.us/wannabes>.*

Ackerman, Diane. *An Alchemy of Mind.* NY: Scribner, 2004.

Anderson, Charles. *The Grunts.* NY: Berkeley Books, 1976.

—*Vietnam: The Other War.* N Y: Random House, 1990.

Anzenberger, Joseph Jr., ed. *Combat Art of the Vietnam War.* Jefferson, NC: McFarland and Co., 1986.

Anthony, Tony. *Life is War But You Can Win.* Wayne, PA: Morgin Press, 1994.

Beattie, Keith. *The Scar that Binds: American Culture and the Vietnam War.* NY: New York University Press, 1998.

Beltrone, Art and Lee, ed. *Vietnam Graffiti.* Charlottesville, VA: Howell Press, 2004.

Bender, David. *The Vietnam War: Opposing Viewpoints.* St Paul, MN: Greenhaven Press, 1984.

—and William Dudley. *The Vietnam War: Opposing Viewpoints.* 2nd Edition. Revised. St Paul, MN: Greenhaven Press, 1990.

Bowman, John, ed. *The Vietnam War Day by Day.* Introduction by Fox Butterfield. NY: Bison Books,1985.

Brown, Margaret C. English 102 Honors, The War in Vietnam. Radford University.

— Radford, VA. Spring 1993, 1994, 1995 & 1996. The four courses, 20 students each, included a film series and weekly meetings with members of the Vietnam Veterans Association as well as other events: including a trip to The Wall and Rolling Thunder with these Veterans, and guest speakers Tim O'Brien, Basil Paquet, and Adrian Cronauer.

—, ed. *Final Papers on Vietnam. English 102H, Spring 1993.* Radford, VA: Radford University Honors Program, 1993.

—Interview with Randy Cribbs. 29 January 2008.

—Interview with Susan Wimmers. January 2011.

Brownmiller, Susan. *Seeing Vietnam: Encounters of the Road and Heart.* NY: HarperCollins, 1995.

Burana, Lily. "The Quiet Side of Being a Soldier's Other Half." *NY Times,* 11 November 2010.

Burkett, B.G. and Glenna Whitley. *Stolen Valor: How the Vietnam Generation Was Robbed of its Heroes and its History.* Dallas, TX: Verity Press, 1998.

Butler, Robert Olen. *A Good Scent from a Strange Mountain.* NY: Henry Holt, 1992.

Carroll, Andrew, ed. *War Letters.* NY: Scribner, 2001.

Chapman, Robert. *American Slang.* New York: Harper and Row, 1987.

Charters, Ann, ed. *The Portable Sixties Reader.* NY: Penguin, 2003.

Chittenden, Varick, ed. *Vietnam Remembered: The Folk Art of Marine Combat Veteran Michael D. Cousino, Sr.* Jackson, MS: University of Mississippi Press, 1995.

Chivers, C.J. "A Sampling from Six Months' Worth of Small-Arms Accidents in Vietnam. *NY Times* 18 February 2007.

Cribbs, Randy. *Were You There: Vietnam Notes Birth, Death, Infinity.* Jacksonville, FL: OCRS, Inc, 2003.

Cronauer, Adrian. Talk on his experience in Vietnam. Radford University. 16 September 1992.

Cummings, Dennis. *The Men behind the Trident.* NY: Bantam, 1997.

Daly, James and Lee Bergman. *Black Prisoner of War: A Conscientious Objector's Vietnam Memoir.* Lawrence, KS: U Press of Kansas, 2000.

Daniel, Clifton, ed. *Chronicle of the 20th Century*. Mt. Kisco, NY: Chronicle Publications, 1987.

Daugherty, Leo and Gregory Mattson. *Nam: A Photographic History*. NY: Barnes & Noble, 2004.

Davies, Anne. "Thunder rolls, tears rain on Vietnam Vets' parade." <theage.com.au/news/world 29 May 2007>.

DeMille, Nelson. *Upcountry*. NY: Warner Books, 2002.

Dickson, Paul. *War Slang*. 2nd ed. NY: Bristol Parks, 2007.

Dorland, Peter and James Nanney. *Dust Off: Army Aeromedical Evacuation in Vietnam*. Washington: US Army, 1982.

Doyle, Edward et al. *The Vietnam Experience*. 18 vol. Robert Manning, Editor-in-chief. Boston: Boston Publishing Co., 1981.

Drake, Ben. "Hall of Shame." <http://www.marine-family.org/ . . . /wannabes.html>.

Duncan, Donald. "The Whole Thing Was A Lie." *Ramparts, Vietnam Primer*. San Francisco: Ramparts, 1966, 76-97.

Dunnigan, James and Albert Nofi. *Dirty Little Secrets of the Vietnam War*. NY: St Martin's Press, 1998.

Duong, Thu Huong. *Novel without a Name*. Trans. Phan Huy Duong and Nina McPherson. NY: William Morrow and Co., 1995.

Durrance, Dick. *Where War Lives: A Photographic Journal of Vietnam*. NY: Noonday Press, 1988.

Ebert, James. *A Life in A Year. The American Infantryman in Vietnam, 1965-1972*. NY: Ballantine Books, 1993.

Edelman, Bernard, ed. *Dear America: Letters Home from the Vietnam War*. NY: Pocket Books, 1985.

Eichler, Thomas and Diana Fecarotta, eds. *Khe Sanh Veterans Book of Poetry.* Wauwatosa, WI: Khe Sanh Veterans, 2005.

Emanuel, Ed. *The Soul Patrol.* NY: Ballantine Books, 2003.

Ezell, Edward Clinton. Introduction. *Reflections on The Wall: The Vietnam Veterans Memorial.* Harrisburg, PA: Stackpole Books, 1987.

Fall, Bernard. "This Isn't Munich, It's Spain." *Ramparts Vietnam Primer.* San Francisco: Ramparts, 1966, 58-70.

Farb, Peter. *Word Play.* NY: Bantam, 1975.

Farquhar, Dudley. "Americal." Poem written in 1982 after attending the dedication of the Vietnam Veterans Memorial in Washington, D.C.

FitzGerald, Frances. *Fire in the Lake.* N Y: Vintage Books, 1989.

Ford, Nick. *Language in Uniform.* Indianapolis, IN: Odyssey Press, 1967.

Gardner, Lloyd. *Approaching Vietnam.* NY: Norton, 1988.

Gaylin, Willard. "What Clinton, Quayle Did Was the Collegiate Norm." *LA Times* 29 October, 1992, B7.

Ghose, Anna, Managing Editor. *Eyewitness Travel Vietnam & Angkor Wat.* NY: Dorling Kindersley, 2007.

Goldman, Peter and Tony Fuller. *Charlie Company: What Vietnam Did To Us.* NY: Ballantine Books 1983.

Gray, J. Glenn. *The Warriors: Reflections on Men in Battle.* Lincoln, NE: University of Nebraska Press, 1998.

Gray, Jim and Richard Olson. *War Poems: a Collaboration.* Gainesville, GA: Georgia Printing Co., 1986.

Green, Joey. *Joey Green's Encyclopedia of Offbeat Uses for Brand Name Products.* NY: Hyperion, 1998.

Greene, Joseph, ed. *The Essential Clausewitz, Selections from On War*. Mineola, NY: Dover Publications, 2003.

Grossman, David. *On Killing*. NY: Little Brown and Co, 1995-96.

Guinta, Peter and Randy Cribbs. *Illumination Rounds*. Jacksonville, FL: OCRS, Inc, 2005.

Hanafin, Bob. *The Definition of a Vietnam Era Veteran*. <http://www. veteranstoday.com 28 July 2009>.

Hasford, Gustav. *The Short-Timers*. NY: Bantam Books, 1979.

Hay, John Jr. *Vietnam Studies: Tactical and Materiel Innovations*. Washington: US Army, 1974.

Hayslip, Le Ly with Jay Wurts. *When Heaven and Earth Changed Places: Vietnamese Woman's Journey from War to Peace*. NY: Random House, 2003.

Hendrickson, Paul. *The Living and the Dead: Robert McNamara and Five Lives of a Lost War*. NY: Vintage, 1996.

Herman, Edward and Noam Chomsky. *Manufacturing Consent: The Political Economy of the Mass Media*. NY: Pantheon Books, 1988.

Herr, Michael. *Dispatches*. NY: Vintage Books, 1991.

Hilsman, Roger. "Vietnam: The Decisions to Intervene." *Superpowers and Revolution, Ed Jonathan Adelman*. NY: Praeger Publishers, 1986, *112-141*.

Holley, Byron Dr. *Vietnam 1968-9: A Battalion Surgeon's Journal*. NY: Ballantine Books, 1993.

Holmes, Richard. *Acts of War: The Behavior of Men in Battle*. NY: Free Press, 1985.

Honda, Katsuichi. *Vietnam: A Voice from the Villages*. Tokyo: Committee for the English Publication of Vietnam, 1968.

Hoover, Paul. *Saigon, Illinois.* NY: Vintage, 1988.

Howell, Terry. "Court Expands Coverage for Vietnam Vets." <http://www. military.com 22 August 2006>.

Hynes, Samuel. *The Soldiers' Tale: Bearing Witness to Modern War.* NY: Penguin Group, 1997.

Isaacs, Arnold. *Vietnam Shadows.* Baltimore, MD: Johns Hopkins U Press, 1997.

Isserman, Maurice. *Witness to War: Vietnam.* NY: Penguin Group, 1995.

Jensen-Stevenson, Monika and William Stevenson. *Kiss the Boys Goodbye: How the US Betrayed its own POWs in Vietnam.* Toronto: McClellan and Stewart, Inc, 1990.

Johannessen, Larry. *Illumination Rounds: Teaching the Literature of the Vietnam War.* Urbana, IL: NCTE, 1992.

Joint Chiefs of Staff. *Dictionary of United States Military terms for Joint Usage.* (JCS Pub 1). Washington, DC: Department of Defense, 1964.

Karnow, Stanley. *Vietnam: A History.* NY: Penguin, 1984.

Katakis, Michael. *The Vietnam Veterans Memorial.* NY: Random House, 1988.

Kissinger, Henry. "Lessons for an Exit Strategy. *Washington Post* 12 August 2005, A19.

Komunyakaa, Yusef. *Neon Vernacular.* Middletown, CT: Wesleyan U Press, 1993.

Kubey, Craig et al. *The Viet Vet Survival Guide.* NY: Ballantine Books, 1985.

Kutler, Stanley, ed. *Encyclopedia of the Vietnam War.* NY: Macmillan, 1996.

Lamb, David. "Revolutionary Road." *Smithsonian,* March 2008, 57-66.

Lanning, Michael Lee and Ray William Stubbe. *Inside Force Recon: Recon Marines In Vietnam.* NY: Ballantine Books, 1989.

Lifton, Robert. *Home from the War.* NY: Simon & Schuster, 1973.

Lippard, Lucy, ed. *A Different War: Vietnam in Art.* Seattle: The Real Comet Press, 1990.

Lowenfels, Walter, ed. *Where is Vietnam? American Poets Respond.* NY: Doubleday, 1967.

Lucas, Jim. *Dateline: Vietnam.* NY: Award House, 1966.

Maclear, Michael. *Vietnam: A Complete Photographic History.* Photographs. Edited by Hal Buell. NY: Tess Press, 2003.

Maga, Thomas. *The Complete Idiot's Guide to the Vietnam War.* NY: Penguin, 2000.

Maraniss, David. *They Marched into Sunlight.* NY: Simon & Schuster, 2003.

Mason, Bobbie Ann. *In Country.* NY: Harper & Row, 1985.

Meyer, Peter and Editors of *Life Magazine. The Wall: A Day at the Vietnam Veterans Memorial.* NY: Thomas Dunne, 1993.

Miller, Henry. "The Alcoholic Veteran with the Washboard Cranium." *The Wisdom of the Heart.* NY: New Directions, 1960, 103-140.

Mooney, James and Thomas West, eds. *Vietnam: A History and Anthology.* St James, NY: Brandywine Press, 1994.

Moore, Harold Gen. and Joseph Galloway. *We Were Soldiers Once and Young.* NY: HarperTorch, 1992.

Nelson, Charles. *The Boy Who Picked the Bullets Up.* NY: Wm Morrow, 1981.

Nguyen, Kien. *The Unwanted: A Memoir of Childhood.* NY: Little Brown and Co., 2001.

Ninh, Bao. *The Sorrow of War: A Novel of North Vietnam.* Trans Phan Thanh Hao. NY: Pantheon Books, 1993.

Niven, Doug and Chris Riley, eds. *Tim Page, Another Vietnam: Pictures of the War from the Other Side.* Washington: National Geographic Society, 2003.

Novak, Marian Faye. *Lonely Girls with Burning Eyes.* NY: Ballantine Publishing Group, 1991.

O'Brien, Tim. *If I Die in a Combat Zone, Box Me Up and Ship Me Home.* NY: Dell, 1973.

—*The Things They Carried.* NY: Penguin, 1991.

—"The Violent Vet." *Esquire*, December, 1979, 96-104.

Olson, James, ed. *Dictionary of the Vietnam War.* Westport, CT: Greenwood Press, 1988.

Orwell, George. "Politics and the English Language." *The Collected Essays, Journalism and Letters. Vol. IV.* Eds. Sonya Orwell and Ian Angus. NY: Harvest, 1968.

Palmer, Laura. *Shrapnel in the Heart: Letters and Remembrances from the Vietnam Veterans Memorial.* NY: Random House, 1987.

Pedigo, Bobbie, former commanding officer of the 68th AHC, ed. *Vietnam Facts vs. Fiction.* Capt Marshal Hanson, researcher. http://www.68thahc. com/K_Vietnam_facts_Truth . . . >.

Phillips, Danny. E-mail correspondence with Margaret Brown, 14 June to 17 June 2009.

Phillips, Thanh and Charles, trans. *Chieu Hoi* program Brochure. 2008.

Pinker, Steven. *How the Mind Works.* NY: Norton, 1997.

Plumb, Charlie as told to Glen DeWerff. *I'm No Hero.* Independence, MO: Independence Press, 1983.

Prochnau, William, ed. *Once Upon a Distant War: Halberstam, Sheehan, Arnett—Young War Correspondents and their early Vietnam Battles.* NY: Random House, 1995.

Puller, Lewis Jr. *Fortunate Son.* NY: Bantam Books, 1993.

Ramsey, Kristi. "Trust." On *Final Papers on Vietnam*, ed Margaret Brown. Radford, VA: Radford University's Honors Program, 1993, 58-69.

Reed, David. "Vietnam Theories Revisited." *Roanoke Times* 17 September 1993.

Reinberg, Linda. *In The Field: The Language of the Vietnam War.* NY: Facts on File, 1991.

Rottman, Gordon. *Fortress 48: Viet Cong and the NVA Tunnels and Fortifications of the Vietnam War.* Botley, England: Osprey Press, 2006.

—*FUBAR Soldier Slang of WWII.* NY: Metro Books, 2010.

Rottmann, Larry, Jan Barry and Basil Paquet, eds. *Winning Hearts and Minds.* New York: McGraw-Hill Book Company, 1972.

Safer, Morley. *Flashbacks.* NY: St Martin's Press, 1990.

Sajak, Pat. E-mail to author, 11 August 2010.

Sampley, Ted. "Democracy for Vietnam is inevitable; join its holy cause." Translated into Vietnamese by Phuc Truong Dao. np: Veterans Alliance for Democracy in Vietnam, nd.

Santoli, Al. *Everything We Had.* NY: Ballantine Books, 1981.

Scheer, Robert. "A View from Phnom Penh." *Ramparts Vietnam Primer.* San Francisco: Ramparts, 1966, 37-50.

—"The Winner's War." *Ramparts Vietnam Primer.* San Francisco: Ramparts, 1966, 70-76.

Schultz, Owen. "Letter," responding to an article by C. Bassford, "Vietnam Protesters Distrusted those who Romanticized War." *Roanoke Times* 3 December 1990.

Seabury, Paul and Angelo Codevilla. *War: Ends and Means.* NY: Basic Books, 1989.

Shafer, Michael, ed. *The Legacy. The Vietnam War in the American Imagination.* Boston: Beacon Press, 1990.

Shawcross, William. Introduction. *Tim Page's Nam.* NY: Alfred Knopf, 1983.

Sheehan, Neil. *A Bright Shining Lie.* NY: Vintage, 1988.

—*After the War was Over: Hanoi and Saigon.* NY: Random House, 1992.

Sherman, Nancy. *Stoic Warriors.* NY: Oxford University Press, 2005.

Sinaiko, Eve, ed. *Vietnam: Reflexes and Reflections, National Vietnam Art Museum.* NY: Harry Abrams, 1998.

Smith, Everett Newman, Colonel. Tape. Thoughts on Vietnam.

Sorley, Lewis. *A Better War.* NY: Random House, 1999.

—"The Vietnam War We Ignore." *NY Times* 18 October 2009.

Soukhanov, Anne. *Word Watch: Stories behind the Words of our Lives.* NY: Henry Holt, 1995.

Souter, Gerry & Janet. *The Vietnam War Experience.* NY: Barnes & Noble, 2007.

Staff, Infantry Magazine. *A Distant Challenge: The US Infantryman in Vietnam 1967-70.* Fort Benning, GA: Infantry Magazine, 1971.

Starry, Donn, General. *Armored Combat in Vietnam.* NY: Arno Press, 1986.

Steinman, Ron, ed. *The Soldiers' Story: Vietnam in their own Words.* NY: Barnes and Noble, 1999-2000.

Stengel, Richard, managing ed. *Time 1969.* NY: Time Books, 2009.

Stoessinger, John. *Why Nations Go to War.* NY: St Martin's Press, 1978.

Summers, Harry Jr. *On Strategy: The Vietnam War in Context.* Carlisle Barracks, PA: US Army War College, 2002.

—*The Vietnam War Almanac.* NY: Ballantine Books, 1985.

Takiff, Michael. *Brave Men, Gentle Heroes.* NY: Perennial, 2004.

Taylor, Telford. *Nuremberg and Vietnam: An American Tragedy.* NY: Bantam, 1971.

Terry, Wallace. *Bloods.* NY: Ballantine Publishing Group, 1984.

Thomas, C. David, ed. *As Seen by Both Sides: American and Vietnamese Artists Look at the War.* Boston: Indochina Arts Project of the William Joiner Foundation, 1991.

Thomas, Claude Anshin. *At Hell's Gate: A Soldier's Journey from War to Peace.* Boston: Shambala Publications, Inc, 2004.

Thomas, Evan et al. "In God They Trust." *Newsweek* 7 May 2007, 27-34.

Thomason, John. *Fix Bayonets.* NY: Scribner, 1970.

Tripp, Nathaniel. *Father, Soldier, Son. Memoir of a Platoon Leader in Vietnam.* South Royalton, VT: Steerforth Press, 1996.

Tuchman, Barbara. *The March of Folly.* NY: Knopf, 1984.

Tully, Matthew, "Less-than-honorable discharge does not have to be permanent." http://www.armytimes.com/community/ask_lawyer/military_askthe lawyer_092208w>.

Tzu, Sun. *The Art of War.* Trans. Samuel Griffith. NY: Oxford U Press, 1963.

Van Devanter, Lynda. *Home Before Morning*. NY: Time Warner, 1983.

—and Joan Furey, eds. *Visions of War, Dreams of Peace: Writings of Women in the Vietnam War*. NY: Warner Books, 1991.

Walt, Lewis. *Strange War, Strange Strategy*. NY: Funk and Wagnalls, 1970.

Weber, Joe. *Rules of Engagement*. NY: Jove, 1992.

Wells, Tom. *The War Within: America's Battle over Vietnam*. Berkeley: U California Press, 1994.

Welsh, Douglas. *The History of the Vietnam War*. London: Bison Books, 1981.

Zaroulis, Nancy and Gerald Sullivan. *Who Spoke Up? American Protest Against the War in Vietnam 1963-1975*. NY: Holt, 1984.

Zumbro, Ralph. *Tank Sergeant*. NY: Pocket Books, 1988.

The following movies and DVDs contributed to my understanding of the Vietnam Conflict. I have indicated those well worth seeing.

▶ *Apocalypse Now* (1979) directed by Francis Ford Copppola.
Born on the 4ᵗʰ of July (1989) directed by Oliver Stone.
▶ *Coming Home* (1978) directed by Hal Ashby.
▶ *Dear America: Letters Home from Vietnam*.
Deer Hunter (1978) directed by Michael Cimino.
▶ *84 Charlie Mopic* (1989) directed by Patrick Duncan. (written, directed by Vietnam vet).
Great premise: videotape a platoon in action to show at basic training, to cut down on casualties in war; send in new cameraman who makes too much noise; great "interviews" with platoon members about race and class and education.
Full Metal Jacket (1987) directed by Stanley Kubrick.
▶ *Gardens of Stone* (1987) directed by Francis Ford Coppola. (respecting and burying the dead).
Good Morning Vietnam (1987) directed by Barry Levinson.
▶ *Go Tell the Spartans* (1978) directed by Fred Post. (about early military advisors).

Hamburger Hill (1987) directed by John Irvin.

▶ *Hearts and Minds* (1974) directed by Peter Davis.

▶ *In Country* (1989) directed by Norman Jewison.

Indochine (1992) directed by Regis Wargnier.

Inside The Vietnam War. VHS. National Geographic.

The Killing Fields (1984) directed by Roland Joffe.

My Lai. DVD. NP: PBS 2010.

Platoon (1986) directed by Oliver Stone.

The Roots of the Vietnam War. The Nation Archives 31 August, 2010.
<http://www.thenation.com/print/learning-pack/roots-vietnam-war>.

▶ *The Scent of Green Papaya* (1993) directed by Hung Tran Anh.

▶ *Southern Comfort* (1981) directed by Walter Hill. (VC as Cajuns; grunts as National Guard).

Vietnam: On the front Line, 4 part series, The History Channel, (2001).

Vietnam: the Women Who Served (1993).

Bombing of Viet Cong Structures along a canal in South Vietnam.
(Notice buildings on right.)

ACKNOWLEDGEMENTS

NONE OF THIS would have happened if not for the support of Radford University's Department of English and the Honors Program. Thank you for letting me teach courses about the Vietnam War and limiting my class-size to 20 students per section. Special thanks to Vietnam Vets of America, Chapter 138, especially George Albright, Jim Bowman, Kathy Bowman, Al Davis, Randall Fletcher, Frank Longaker, Carolyn Parsons, Diane Phillips, Johnny Phillips, Dee Phillips, James Ratcliff, Lee Thacker, Bobby Ward, Joyce Ward, and Banjo Williams. They gave up their Thursday evenings to speak freely with my students and to answer questions they seemed to expect but I did not anticipate. No question went unanswered, no matter what it was. They were honest and patient, and my students loved them for it. So did I.

Heather Casto, thanks for being one of my students. You asked Johnny how you could get your father, a veteran, to talk with you about the war. "Welcome him home." You walked over to Johnny and welcomed him home. That moment is on tape somewhere at Radford University; Chris Shell, where are you? Thank you, Chris Armes, for believing me when I said you belonged in the RU Honors Program. You did, and you have the academic and professional successes you once thought impossible. You asked the same question of each vet, "How do you think the war changed you?" not because you couldn't think of any other, but because you gave us a comparison of our vets' lives. We learned a lot from their different answers.

Welcome home to all Vietnam veterans, especially to Doc Holley (*Vietnam 1968-1969: A Battalion Surgeon's Journal*) who kept me working, gave me good feedback, and is my friend even though we've never met face to face. Randy Cribbs, vet and poet, for the generous use of his poetry and for being an all-around good guy. Tim O'Brien, vet, fine writer, and genuine speaker; your *The Things They Carried* pushed my freshmen to rethink how they saw truth and the world. Special thanks to Danny Phillips for his pictures and his willingness to share them.

None of this would have happened if not for my neurosurgeon, Dr. Carlos Arce (Shands Hospital in Jacksonville) who fixed my brain, and Dr. Joann Gates, my neuropsychologist in St. Augustine, who taught me what I could do with my new brain. (Me, write a book? Now?)

Thank you, thank you to all my friends at the duplicate bridge clubs in St. Augustine, Palm Coast, Daytona Beach, and Jacksonville who worried about me, who didn't mind my forgetfulness, and who partnered Earl when I couldn't play. To Temple Bet Yam members that watched over our daughter and prayed for all of us during a difficult surgery. And what to say about the late, great Harvey Wolf? I miss you—your truth, your laughter, and your "So"? To Ron Link who sent me wonderful books by Vietnamese writers. To Candice and Dan Gulden and to Hew and Martha Joiner who have enriched my life for years by your strength, kindness, and good sense. To special friends, Barbara Nailer, Nancy Mitchell, Frankie Dittman, and Lois Pearson for their courage. And my mothers, Margaret and Gertrude, my fathers, Robert and Earl, Sr. The best is last. Rosie Rose, my 18 pounds of tabby cat that saved my life. My first and only husband, Earl, and our daughter, Emily, who kept me fed and watered, fixed my laptop, got rid of paper jams, and introduced me to thumb drives, fingernail drives, and wireless wonders. My tour is over, my dear friends.

The infamous Rosie Rose.

Copyright Page

From Chieu Hoi Program Brochure, Translated by Thanh and Charles Phillips, copyright © 2008. Used by permission of the translators.

From a tape entitled, Thoughts on Vietnam, by Colonel Everett Smith. Used by permission of his daughter, Evangeline Smith.

Margaret Brown would like to thank Susan Wimmers for allowing her to publish material from an interview in January 2011 and to use photographs from her experience with the USO in Vietnam.

Dudley Farquhar "Americal Division" and picture of the Vietnam Memorial Wall. Used by permission of Dudley Farquhar.

E-mail correspondence between Danny Phillips and the author. Used by permission of Danny Phillips.

From *Charlie Ration Cookbook* Copyright ©1966 by McIlhenny Co. Used by permission of TABASCO®.

Charles Ward for permission to use pictures on the Vets With a Mission website.

Picture Credits:

Bettman/Corbis National Archives: 262.

Brown, Dr Earl: 255 (3).

Brown, Earl Jr.: 15, 22, 52, 79, 106, 112, 116, 118, 125, 132, 151, 204, 257, 297, 300, 310 (2), 314, 332, inside back cover.

Dorling Kindersley: 254 (4).

Farquhar, Dudley: 293.

Falk, Jim: 121.

Free-photos.biz: 130, 150.

Goldman, Meryl: 64.

Halverson, Paul D.: 140.

Hoa Lo Prison Historic Vestige Brochure: 125, 126.

Lindsay, Steve <*http://pbase.com/Jerry9204/image/115508041*>: 222.

Nickerson, F. C. III: 201.

Olson, John (for "Stars and Stripes" in *Eyewitness Travel Vietnam & Angkor Wat*)): 254.

O'Neal: Norman (Reggie): 16, 74, 249.

Phillips, Sgt. Danny: 23, 26, 32, 42 (2), 46, 57, 58, 71, 75, 94, 97, 108, 111, 112, 117 (2), 136, 139, 141, 143 (2), 146, 149, 157 (2), 162, 165 (2), 169, 170, 171, 178, 209, 210, 223, 225, 240, 251, 252, 261, 265, 267 (2), 268, 280 (3).

Sheridan, Autumn: 296 (2).

Strattan, Chris: 191.

USO Photo/Vietnam: 258.

Vets with a Mission: 10, 25, 41, 58, 60, 80, 96, 139, 192, 201, 208, 210, 212, 217, 228, 244, 279, 282, 290, 308.

Vietnam Helicopter Pilots Association: 230, 277.

Wimmers, Susan: 27, 259 (2).

Cover idea courtesy of Radford University

Every effort has been made to contact the copyright holder of the following work. If the copyright holders consider that my use of their work does not meet fair use guidelines, please contact me. I'll be most pleased to discuss arrangements.

Eichler, Thomas and Diana Fecarotta, eds. *Khe Sanh Veterans Book of Poetry.* Wauwatosa, WI: Khe Sanh Veterans, 2005.